The Cambridge Introduction to Intercultural Communication

Uniquely interdisciplinary and accessible, *The Cambridge Introduction to Intercultural Communication* is the ideal text for undergraduate introductory courses in Intercultural Communication, International Communication and Cross-cultural Communication. Suitable for students and practitioners alike, it encompasses the breadth of intercultural communication as an academic field and a day-to-day experience in work and private life, including international business, public services, schools and universities. This textbook touches on a range of themes in intercultural communication, such as evolutionary and positive psychology, key concepts from critical intercultural communication, postcolonial studies and transculturality, intercultural encounters in contemporary literature and film, and the application of contemporary intercultural communication research for the development of health services and military services. The concise, up-to-date overviews of key topics are accompanied by a wide variety of tasks and eighteen case studies for in-depth discussions, homework, and assessments.

Guido Rings is Emeritus Professor of Postcolonial Studies, co-director of the Anglia Ruskin Research Centre for Intercultural and Multilingual Studies (ARRCIMS), and co-founder of iMex and German as a Foreign Language, the first internet journals in Europe for their respective fields. Professor Rings has widely published within different areas of critical intercultural and postcolonial studies. This includes, as editor, the acclaimed *Cambridge Handbook of Intercultural Communication* (with S. M. Rasinger, Cambridge University Press, 2020) and, as author, the world-leading scoring *The Other in Contemporary Migrant Cinema* (Routledge, 2016) and the celebrated *La Conquista desbaratada* (The Conquest upside down, Iberoamericana, 2010), next to more than fifty distinguished refereed articles.

Sebastian M. Rasinger is Associate Professor of Applied Linguistics at Anglia Ruskin University. His research focuses on language and identity, with a particular focus on multilingual and migration contexts. He has extensive experience in teaching courses in these areas at all levels. His textbook *Quantitative Research in Linguistics: An Introduction*, published in two editions (Bloomsbury 2008 and 2013), has sold several thousand copies and has been published in its Spanish translation by Ediciones Akal. Sebastian has a strong interest in equality and diversity in higher education, and is currently the vice chair of the QAA Advisory Group for linguistics, overseeing the review of the linguistics subject benchmarks in UK HE.

This interdisciplinary text offers valuable insight into a wide range of intercultural communication concepts and issues that are a concern in today's increasingly interconnected and interdependent world. The chapters underscore societal imperatives for intercultural competence and provide a useful survey of diverse approaches to the study of intercultural communication.

Professor Emerita Jane Jackson, The Chinese University of Hong Kong

This is an excellent textbook. It is comprehensive in approaching intercultural communication from different theoretical perspectives. It also pushes forward our understanding of intercultural communication in real life using the latest cases. It is a must-read for any training involving intercultural communication competence.

Dr Xin Zhao, Bournemouth University

The authors of this entry-level textbook are uniquely positioned to provide this comprehensive overview of intercultural communication. This cutting-edge and multi-disciplinary exploration of such a critical area of communication provides a strong foundation upon which to develop further.

Dr Darla K Deardorff, Duke University (Author and Founding President, World Council on Intercultural and Global Competence)

Coursebooks at their best provide a readable, thought-inviting, extensive, state-of-the-art and future-relevant introduction to a field. *The Cambridge Introduction to Intercultural Communication* convincingly meets all these requirements. The authors give insight into manifold subject-relevant theories and areas of application by inviting their readers to critically move beyond established notions of intercultural communication.

Professor Werner Delanoy, University of Klagenfurt

This beautiful book offers readers of all levels an excellent overview of research on intercultural communication, including its very latest, exciting developments. What Capability Brown once did for the British garden, Rings and Rasinger have done for intercultural communication.

Professor Jean-Marc Dewaele, Birkbeck, University of London

The textbook provides a lucid and refreshing introduction to intercultural communication. It has an impressive coverage of key and current practical and theoretical issues, from postcolonial studies to psychology perspectives and from digital spheres to military services. It is a must read for those new to the field.

Professor Zhu Hua, University College London

Rings and Rasinger bring a novel and nuanced transcultural approach to intercultural communication, addressing limitations of contrastive, essentialist perspectives, as well as critical research. They combine up-to-date issues (digital and gig work, hyper-nationalistic trends, social media) and new approaches (positive psychology, storytelling, film and narrative) with world-wide examples, to deeply consider intercultural communication within larger power, business, and political relations.

Professor John Baldwin, Illinois State University

This textbook offers a thorough overview of intercultural communication as a field of study that transcends geographical and academic borders. The authors track the development of intercultural approaches and applications across a wide variety of disciplines and contexts, showing the potential of a critical intercultural communication perspective to help us understand and act upon our everyday individual and communal experiences.

Professor Susana Martinez Guillem, University of New Mexico

A didactically excellently designed introductory volume in Intercultural Communication! Each chapter contains aims, key terms and tasks to introduce the subject matter as well as discussion questions and a case study to conclude. In terms of content, the book also meets all expectations: it introduces the current state of the most important theoretical and methodological discussions and provides a multidisciplinary overview of current research on the subject area.

Professor Jürgen Bolten, Jena University

Presenting an integrative reorientation of intercultural communication, this book offers new and expansive interdisciplinary insights that reach beyond the commonly researched social domains. The book takes the reader on a journey that starts with discussing concepts, theories, and approaches in ways that are both provocative and accessible before introducing a wide range of contemporary applications with examples and discussions. It is beautifully written and it makes a vital and much-needed contribution to the teaching and research of intercultural communication.

Dr Khawla Badwan, Manchester Metropolitan University

The Cambridge Introduction to
Intercultural Communication

GUIDO RINGS

Anglia Ruskin University

SEBASTIAN M. RASINGER

Anglia Ruskin University

CAMBRIDGE
UNIVERSITY PRESS

CAMBRIDGE
UNIVERSITY PRESS

Shaftesbury Road, Cambridge CB2 8EA, United Kingdom

One Liberty Plaza, 20th Floor, New York, NY 10006, USA

477 Williamstown Road, Port Melbourne, VIC 3207, Australia

314–321, 3rd Floor, Plot 3, Splendor Forum, Jasola District Centre, New Delhi – 110025, India

103 Penang Road, #05–06/07, Visioncrest Commercial, Singapore 238467

Cambridge University Press is part of Cambridge University Press & Assessment, a department of the University of Cambridge.

We share the University's mission to contribute to society through the pursuit of education, learning and research at the highest international levels of excellence.

www.cambridge.org
Information on this title: www.cambridge.org/9781108842716

DOI: 10.1017/9781108904025

First published 2023

A catalogue record for this publication is available from the British Library

Library of Congress Cataloging-in-Publication data
Names: Rings, Guido, 1964– author. | Rasinger, Sebastian M.
(Sebastian Marc), 1977– author.
Title: The cambridge introduction to intercultural communication /
Guido Rings, Anglia Ruskin University, Cambridge, Sebastian M. Rasinger,
Anglia Ruskin University, Cambridge.
Description: New York : Cambridge University Press, 2023. |
Includes bibliographical references and index.
Identifiers: LCCN 2022023676 | ISBN 9781108842716 (hardback) |
ISBN 9781108904025 (ebook)
Subjects: LCSH: Intercultural communication. | Communication and culture. |
BISAC: LANGUAGE ARTS & DISCIPLINES / Linguistics / General
Classification: LCC HM1211 .R564 2022 | DDC 303.48/2–dc23/eng/20220613
LC record available at https://lccn.loc.gov/2022023676

ISBN   978-1-108-84271-6   Hardback
ISBN   978-1-108-82254-1   Paperback

CONTENTS

FIGURES

PREFACE

Why Intercultural Communication?

In our increasingly globalised world, interactions with people from other cultures are on the rise. Particularly in cities, but increasingly also outside urban areas, schools, universities, workplaces, neighbourhoods and health services are becoming more culturally mixed, and there is significant interest from other public services such as police, firefighters and the military reflecting these demographic developments. In the virtual realm, we see a comparable growth in cultural encounters, for example in social media like Facebook, Twitter and Instagram, while mass media confronts us daily with images of – and often also perspectives from – other cultures.

Interculturally competent people have a huge advantage in that context, because the ability to work in teams effectively is key to success in most social environments. The workplace is an obvious example, because most employers want outstanding team players, for which excellent communication skills are essential. In a culturally mixed workplace this means having intercultural communication skills, and employability may very much depend on them. However, 'culture' should be defined in a wider sense than ethnicity, race and nationality, to include, for example, educational differences and similarities, class, gender and age (see Chapters 1 and 2). In this context, intercultural competence must be discussed as a wider social competence (Chapter 3), which can be extremely helpful in the development of most personal relationships.

Interest in intercultural competence has led to the creation of new jobs, from intercultural coaches for international companies to intercultural trainers for the police and military, and many interculturalists have established their own companies, managing coaches and trainers. However, not everything should be seen through the lens of employability and job prospects, because great social contacts, friendships and partnerships might depend on intercultural communication skills too. Finally, the ability to experience the world through other perspectives can be very enriching in the sense that it can help solve personal and social problems, identify better ways of living, or simply make people feel better. It is no coincidence that in intercultural business communication, there is now a strong movement towards including the emotional wellbeing of employees as a factor as important as economic aims, and that should certainly also be a goal outside corporate life.

Why This Book?

We have both taught and supervised intercultural communication at undergraduate, postgraduate and doctoral level, and have approached the topic from the perspectives of cultural studies, linguistics, postcolonial studies, psychology and other social sciences. Having edited *The Cambridge handbook of intercultural communication* (Rings & Rasinger, 2020) and published widely on cultural topics, we saw an opportunity to write an entry-level textbook that not only truly reflects the multidisciplinary and interdisciplinary nature of the field, but also provides a state-of-the art introduction to it. The book is designed to provide (i) a thorough discussion of key theoretical and conceptual discussions, (ii) a survey of the various methodological approaches to intercultural communication, and (iii) a multidisciplinary overview of current research in intercultural communication with a particular focus on intercultural theory in various domains of application. In particular, the book addresses the relationship between intercultural communication and power, and provides a balanced exploration of contrastive, interactional, imagological, psychological and digital aspects. The book can be used as either a standalone text or a companion to the collection of original research work in the *Handbook*.

Unlike existing introductions, the book encompasses the full breadth of the field of intercultural communication. It includes themes which to date have found comparatively little consideration in books of this type, such as evolutionary and positive psychology, key concepts from critical intercultural communication, postcolonial studies and transculturality, intercultural encounters in contemporary literature and film, and the application of contemporary intercultural communication research for the development of health services and military services. It therefore has the potential to be used in a wide variety of courses whether intercultural communication plays a central or only peripheral role in them.

Although there is a progressive narrative underlying the book, with parts and chapters well connected, each chapter can be used and understood in isolation, and there is no strict sequence that needs to be followed, allowing tutors to fit the book into their own syllabi and independent readers to select those chapters that are most appropriate for them.

What Does This Book Offer?

The book contains eighteen chapters, which cover – as an introduction to intercultural communication – the programme of a full academic year or, alternatively, provide a substantial selection of key themes for specialist single-semester, trimester or intensive courses. Such courses could, for example, focus on intercultural awareness, competence or coaching and training, intercultural business communication, cultural diversity and integration, international assignment or year abroad preparation (and repatriation), as well as intercultural leadership and management, linguistics, literature or film.

Each chapter presents topics that could be covered in a single session or week. However, the first chapter in each of the three parts deserves to be given more time if available: in a one-year teaching programme, we would recommend devoting two sessions or weeks to the topics of Chapters 1, 4 and 12, because they serve as introductory chapters to their respective parts and cover more ground (e.g. Chapter 1 on culture and cultural identity constructs). Depending on the focus lecturers would like to give their courses, the relevant key chapters would also benefit from a slightly more generous time frame. For example, in a programme in which students are expected to apply contrastive, interactive and psychological approaches in different scenarios in full depth, it would be advisable to devote two sessions or weeks each to the topics of Chapters 5, 7 and 10, bearing in mind that lecturers might want to add a week for a general introduction and leave sessions for the preparation of assessments.

While the book presents all themes in a 'natural progression', from basic discussions of culture and cultural identity to specific applications of intercultural communication in business, health care and military settings, each chapter can also stand independently, potentially serving as the basis for specialist courses. For example, for a single-semester (or intensive) course in intercultural business communication, lecturers might want to choose the three chapters of Part I, followed by Chapter 14 and then 5, 7 and 10 as analysis chapters, before Chapter 17 provides preparation for course assessment. If more time is available, then intercultural communication in health and military settings would also deserve to feature in such a course, as publicly funded systems are very much interconnected with the private sector, in that they are important areas for many companies. There are also numerous structural parallels, for example, of an increasingly more culturally mixed workforce in intercultural leadership and management, or in the cultural integration and intercultural competence development of that workforce.

We have structured each chapter in such a way that it scaffolds students' learning. Each chapter starts with clearly stated learning aims and a set of keywords. Early on in each chapter, there are tasks to set the scene and ease students into the topic. As the chapter progresses, tasks become more complex. These tasks might be points for discussion, small data collection and analysis pieces, or creative elements, allowing students and tutors to check their understanding and critically reflect on their own personal experiences of the topic. We end each chapter with more complex discussion questions that draw the key issues of the chapter together, and an authentic case study that allows students to apply what they have learned in a clear and precise but challenging cultural encounter.

While the learning aims provide guidance, questions and case studies allow for an in-depth exploration of theoretical concepts or the application of newly acquired skills in an interactive learning environment. Each chapter also contains a brief summary of key issues, and reference lists are at the end of each chapter rather than the end of the book to facilitate further reading, which tutors might want to link to additional tasks and/or recommend as preparation for assessments. Key terms are explained and discussed in their respective chapters, but a glossary is also provided at the end of the book.

Part I introduces students to different key concepts of culture before discussing recent assumptions regarding developments from monocultural and traditional multicultural concepts to intercultural and transcultural perspectives. A working definition of intercultural communication is then provided and new dynamic and inclusive concepts of intercultural competence are explored.

In Part II, we guide students through key theories, concepts and approaches that have shaped the field of intercultural communication and continue to inform it. We start with concepts established in most recent research on 'critical intercultural communication', which correlate with postcolonial theory and can be traced to imagological explorations in literature and media studies. We compare such approaches with the contrastive theories that laid the ground for intercultural communication as an academic field and continue to shape intercultural training. Unlike other introductions to intercultural communication, our aim is not simply to reject contrastive approaches as outdated, but to examine their potential within the new framework set by critical intercultural communication.

Part II will also familiarise students with the different methodological approaches to studying intercultural communication, drawing upon the various disciplines that contribute to the field to reflect its diversity. From a linguistic angle, it will discuss issues such as politeness in an intercultural context, taking into account recent research on contrastive pragmatic work. Anthropological approaches trace the origins of intercultural communication as a discipline, with a focus on culture in everyday life. Sociological approaches will explore themes such as gender and feminist angles, but also highlight the concept of intersectionality, to allow students to understand the complexities of modern societies. Unlike many other introductory volumes, we then turn towards more recent developments in the field, by exploring how positive psychology concepts can be used to understand and develop intercultural relations better before moving to a discussion of how storytelling has the potential to create and enhance intercultural understanding.

Part III addresses the different communicative contexts, or domains, in which intercultural communication plays a substantial role. Chapter 12 starts the discussion with the exponential expansion of digital technology and social media over the last two decades, and addresses intercultural encounters in the digital sphere. Chapter 13 explores intercultural communication in the context of migration, taking into account increases in global mobility where people live in more than one place and culture during their lifetimes. Chapters 14, 15 and 16 are dedicated to intercultural communication in three different professional contexts: the business world, medical and health services, and the military. Chapter 17 looks at a set of tools to assess intercultural competence, such as the Developmental Model of Intercultural Sensitivity (DMIS). Chapter 18 concludes the book by discussing future developments in intercultural communication, and intercultural communication research.

 PART I

INTRODUCING INTERCULTURAL COMMUNICATION

1 From Culture to Cultural Identity Concepts

In this chapter, we develop a working definition of culture that outlines its key aspects and notes important links between culture and other dimensions that can shape behaviour in cultural encounters. We then examine four popular cultural identity concepts that partially draw on very different values.

AIMS
By the end of this chapter, you should be able to:

1. define key aspects of culture;
2. distinguish between four popular cultural identity constructs;
3. describe the potential impact of these constructs on cross-cultural life and work;
4. explain the extent to which these constructs are connected to questions of power.

> **KEY TERMS**
> culture – cultural identity – monocultural – traditional multicultural – traditional intercultural – transcultural – intercultural identity

1.1 Approaching Culture

> **TASKS**
>
> – How would you define culture?
> – Would you limit this to the literature, music and similar products of a nation, or does it go beyond that?
> – Does your local football club have a culture, or does culture start at national level?
> – Does culture exist at a wider geographical (e.g. European) or religious (e.g. Christian) level?
>
> – Think of examples that could help us understand the concept and compare these examples with Figure 1.1, which shows culture as a blend of three women dressed in traditional East Asian, Indian and Arab attire beside a globe symbolising connection and unity, yet also differences across the world.

Figure 1.1 *Culture* by Alíz Kovács-Zöldi

In our global and increasingly virtual world, encounters with people from other cultures often occur on a daily basis. This might be face to face, for example at university, the workplace and in the neighbourhood, or on Instagram, Facebook or other social media networks. It also happens in a more mediated way, for example through the cultural interactions seen in television series, films and advertising. Yet, what culture actually is, remains difficult to define. Little has changed since Raymond Williams noted that it is 'one of the three most complicated words in the English language' (1985, p. 87), with discussions connected to questions of power hierarchies continuing (see Delanoy, 2020; Nakayama, 2020). Nevertheless, we aim to provide a working definition that you might want to build on and amend as you continue with your studies, read new articles on the topic and explore your own experiences.

1.1.1 Hofstede's Pyramid

A good starting point for the development of that working definition is the widely disseminated pyramid of 'mental programming' (Hofstede et al., 2010, p. 6), which is divided into three parts: the top level is entitled 'personality', the middle 'culture' and the bottom 'human nature', with black lines clearly separating each of these parts from the others. The pyramid highlights that our behaviour, which might lead to challenges in encounters with other people and/or to the development of new social relationships, is not exclusively shaped by 'culture'. Factors like 'personality' and 'human nature' have to be taken into account as well. Personality includes traits such as 'the Big Five': extraversion, conscientiousness, openness to experience, agreeableness and neuroticism (Marsh et al., 2010), all of which could be inherited and/or learned. Human nature refers to instincts and basic emotions like fear, anger, sadness and shame, which are inherited, but we might want to add cognitive and storytelling abilities too (Harari, 2015, pp. 36–41; Gottschall, 2012). At the middle of the pyramid, we find 'culture' as something *learned* and *specific to a group*, and that is certainly a good starting point for a working definition.

The fixed boundaries indicated by black lines in Hofstede's pyramid should however be questioned: you might know from experience that cultural contexts can have an impact on both the expression of personality traits and the stories that we tell each other. Extraversion, for example, could be supported or met with scepticism: Ferraro describes numerous case studies in which US American individual extraversion was regarded as problematic by Japanese participants in joint business meetings (e.g. 2010, p. 64). On the other hand, individuals and stories can shape culture, especially if they become popular. For example, Van Assche et al. (2019) highlight clear parallels in xenophobic, ultraconservative and ultranationalist re-imaginings of the US, UK and France, when they compare the social-psychological underpinnings of Trumpism, Brexit and far-right parties on the European continent. In particular, the authors link this to a revival of tendencies towards prejudice, social dominance orientation and authoritarianism (2019). While this should not be misunderstood as a simple return to the early twentieth-century fascism that led to WWII, it shares key aspects with that fascism (Griffin, 2008, p. 186). At the same time, it shows even more similarities with late nineteenth- and early twentieth-century European nationalism, which culminated in WWI and allows for a transfer of such social-psychological research to forms of extreme nationalism in other parts of the globe, including Xi Jinping's China and especially Putin's Russia. The renewed dissemination and internalisation of aggressive 'My country first' stories by politicians like Donald Trump, Nigel Farage, Marie Le Pen, Xi Jinping and Vladimir Putin stand in contrast to earlier more intercultural and transcultural images of these cultures as well as alternatives (such as from Biden in the US), but it connects with colonial, neo-colonial and/or other imperialist heritages. Overall, this highlights a substantial degree of *imagination* and *mediation* in the construction of culture (Jackson, 2014, pp. 66–68), to which we will return in our discussion of different cultural identity constructs in this chapter.

Finally, depending on the context, each of the three basic aspects of mental programming in Hofstede's graph might become more or less important depending on the situation. For example, if an ultranationalist mob decides to hunt you and your friends on the streets because you said that you would like to bring down a statue of a historic racist who continues to be celebrated as a national hero by that mob, then instincts (human nature) might guide your behaviour more than culture or personality. On the other hand, in academic discussions at university, personality and culture might be much more in the foreground than human nature. This highlights *dynamics* that we would like to add to our working definition of culture.

Overall, these examples indicate that boundaries between personality, culture and human nature should be imagined as fluid, dynamic and open, rather than static, which might be better expressed with a dotted curved and not a straight line.

TASKS

Prepare a presentation with one example each for the impact of a personality trait, a cultural aspect and human nature on an encounter that you have had with another person, or that you have seen or heard of. Then explain to what extent and exactly how the encounter was shaped by the factor mentioned, and which other factors may have played a role.

1.1.2   Other Key Aspects

Think of an *iceberg*: you can only see a small part, which is out of the water, while most of it remains hidden beneath the water. Frequent illustrations of culture, so-called 'iceberg models' (e.g. Matejovsky, 2011), draw on this image to stress that most cultural features remain *invisible* – like most parts of an iceberg. These invisible features include norms, beliefs, assumptions and, above all, values. One reason for their invisibility is that they are not always consciously learned (like writing usually is), but programmed or conditioned through model behaviour that you follow or sanctions that you try to avoid. Unlike behaviour or cultural artefacts, which tend to form the *visible* part of cultural icebergs, values cannot be directly (e.g. photographically) captured, but need to be deducted, for example through surveys and interviews, or observation of behaviour.

Now, think of an *onion*: it has a core and then different layers until you reach the peel. Popular 'onion diagrams' build on this image to highlight the links between different aspects of culture. Most of them show cultural values as core because they are considered key for cultural practices that tend to be linked to beliefs, attitudes, behaviour and rituals, but also for the development of systems and institutions. All this can be put into the different layers, and there is a variety of onion diagrams to choose from (see Spencer-Oatey, 2004, p. 5; Hofstede Insights, 2020). While the cultural aspects of these layers have to be imagined in dynamic interaction (rather than stable as they are in popular onion diagrams), there can be little doubt that core values, or 'shared ideas about what is right or wrong' (Jackson, 2014, p. 53), tend to remain relatively stable if compared with actual behaviour and artefacts. In this sense, we want to amend Benessaieh's summary of culture as 'a stable system of practices and beliefs' (2010, p. 13) by adding *values* as key aspects and highlighting that we also have to expect *dynamics*, which are a result of people's interaction, their negotiation of meaning and contributions to (or interventions against) particular cultural aspects (i.e. beliefs, attitudes, behaviours and rituals).

Finally, the association of culture with a particular collective deserves to be considered in more detail: if that collective could be defined as 'a community or population large enough to be self-sustaining' (Jandt, 2010, p. 15), then we have to imagine a broad spectrum of cultures. From a territorial perspective, we might have to distinguish between local (Hong Kong in China, New York City as 'the Big Apple'), regional (e.g. Bavaria in Germany and Andalucía in Spain), national and supranational cultures (the United Kingdom and the European Union), and consider the tensions that come with that. Cultural identification can, however, also be linked to different affiliations within a territory, for example in football with 'São Paulo FC' rather than 'SE Palmeiras' (both of which are in São Paulo), or 'Seville' instead of 'Betis' (both in Seville). Such affiliations would traditionally be summarised as 'subcultures', but there is growing acceptance that for the development of intercultural competence as 'social action competence' the difference between 'intercultural' and 'intracultural' tendencies is at best a gradual one, because very similar principles apply (see Bolten, 2020).

TASK

Take some time to reflect on yourself: to which cultures at local, regional, national and supranational level do you belong? To what extent do these cultures complement each other and where do you see conflicts? In which way and how exactly have you contributed to (or against) cultural identity constructs at these levels? Now, exchange these ideas in smaller groups with members of your class. What are the differences, and what is the common ground?

1.1.3 In Summary

We can now argue that **culture** refers to learned, programmed or conditioned values, beliefs, assumptions and norms common to a larger (self-sufficient) population that expresses these characteristics in particular patterns of behaviour, rituals, artefacts and institutions. Due to its largely unconscious and conflictive acquisition, which is a consequence of priming through a wider spectrum of stories, it is predominantly mediated, invisible and imagined. At the same time, culture is dynamic, because people contribute to (or intervene against) these stories, that is retell, rewrite, adapt and negotiate them, or try to develop alternatives.

Understood as such, cultures can be described in their historical continuities, for example you could say that from the eighteenth century until the early 1960s, racial segregation norms were a key feature of US American culture. They should, however, also be discussed in their discontinuities, because norms can be learned, questioned and replaced by other norms. For example, racial segregation was declared unlawful in the US Civil Rights and Voting Rights Acts of 1964/1965, which had an impact on the lives of black people, though it did not end discrimination, as has been highlighted by the Black Lives Matter movement more recently.

With focus on such learning experiences, Welsch reminds us that 'our understanding of culture is an active factor in our cultural life':

> If one tells us that culture is to be a homogeneity event, then we practice the required coercions and exclusions. [...] Whereas, if one tells us [...] that culture ought to incorporate the foreign and do justice to transcultural components, then we will set about this task, and then corresponding feats of integration will belong to the real structure of our culture. The 'reality' of culture is [...] always a consequence too of our conceptions of culture.
> (Welsch, 1999, p. 201)

It might be worth adding that we do not always do what we are told. For example, in National Socialist Germany, Stalin's Soviet Union and Pinochet's Chile, many people rejected the regime's coercions and exclusions and fought for a more inclusive transcultural society, although they knew that this could mean jail, concentration camp or death penalty. Similarly, numerous people challenge the coercions and exclusions of contemporary authoritarian and non-authoritarian regimes, despite the knowledge of the regimes' power to put them in jail, indefinitely prolong these jail sentences and/or kill them, even if they are in exile in other countries. The treatment of Uyghurs by the Chinese authorities, critics and dissidents by the Russian and Belarusian governments, and foreign suspects by the US military at Guantanamo are just a few examples that critical interculturalists might want to consider in this context.

Drawing on our basic working definition of culture in context, we would now like to explore common ground and key differences in cultural values in greater depth. They tend to culminate in different identity constructs, that is, different concepts of self that define how we see ourselves and our place in the world.

TASK

Define your identity in three words. Compare your answer with that of your classmates.

Between you, the answers to the above tasks will probably fall into several categories: some of you may have put references to your sex or gender, or your nationality, or your ethnic background; others will have put religious affiliation, marital status, or character traits. The concept of **cultural identity** is a complex one, but one that is important for the study of intercultural communication. Reginald Byron provides a basic definition, according to which identity relates to the 'properties of uniqueness and individuality, the essential differences making a person distinct from all others, as in "self-identity"' but also to 'qualities of sameness, in that persons may associate themselves, or be associated by others, with groups or categories on the basis of some salient common feature, e.g. "ethnic identity"' (Byron, 2002, p. 441).

Identities are not, however, monolithic, fixed or static: Tope Omoniyi reminds us that identities are dynamic and constructed in interaction (Omoniyi, 2006). Bonny Norton similarly defines identity as 'the way a person understands his or her relationship to the world, how that relationship is constructed across time and space, and how the person understands possibilities for the future' (Norton, 2013, p. 4). In other words, the way you have defined your identity in the task above will very much have been influenced by how you saw yourself in the context you have completed this task in, and in relation to others around you.

In the next sections of this chapter, we will dissect identity construction in more detail, in particular with reference to different approaches to culture. This will lead us to distinguish between monocultural, traditional multicultural, traditional intercultural and transcultural identity constructs, the last of which are in line with leading intercultural perspectives today.

1.2 Back to Our Island: Monocultural Identity Constructs

In his reference to perceptions of culture as 'a homogeneity event' linking up to 'coercions and exclusions', Welsch (1999, p. 201) highlights key features of **monocultural identity** constructs, which are also known as 'island' or 'container' concepts of culture (Eriksen, 1993; Moses & Rothberg, 2014, p. 31). These concepts shaped European colonialism and nationalism in the nineteenth and twentieth centuries and the construction of most new nation states in the twentieth century. They continue to inform neo-colonialism in different parts of the globe and, above all, the rise of populist ultranationalism in different shapes and forms, for example in the underpinning of far-right parties on the European continent, English Brexit, Trumpism in the United States, Xi Jinping's China and Putin's Russia. Characteristic is the link to populist images of 'the people' forming in 'their' national culture a *separate*, *homogeneous* and *essentialist* community with boundaries with other cultures clearly demarcated (Benessaieh, 2010, pp. 13–14).

The island metaphor captures that concept particularly well, because islands have clear boundaries (surrounded by water) and – if left untouched (think of Robinson Crusoe's island in Defoe's novel) – tend to develop their own fauna and flora, which links up to ideas of difference of the whole. From there, it is only a

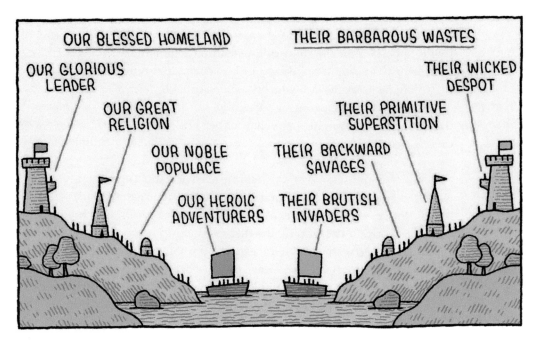

Figure 1.2 'Us vs. Them' by Tom Gauld

small step to assume that one's island will continue to develop in its own way, that is, remain fundamentally different from other islands, which connects to essentialist ideas (focusing on an imagined essence).

If such a simplistic island image is naively transferred to human cultures, we tend to end up with rigid oppositions (e.g. 'the Mexicans' as completely different to 'the Americans' in former US American president Donald Trump's tweets; see the discussion in Chapter 4), and from there it is only a small step to invent cultural hierarchies, because people tend to claim superiority for their 'own' culture. Evolutionary psychologists explain this rigid in-group thinking as 'tribalism' and link it to a stone-age mindset that modern humans have still not managed to overcome: 'We are genetically primed and culturally shaped to alert, defend, and aggress [...]. This extends to the protection of our way of life' (Hobbs, 2018, p. 1). This 'priming' can be explained by the sheer length of the era of tribal life of humans and their evolutionary ancestors, which was formed through several million years of close face-to-face contact in groups that did not usually exceed 75 individuals (Cosmides & Tooby, 1997; Keltner, 2009, p. 57; Clark & Winegard, 2020). Tom Gauld's caricature (Figure 1.2) illustrates the hierarchy and conflict-drive linked to monocultural 'priming', which was finally – in the last few thousand years – extended to much larger 'imagined communities' (Anderson, 1983) as, for example, kingdoms and nations. This cooperation between large numbers of strangers through fictional stories (Harari, 2015, p. 41) has cleared the way for large-scale wars and genocides.

Key for cultural 'island' thinking is a paradigm of assimilation and exclusion that does not accept a 'middle ground'. The German philosopher Johann Gottfried Herder (1744–1803) summarised this for the European nationalism of his time as follows: 'Everything which is still the same as my nature, which can be assimilated therein, I envy, strive towards, make my own; beyond this, kind nature has armed me with insensibility, coldness and blindness; it can even become contempt and disgust' (Herder, 1967, p. 45).

TASK

Have you, a member of your family or one of your friends, experienced cultural discrimination? If not, can you think of an example highlighted in the news, or a film that you have seen? Share your experiences with people sitting next to you. Which monocultural patterns can you identify?

That disgust connects to ideas of *national purity* based on the imagined threat of *contamination* through 'others', which is particularly characteristic for race ideologies in eighteenth- and nineteenth-century colonialism, and twentieth- and twenty-first-century fascism, but also racial segregation after World War II, for example in South Africa until the early 1990s, and contemporary racism (see Dave's song *Black* in 2020). Hobfoll highlights the common ground in this drive for separation and exclusion that accompanies the wide spectrum of 'contamination' stories when he starts his book about **tribalism** with a quote from Hitler on the dangerous nature of Jews and another from Trump on the dangerous nature of Mexican migrants (2018, p. 1), though the differences between these cases and their link to other forms of aggressive nationalism, including Putin's Russia, remain underexamined.

1.3 Coexistence Is Key: Island Images of Multiculturality Revisited

By stressing the need for *peaceful coexistence* of different cultures within a society, **traditional multicultural identity** constructs – as we would call them because they too draw on island images of cultures (see Rings, 2018, p. 9) – establish some distance from monocultural principles of cultural and racial purity. As such, they could be seen as reactions to racial discrimination in the context of mass post-WWII labour recruitment from abroad, for example in England, France and Germany in the 1950s and 1960s. This was a time when Enoch Powell gave his famous 'Rivers of blood' speech (1968) that declared the post-war recruitment of black men as 'madness', because 'in this country in 15 or 20 years' time the black man will have the whip hand over the white man' (ODN, 2018).

Multiculturalists fight these aggressive forms of racial exclusion, but their frequent insistence on clearly definable cultural borders, and the presentation of diaspora cultures from the Caribbean (in England), Algeria (in France) and Turkey (in Germany) as autonomous, self-sufficient and coherent, links back to an island concept of culture that is characteristic of monocultural constructs. Epstein describes the result as 'cocoonization of each culture within itself' (2009, p. 329), while Neubert et al. stress the visibility of cultural separation in communitarian left-wing multiculturalism (2013, pp. 16–17).

One example for that 'cocoonization' within traditional multiculturalism is the German radio station 'Multikulti', which was inaugurated in 1994 and provided broadcasts in Turkish, Spanish, Italian and other languages of people who had arrived as *Gastarbeiter* (guest workers) in Germany in the 1950s and 1960s and stayed. These broadcasts were originally made without any translation, and while they could be regarded as expressions of respect and welcome for migrants who had experienced discrimination, they do not show the focus on communication, exchange and integration that manage to cross and blur cultural boundaries and that could be regarded as key for life and work in the multi-ethnic communities and workplaces of the twenty-first century (for a discussion of 'dialogic communicative competence' as a way forward see Antor, 2020, pp. 78–80).

TASK

Describe another example from mass media or politics that focuses – like Radio Multikulti – on living next to each other, but does not fully support life together.

In contrast to Welsch (1999 and 2017), we would like to categorise this pattern of identity construction as 'traditional' or an 'island' form of multiculturality, rather than multiculturality per se. After all, a fast-growing number of scholars who regard themselves as multiculturalists (e.g. Neubert et al., 2013, quoted above) propose concepts of multiculturality that are more in line with the transcultural perspectives that will be discussed in Section 1.5 than with the concept outlined in this section.

1.4 Interaction Based on Difference: Island Images of Interculturality

Traditional intercultural identity perspectives promote interaction and exchange between people from different cultural backgrounds, but continue to draw on island concepts of cultures that characterise the monocultural and traditional multicultural constructs described in Sections 1.2 and 1.3 (Rings 2018, p. 10).

Only one example for the dissemination of traditional intercultural perspectives is Gudykunst's acclaimed study book *Bridging differences* (2004), which goes well beyond traditional multicultural work in that it focuses on exercises to improve dialogue in a multi-ethnic world. Like Schmidt's *In search of intercultural understanding* (2007), *Bridging differences* marginalises, however, cultural similarities and remains instead fixated on differences. As such, it continues to draw – like the traditional multicultural constructs discussed above – on images of cultures as largely autonomous, self-sufficient and coherent islands. For Huggan, such a focus on difference implies a 'back-door to cultural essentialism' (2006, p. 58) that highlights monocultural continuities.

Welsch regards all intercultural approaches as connected to separatist and homogeneous ideas and asks scholars to give up on the misleading concept of interculturality (1999, p. 2; 2017, p. 24). Yet this does not take into account that contemporary interculturalists tend to define their discipline with a much greater focus on 'cultural interdependence' (Delanoy, 2006, p. 239; Bolten, 2020). This includes an understanding of 'culture' that goes well beyond the national cultural or ethnic realm and instead highlights what people tend to have in common, such as 'global networks, multiple identities and a large number of cultural reference points' in people's 'micro-worlds' (Bolten, 2020, p. 64). Consequently, we prefer to categorise the concept outlined in this section as 'traditional' or an 'island' form of interculturality, while the now dominant trend in intercultural research leads us into Section 1.5.

TASK

Describe an exercise, strategy or policy that aims to increase the interaction of people with different cultural backgrounds, but does not convincingly consider common ground and overlap between these backgrounds.

1.5 Leaving that Island: Transcultural Push and Interculturality Today

Transcultural identity constructs focus on the interconnectedness of our increasingly global environment. Key is the idea that all cultures overlap in some respects, which means there is always some common ground that can support interactions, cultural exchange and the negotiation of meaning and identity constructs.

That common ground may appear different in size, depending on the cultures in question (in line with territorial distance and historical developments, some are closer than others) and context (e.g. periods are shaped by conflict). However, its existence (even in most adverse contexts) highlights that cultural boundaries are blurred, which opens up a 'Third Space' as 'in-between space' (Bhabha, 2004, p. 56) in which cultural identities can be negotiated. Transcultural debates can build on well-established ideas of hybrid cultures (Bhabha, 2004; García Canclini, 1990), but they tend to concentrate more on questions of agency and often remain more process-oriented than discussions of hybrid cultures. All this breaks with the monocultural paradigm of assimilation and exclusion, and it goes well beyond monocultural continuities in traditional multicultural and traditional intercultural island concepts.

Excellent examples for transcultural dialogue and exchange resulting in hybridity can be found in food culture. In a well-stocked supermarket or through online shopping you might be able to pick what you like to mix for lunch or dinner: perhaps Italian pasta, aubergines imported from Spain, Indian Madras curry powder, local fresh tomatoes and tomato ketchup from a US company to make your favourite spaghetti? Or better Japanese yasai katsu curry with Korean kimchi and Chinese noodles? In most cases, we are not even aware of the cultural origin of the different ingredients or entire dishes anymore. We simply pick and mix what we think might taste nice (or what is left in the fridge), and in this way we often create something new. This highlights how we blur cultural boundaries in food culture, sometimes on a daily basis, and can serve as an example of more transcultural agency in a global world.

Musicians tend to do the same if they want to develop their own music: Shakira, herself a Colombian singer with Lebanese grandparents and a father born in the United States, became one of the world's best-selling musicians with songs that mix – as she highlights for her album *Shakira* (2014) – 'a little bit of rock, a little bit of folk, a little reggae' (Vena, 2014). Similarly, the Turkish musicians interviewed in Akın's documentary *Crossing the bridge* declare their music as a mix of different styles, especially 'traditional Turkish' music and 'Western pop' to create something new (2005). This new style tends to be the result of ongoing explorations and negotiations and as such is never complete. In principle, it cannot culminate in a harmonious entity because it is never free of tensions, but it blurs traditional boundaries when joining different cultural elements within a shared cultural framework. Both Shakira and the Turkish musicians remind us that transcultural agency depends on the ability to understand culture as a highly dynamic, interconnected and transitory 'relational web' (Benessaieh, 2010, p. 11).

TASK

Write down the names of three of your favourite musicians. Which music do they produce and to what extent can that music be linked to one or more cultures?

Contemporary **intercultural identity** concepts tend to build on that 'interlocking interdependence of cultures in the age of globalization' (Antor, 2010, p. 12). This is enhanced through social networking, virtual communication by Skype, Teams or Zoom, and research by internet with e-publications potentially reaching a far wider readership than most hardbacks and paperbacks. One recent example is the Black Lives Matter movement, which fights racism worldwide on the basis of elaborated social networks, within which people of all nationalities and skin colours tend to organise a wide spectrum of activities, from online petitions to mass protests on US streets (see also Chapter 4). In a context in which cultures are understood as 'interlinked networks', even transculturalist Welsch now admits that the difference between interculturality and transculturality is at best gradual (2017, p. 27). Antor highlights that this is due to 'theorists of transcultural competence establishing not a counter-position to that of interculturalists, but stressing to a lesser degree the concept of difference and emphasizing what links and unites us within the global networks that characterize the world today' (2020, p. 136).

1.6 In Summary

Some scholars simply assume that we can expect a development from monoculturality to transculturality in the context of enhanced globalisation (see Welsch, 1999). However, given the rise of populist ultranationalism in recent decades, it is by no means self-evident that this will follow.

History shows that open cultures can close down in a relatively short time span and vice versa, and all this tends to be connected with questions of power. Monocultural tribal politics brought Hitler and his supporters to dictatorial power, but they are also key to understanding the advance of far-right parties on the European continent today, Trumpism in the US and the UK's Brexit. Furthermore, they helped Xi Jinping in the recent past remove the two-term limit on his presidency, which allows him to remain in power for life. Even more recently, Vladimir Putin managed to break the constitutional limits for the Russian presidency and his invasion of the Ukraine was driven by an assimilationist policy and an essentialist notion of Russian identity, both of which are characteristic of monocultural tribal aggression. On the other hand, representatives of traditional multicultural, traditional intercultural and transcultural societies are also likely to have individual and/or collective power-related agendas.

Consequently, rather than imagine cultural boundaries as 'natural' or 'rational', we have to question the reasons behind the push for particular cultural identity constructs, decide which construct we would like to support and act upon it. After all, if culture is learned, we can help shape the learning process, be it in the classroom, seminar or workplace, through TED talks, websites, blogs or numerous other means. And for such a critical intervention there is no time to waste. If, for example, we prefer intercultural societies to a monocultural world, then we better start work on becoming influencers now.

DISCUSSION QUESTIONS

Write a short text for an intercultural blog about the portrayal of an ethnic minority in your country. How is this minority being presented by representatives of different political parties, churches and/or in the mass media? Do you see monocultural, traditional multicultural, traditional intercultural and/or transcultural/contemporary intercultural perspectives here?

CASE STUDY

Please analyse the following excerpt from an article by three-times Pulitzer Prize winning journalist Thomas Friedman. How does he present Arabs, and which cultural identity perspective does that portrayal reflect?

> The profound differences between the West and the Arab world can be highlighted by looking at the symbols that represent each. The symbol of the West is the cross – full of sharp right angles that begin and end. But the symbol of the Arab East is the crescent moon – a wide ambiguous arc, where there are curves, but no corners. What Westerners fail to understand is that Arabs just don't think like we do: whereas we are rational and say what we really mean, for Arabs things are often not what they seem; they say one thing but mean and do another. In the Middle East truth and reality are always relative, even dreamlike, just like the desert landscape. Unfortunately, the U.S. lack enough trained and experienced Foreign Service and intelligence personnel who really understand how the Arabs think.

(Friedman, 1990)

References

Akın, F. (2005). *Crossing the bridge: The sound of Istanbul.* Germany: Corazón International/Intervista Digital Media/NDR.

Anderson, B. (1983). *Imagined communities: Reflections on the origin and spread of nationalism.* London: Verso.

Antor, H. (2010). From postcolonialism and interculturalism to the ethics of transculturalism in the age of globalization. In H. Antor, M. Merkl, K. Stierstorfer, & L. Volkmann (eds.), *From interculturalism to transculturalism: Mediating encounters in cosmopolitan contexts* (pp. 1–14). Heidelberg: Universitätsverlag Winter.

Antor, H. (2020). Interculturality or transculturality? In G. Rings & S. M. Rasinger (eds.), *The Cambridge handbook of intercultural communication* (pp. 68–82). Cambridge: Cambridge University Press.

Benessaieh, A. (2010). Multiculturalism, interculturality, transculturality. In A. Benessaieh (ed.), *Transcultural Americas/Amériques transculturelles* (pp. 11–38). Ottawa: Ottawa University Press.

Bhabha, H. K. (2004 [1994]). *The location of culture.* Abingdon: Routledge.

Bolten, J. (2020). Rethinking intercultural competence. In G. Rings & S. M. Rasinger (eds.), *The Cambridge handbook of intercultural communication* (pp. 56–67). Cambridge: Cambridge University Press.

Byron, R. (2002). Identity. In A. Barnard & J. Spencer (eds.), *Encyclopedia of social and cultural anthropology* (p. 292). Abingdon: Routledge.

Clark, C. J., & Winegard, B. M. (2020). Tribalism in war and peace: The nature and evolution of ideological epistemology and its significance for modern social science. *Psychological Inquiry,* 31(1), 1–22.

Cosmides, L., & Tooby, J. (1997). Evolutionary psychology: A primer. Center for Evolutionary Psychology. Online. www.cep.ucsb.edu/primer.html (last accessed 7 April 2022).

Dave, S. (2020). Black. BRIT Awards 2020. Online. www.youtube.com/watch?v=mXLS2IzZSdg (last accessed 20 April 2022).

Delanoy, W. (2006). Transculturalism and (inter-)cultural learning in the EFL classroom. In W. Delanoy & L. Volkmann (eds.), *Cultural studies in the EFL classroom* (pp. 233–248). Heidelberg: Winter.

Delanoy, W. (2012). From 'inter' to 'trans'? Or: Quo vadis cultural learning? In M. Eisenmann & T. Summer (eds.), *Basic issues in EFL teaching and learning* (pp. 157–167), Heidelberg: Winter.

Delanoy, W. (2020). What is culture? In G. Rings & S. M. Rasinger (eds.), *The Cambridge handbook of intercultural communication* (pp. 17–34). Cambridge: Cambridge University Press.

Epstein, M. (2009). Transculture: A broad way between globalisation and multiculturalism. *American Journal of Economics and Sociology*, 68(1), 327–351.

Eriksen, T. H. (1993). In which sense do cultural islands exist? *Social Anthropology*, 1(1B), 133–147.

Ferraro, G. P. (2010). *The cultural dimension of international business* (6th edition). Upper Saddle River, NJ: Prentice Hall.

Friedman, T. (1990). A dreamlike landscape, a dreamlike reality. *The New York Times.* 28 October. https://nyti.ms/3ra0cQG (last accessed 7 April 2022).

García Canclini, N. (1990). *Culturas híbridas: Estrategias para entrar y salir de la modernidad*, Mexico City: Grijalbo.

Gottschall, J. (2012). *The storytelling animal. How stories make us human.* Boston and New York: Houghton Mifflin Harcourt.

Griffin, R. (2008). *A fascist century.* London: Palgrave Macmillan.

Gudykunst, W. B. (2004). *Bridging differences: Effective intergroup communication* (4th edition). London: Sage.

Harari, Y. N. (2015). *Sapiens: A brief history of humankind.* London: Penguin.

Herder, J. G. (1967 [1774]). *Auch eine Philosophie der Geschichte zur Bildung der Menschheit.* Frankfurt am Main: Suhrkamp.

Hobfoll, S. E. (2018). *Tribalism: The evolutionary origins of fear politics.* London: Palgrave Macmillan.

Hofstede Insights (2020). What do we mean by culture? Online. https://news.hofstede-insights.com/news/what-do-we-mean-by-culture (last accessed 7 April 2022).

Hofstede, G., Hofstede, G. J. & Minkov, M. (2010). *Cultures and organizations: Software of the mind* (3rd edition). New York: McGraw Hill.

Huggan, G. (2006). Derailing the 'trans'? Postcolonial studies and the negative effects of speed. In H. Antor (ed.), *Inter- und Transkulturelle Studien: Theoretische Grundlagen und interdisziplinäre Praxis* (pp. 55–61). Heidelberg: Winter.

Jackson, J. (2014). *Introducing language and intercultural communication.* New York: Routledge.

Jandt, F. E. (2010). *An introduction to intercultural communication: Identities in a global community* (6th edition). Los Angeles: SAGE.

Keltner, D. (2009). *Born to be good: The science of a meaningful life.* New York: Norton.

Marsh, H. W., Lüdtke, O., Muthén, B. O., Asparouhov, T., Morin, A. J. S., Trautwein, U., & Nagengast, B. (2010). A new look at the big-five factor structure through exploratory structural equation modelling. *Psychological Assessment*, 22, 471–491.

Matejovsky, S. (2011). Understanding culture and managing culture awareness: A paradox. *La Revue Géopolitique*. 18 March. www.diploweb.com/Understanding-culture-and-managing.html (last accessed 7 April 2022).

Moses, D. & M. Rothberg (2014). A dialogue on the ethics and politics of transcultural memory. In L. Bond (ed.), *The transcultural turn: Interrogating memory between and beyond borders* (pp. 29–38). Berlin: De Gruyter.

Nakayama, T. K. (2020). Critical intercultural communication and the digital environment. In G. Rings & S. M. Rasinger (eds.), *The Cambridge handbook of intercultural communication* (pp. 85–95). Cambridge: Cambridge University Press.

Neubert, S., Roth, H.-J., & Yildiz, E. (2013). Multikulturalismus: – ein umstrittenes Konzept. In S. Neubert, H.-J. Roth & E. Yildiz (eds.), *Multikulturalität in der Diskussion: Neuere Beiträge zu einem umstrittenen Konzept* (pp. 9–29). Wiesbaden: Springer.

Norton, B. (2013). *Identity and language learning: Extending the conversation* (2nd edition). Bristol: Multilingual Matters.

ODN (On Demand News) (2018). Enoch Powell's 'rivers of blood' speech: 50 years on. Online. www.youtube.com/watch?v=qjbZi2hTLVw (last accessed 7 April 2022).

Omoniyi, T. (2006). Hierarchy of identities. In T. Omoniyi & G. White (eds.), *Sociolinguistics of identity* (pp. 11–33). London: Continuum.

Rings, G. (2018). *The other in contemporary migrant cinema: Imagining a new Europe?* New York: Routledge.

Schmidt, P. (2007). *In search of intercultural understanding: A practical guidebook for living and working across cultures*. Montreal: Meridian.

Shakira (2014). *Shakira*. Nashville: RCA Records.

Spencer-Oatey, H. (2004). *Culturally speaking: Managing rapport through talk across cultures*. London: Continuum.

Van Assche, J., Dhont, K. & Pettigrew, T. F. (2019). The social-psychological bases of far-right support in Europe and the United States. *Journal of Community & Applied Social Psychology*, 29(5), 385–401.

Vena, J. (2014). Shakira's new album title sounds familiar. MTV News. 22 January. Online. www.mtv.com/news/1720866/shakira-new-album-announcement

Welsch, W. (1999). Transculturality: The puzzling form of cultures today. In M. Featherstone & S. Lash (eds.), *Spaces of culture: City, nation, world*, pp. 194–213. London: Sage.

Welsch, W. (2017). *Transkulturalität: Realität – Geschichte – Aufgabe*. Wien: New Academic Press.

Williams, R. (1985). *Keywords: A vocabulary of culture and society*. London: Fontana.

2 What Is Intercultural Communication?

Drawing on key features of culture discussed in Chapter 1, we would now like to establish a working definition of intercultural communication. We will then give a brief historical outline of key contributions to the field and outline their links to power hierarchies.

AIMS

By the end of this chapter, you should be able to:

1. **define intercultural communication;**
2. **distinguish between key contributions to the field;**
3. **explain the extent to which these contributions are connected to questions of power.**

> **KEY TERMS**
> intercultural communication – mediation – integrative intercultural communication

2.1 Defining Intercultural Communication

2.1.1 Starting from Popular Definitions

In Section 1.5, we stressed that contemporary notions of interculturality focus on cultural *interaction*, *exchange* and the *negotiation of meaning* in the context of interconnected and dynamic identity constructs. Working definitions of intercultural communication should therefore cover all these aspects. However, unfortunately, the most popular definitions stop at the level of interaction. One example is Jandt's *Introduction to intercultural communication*, which even in its sixth edition continues to summarise the concept as referring to 'face-to-face interactions of people from different cultural backgrounds' (Jandt, 2010, p. 45).

In many aspects more convincing is Jackson's definition of intercultural communication as 'interpersonal communication between individuals or groups who are affiliated with different cultural groups and/or have been socialised in different cultural [...] environments' (Jackson, 2014, p. 3). In particular, there is no attempt to limit intercultural communication to 'face-to-face' interactions in a world shaped by Skype, Zoom, Microsoft Teams and numerous other online communication tools. Such a limitation is now clearly unacceptable given the fact that online forms of intercultural communication are thanks to these tools quickly increasing in popularity and have often become the preferred means of communication. After all, online communication helps to reduce travel costs, saves valuable time and avoids the risk of infection, for example in the recent coronavirus pandemic. Also, by highlighting that cultural differences may relate to questions of 'age, class, gender, ethnicity, language, race, nationality and physical/mental ability', Jackson (2014, p. 3) breaks convincingly with the rigid binary construct of *inter*culturality versus *intra*culturality (see Section 1.1).

That binary is further questioned by **critical intercultural communication** research, which suggests interrogating 'the ways in which structures and contexts of power impact our lives and experiences, including the taken-for-granted shapers of intercultural relations: the media, government, economy, history, global markets, and popular culture' (Halualani, 2014). While we will return to the latter towards the end of Chapter 3, it is worth summarising that the focus in most introductions to intercultural communication, including Jandt (2010) and Jackson (2014), remains on interaction, which marginalises cultural exchange and the negotiation of meaning within power contexts. We will therefore offer our own working definition towards the end of this chapter.

TASKS

– From what you have heard so far, how would you define intercultural communication?

– Think of examples that could help us understand the concept and compare these with the illustration of intercultural communication in Figure 2.1.

2.1.2   Intercultural Communication as Mediation

Rehbein is one of the scholars who goes the extra mile, when he defines intercultural communication as 'the mediation of cultural differences between social groups through verbal or nonverbal interaction' and amends that 'this kind of bridgeover requires specific techniques necessary for creating the participants'

Figure 2.1 *Intercultural Communication* by Alíz Kovács-Zöldi

mutual understanding' (Rehbein, 2013, p. 2758). He builds here on his detailed discussion of the 'emergence of the cultural apparatus', within which a process of 'reflection' facilitates the emergence of new action practices, thought patterns and forms of imagining that ultimately modifies previously acquired presuppositions and action systems (Rehbein, 2006, p. 73). However, research that examines contemporary migrant cinema as a 'laboratory' for intercultural communication suggests that a similar impact might be achieved by 'affect' or by a combination of 'affect' and 'reflection', in which for example the former triggers new behaviour and the latter helps to understand and implement it more permanently (Rings, 2018, pp. 86–91; 2020).

In an exploration of intercultural communication as mediation, Ten Thije (2020) draws directly on Rehbein's ideas. There is evidence for a wider shift towards aspects of exchange and negotiation of meaning that could be summarised as intercultural mediation, although sometimes affiliated concepts are being used. For example, Chikudate was already discussing the role of 'cultural interpreters' for adaptation in Japanese–European business environments in the 1990s (Chikudate, 1995), Yu et al. (2002) highlight the importance of 'intercultural mediation' for the work of Chinese tour guides, and Gültekin argues for a significant shift towards mediation in education from elementary schools to universities so that students can become intercultural 'negotiators' (Gültekin, 2012).

In line with our argument to consider common ground as much as differences in intercultural communication (Section 1.4), we follow McConachy & Liddicoat (2016), who suggest that participants should compare cultural frames and aim for common ground in their negotiation of differences. They call this process 'mediation' and define it as:

> constituted by a process where the individual makes a conscious effort to consider the cultural frames that shape interpretation of pragmatic acts in each language, how these differ across languages, and what the consequences of these differences are for the use of these languages in intercultural communication.
>
> (McConachy & Liddicoat, 2016, p. 17)

Ten Thije adds that such remarks on mediation are valid for coping with cultural diversity in general, and highlights that mediation does not have to lead to an inclusive understanding: 'Interlocutors can also agree to disagree since power relations determine their asymmetric interaction which may end up in exclusion' (Ten Thije, 2020, p. 39). However, the negotiation of meaning should always include a critical interrogation of own social norms and identity constructs, which might help to prepare the ground for mutual understanding and a potential compromise. Not by coincidence, Martin and Nakayama highlight in the first chapter of *Intercultural communication in contexts* the importance of intercultural communication for the development of self-awareness, skills for the management of increasing diversity and, ultimately, peaceful coexistence (Martin & Nakayama, 2010, pp. 3–43). Similarly, Hua ends *Exploring intercultural communication* with a chapter on self-awareness in the context of conflicting identity construction and summarises intercultural communication as 'concerned with how individuals [...] negotiate cultural or linguistic difference' (Hua, 2014: 200).

TASKS

Think of encounters that you had with people from other cultures – be it in person, through emails, over the phone or in social networks: In which cases was mediation involved? What exactly was mediated and what was the result?

2.1.3   Encounters with and without Intercultural Communication

As an example of cultural exchange based on reflection, Rehbein discusses the royalty negotiation between an American author and a German publisher's representative (Rehbein, 2006, pp. 53–59). While the American author – Mrs S. – starts from an American publishing convention and insists on royalties being paid from the first copy sold, the agent – Mr P. – starts from the standard German publishers' convention that requires sales to cover some (or all) of the publisher's expenses first before any royalties are paid. In the course of the conversation, the publisher's agent takes on both roles and predominantly through an inner dialogue negotiates the basis for a royalty agreement that is ultimately very much in line with the American standard. In this context, the publisher's representative appears as intercultural mediator who questions and finally revises cultural presuppositions to secure the contract, and it is this negotiation of meaning that allows us to examine this interaction as intercultural communication.

Understood in this sense, as cultural exchange and negotiation of meaning, intercultural communication *does not cover all of the forms of communication in which members of different cultures happen to be involved*. However, in line with the different cultural identity constructs explored in Chapter 1, it seems important to limit its use in that way. Taken within a monocultural colonial context of the 1940s, for example a simple order from a Japanese official to his Korean servant to bring him tea, and the Korean servant's prompt preparation and delivery of the tea would qualify as an interaction between people from different cultural backgrounds, but categorising it as intercultural communication would be misleading because there is no negotiation of meaning. Instead of a cultural exchange based on reflection, we are dealing predominantly with a response by the Korean servant to the stimulus (order) by the Japanese official. All this is framed by a rigid power hierarchy (e.g. Japanese = coloniser and employer, Korean = colonised and employee), which enhances assimilation of the Korean to the Japanese environment. At the same time, the Japanese official has a wide range of sanctions and punishments at his disposal if orders are not satisfactorily fulfilled.

Finally, the clash of different social groups in the following example provided by Gumperz shows interaction that could be examined as a consequence of traditional multicultural coexistence, but not convincingly as an intercultural encounter. It describes the tension between a black graduate student, who was – after initial phone contact – asked to interview a black housewife in a poor neighbourhood, and the housewife's husband, who answers the door:

> HUSBAND: So y're gonna check out ma ol lady, hah?
> INTERVIEWER: Ah, no. I only came to get some information. They called from the office.
> (Husband, dropping his smile, disappears without a word and calls his wife.)
> (Gumperz, 1982, p. 133)

Rehbein discusses this encounter as an example of a gap between two social groups with different assumptions and actions systems, all of which remain in this situation without reflection and/or mediation, and that tends to enhance rather than reduce cultural boundaries: 'If cultural action is suppressed [...], because there is no restructuring of the mental processes involved, the cultural load [...] leads to a process of reifying which insulates the action systems even more strongly against reflection' (Rehbein, 2013, p. 2763). More focus on coexistence is likely to be a consequence of such encounters, although the interview might be a chance to question some mediation boundaries.

TASK

How do your personal examples of mediation in cultural encounters (see the previous task) compare to these examples? Which mediation boundaries did you come across?

2.1.4 In Summary

In this context, we would like to define intercultural communication as:

> mediation aimed at creating mutual understanding between individuals or groups of different cultural backgrounds. That mediation includes exchange and negotiation of common ground and differences with particular focus on the cultural frames that shape interpretations of verbal and non-verbal behaviour as well as the results of that behaviour, e.g. particular norms, beliefs, products, systems and institutions.

The mediator, who might be a participant or a third person, has to consider that these frames could be shaped by numerous factors, including nationality, ethnicity, race and language, which have so far been the focus of research, but also class, age, gender, physical or mental abilities and – above all – powerful societal forces, which deserve more attention.

2.2 Contributions from Different Disciplines around the Globe

2.2.1 Intercultural Communication in Academia

While there have been well before the twentieth century numerous individual studies on cultural similarities, differences and ways to overcome such differences, there is agreement that wider, systematic and academic research of intercultural communication developed after World War II (Jackson, 2014, p. 30, Martin & Nakayama, 2010, p. 46). Key is the work of the Foreign Service Institute (FSI), which was founded in 1947 to enhance the intercultural communication skills of US diplomats and government officers sent to develop US relations abroad. One of the institute's educators was Edward T. Hall (1914–2009), an anthropologist who became famous for publications like *The silent language* (1959), *The hidden dimension* (1966) and *Beyond culture* (1976). In *The silent language*, Hall develops key ideas regarding the impact of culture on everyday behaviour, which includes observations of different time concepts, e.g. sequential and synchronous notions of time that are still key for intercultural training today. More long-term impact comes through his detailed observation of social distancing rules in *The hidden dimension* and differences between low and high context cultures in *Beyond culture*. Such essayistic work, in which he also draws on the study of animal behaviour, linguistics and psychoanalytic theory, led to his consideration as a founder of intercultural communication with *The silent language* being proposed as a 'founding document' (Rogers et al., 2002, p. 3, 1; see Chapter 10 for more on Hall's work).

Inspired by the impact of the Foreign Service Institute and then Hall's work, the Japan Center for Intercultural Communications (JCIC) was founded in 1953. Of particular interest is the work of Japanese linguists Mitsuko Saito and Masao Kunihiro, who translated Hall's *The silent language* into Japanese. Even Kitao & Kitao's volume *Intercultural communication: Between Japan and the United States* (1989) draws still very much on Hall's work. However, beyond the USA and Japan, there was until the late 1970s relatively little systematic and specific academic research in intercultural communication beyond individual scholars' work (see Martin et al., 2020).

TASK

In his classic *The hidden dimension*, Hall starts his chapter on 'The Arab World' with the statement: 'In spite of over thousand years of contact, Westerners and Arabs still do not understand each other' (1966: 154). If you had to write an essay about people with an Arab cultural background, would you start it like that? If yes, why? If not, why not – and how would you start instead?

2.2.2 Intercultural Business Communication

Intercultural communication shifted in the following decades more towards applications for international business relations, for example through the work of social psychologist Geert Hofstede (1928–2020) and management consultants Fons Trompenaars (born 1953) and Charles Hampden-Turner (born 1934). Hofstede's *Culture's consequence* (2001; first published in 1980) achieved particular impact and laid the foundations for his six-dimensional model, which is still being used widely in intercultural training. Unlike most other applications, key definitions and country scores of the 6D model can still be accessed for free through the Hofstede Insights webpage (www.hofstede-insights.com). Trompenaars and Hampden-Turner countered with a seven-dimensional model in *Riding the waves of culture* (1997) (see Chapter 6), though this is not available as free open access material.

Hofstede, Trompenaars and Hampden-Turner's studies compare – like Hall – cultural values in different cultures and are therefore often summarised as cross-cultural or contrastive research. Despite the frequently polemical debate between representatives from both sides, the GLOBE leadership study founded by Robert J. House in 1991 (GLOBE, 2020) managed to bring key ideas from the two models together, but never achieved comparable impact. In Japan, Hofstede gained significant popularity in the 90s, and cross-cultural research with business focus was advanced by Ito (1992, 2000) and Yoshino (1992). In the same period, intercultural communication research gained popularity in China, e.g. through the foundation of the China Association for Intercultural Communication (CAFIC) in 1995, the development of intercultural studies courses in several universities and the work of CAFIC co-founder Hu (1994; Hu & Grove, 1999). Hofstede's dimensions became very popular in this context and there have been different attempts at updating his country scores, for example by Zhang and Wu (2014). Comparable business studies applications can be found on all other continents, including Australia (Leo et al., 2005) and Africa (e.g. Schutte, 2009). In addition, applied intercultural communication research developed particularly in education, national health services and legal systems, to name just a few areas shaped by growing multi-ethnicity.

TASK

Readers tend to find lists of things to do and not to do in a foreign culture, especially in older introductions to international business, e.g. bowing instead of hand-shaking in greetings.

Why can we not limit intercultural communication training to the development and dissemination of such lists? What are the possibilities and limits of those lists?

2.2.3   From Multi-disciplinarity to Interdisciplinarity

Since the early years of intercultural communication research, the field has overall become more multidisciplinary, but unfortunately not always more interdisciplinary, hence Salo-Lee's recent request to embark on a reorientation towards *integrative intercultural communication* (Salo-Lee, 2020). The disciplines that have been encouraged to overcome disciplinary boundaries and work closer together to achieve common intercultural aims are especially those that shaped the first decades of intercultural studies, that is, anthropology, linguistics, business studies, psychology and sociology (see Chapters 6, 9, 10 and 11). However, we argue that such a reorientation should also include contributions to the further development of the field, which come these days also from literature, film studies, law, media and communication, gender studies and postcolonial studies (see Chapters 4, 5, 8, 14, and 17), with the last three disciplines providing particular support for the advance of *critical intercultural communication*. Examples for this focus in research are studies from Martin & Nakayama (1999) and Nakayama & Halualani (2012) in the United States, as well as Byram (1997), Scollon & Scollon (2007) and Rings (2010, 2018) in Europe. It discusses questions of power in cultural encounters that have been marginalised in the push towards immediate diplomatic and/or business and management related applications.

TASKS FOR GROUP WORK

Discuss examples of cultural encounters in which social, economic, political or military power

matters. Why should we examine the impact of that power?

Similar developments can be observed in other parts of the globe, e.g. by Ishii (2004) and Miike (2007) who both argue for critical distance from US-centrism and Eurocentrism in intercultural research and propose alternatives. In New Zealand, there is path-breaking Māori research that questions Western notions of knowledge and culture (Walker et al., 2006), while South Africa continues to lead critical intercultural communication on the African continent, for example through the South African Communications Association (SACOMM). In the Middle East, large scale intercultural communication teaching and research have only recently advanced through the introduction of specialised studies in higher education institutions like Cairo University, King Saud University and Qatar University (Alkharusi, 2018, p. 1162). While these study programmes tend to focus on applications for future employment, they also raise comprehensive awareness of discrimination against Arabs in Western countries, which is likely to enhance critical intercultural communication research (Alkharusi, 2018, 1163). Important individual contributions to the field could also already be found in the 1990s, including studies that question the homogeneous, essentialist and above all separatist tendencies in Hall's and Hofstede's discussion of 'the Arab world' (e.g. Feghali, 1997; Ayish, 1998). Finally, there is active interest in interculturality in Latin America, promoted for example by the journal *Cultura Latinoamericana: Revista de Estudios Interculturales*. However, most research with a focus on power relations can still be found in related disciplines, above all anthropology (e.g. García Canclini, 1995, 2001, 2014), philosophy and postcolonial studies (Dussel, 1994, 2013; De Toro, 1997, 2013, 2019).

2.2.4 In Summary

The reflective dimension involved in intercultural mediation is key for intercultural communication, because there is a need to consider – before, during and/ or after the exchange – 'how different power structures and interests have framed conversations across groups in ways that benefit those very interests' (Halualani, 2014). The challenge is then 'how to reshape a dialogue so that greater understanding and connection can occur across those involved and impacted' (2014). While this might be obvious for the mediation of Palestine–Israeli or US–Russian encounters in international politics for example, it is worth considering for all encounters, including everyday contact between employees and employers/ line managers, doctors and patients, teachers and students as well as men and women, especially in the military, police and other professions in which women tend to be heavily underrepresented. Intercultural communication research itself has to be questioned in this context as well, especially when it serves to enhance the success of diplomats or business people from one side of the negotiating table. The good news is that there is already significant research on issues of power in related fields, which can help to raise intercultural mediators' awareness, for example in postcolonial and decolonial studies (Dussel, 2013, de Toro &

Tauchnitz, 2019, Mignolo, 2002, 2011), precariat research (Standing, 2011, 2016) and studies on the impact of power in humanitarian aid (Smirl 2015).

2.3 In Summary

Simply labelling all forms of interpersonal interaction between members of different cultural backgrounds as 'intercultural communication' would mean a gross over-generalisation of the concept, which breaks with key ideas in intercultural studies and marginalises or even suppresses the impact of a wide range of contextual factors. Therefore, we suggest applying the concept only to situations of *mediation aimed at creating mutual understanding between individuals or groups of different cultural backgrounds*.

That mediation should include *exchange and negotiation of common ground and differences* with a focus on the cultural frames that shape interpretations of behaviour and the results of that behaviour, for example particular norms and beliefs. The mediator, who might be a participant or a third person, has to consider that these frames could be shaped by numerous factors. Intercultural communication research has so far focused predominantly on the importance of nationality, ethnicity, race and language.

However, we have made the point that – next to class, age, gender and abilities – *power structures and interests deserve particular attention*, which leads us to join critical intercultural communication scholars like Martin, Nakayama and Halualani. All this links up directly to our discussion of the link between individual and collective power interests and particular identity constructs in Chapter 1, starting with monocultural, that is homogeneous, essentialist and separatist notions of nationalism, which are shaped by populist ultranationalists worldwide. Reducing intercultural research in such a context to questions of misunderstandings related to different cultural values or verbal and non-verbal behavioural norms would be misleading.

DISCUSSION QUESTIONS

Team up with another participant in your course who has a different cultural background – ideally a background that you have some knowledge of, and then address the following tasks:

1. Independently from each other, write down key differences and similarities between your own and the other person's culture that spring to mind (e.g. very individualist/collective, conservative/open, affective/neutral ...).
2. Exchange documents and discuss which points you can agree on and which you do not. Try to explain the reasons for agreements and disagreements with precise examples.
3. Prepare a short presentation for the rest of the course, in which you summarise with examples the agreed points and remaining disagreements regarding both cultures. How far were you able to agree on these points?

CASE STUDY – ROLE PLAY FOR YOU, 'ADVIK' AND 'JOHN'

As coordinator of a team of international software developers based in Jerusalem, you have been asked to mediate in a conflict within your company, a globally operating US American publishing house.

Background: Both your manager and Human Resources have received requests from your best software developers in India, China and the US to take holidays over important festivals for them, that is, Diwali, Chinese New Year and Christmas. In exchange, they offered to work during festivals that they do not celebrate. However, software development is done in international teamwork, so to work effectively, they always need colleagues to be present in the other national headquarters.

Conflict: Indian (Hindu) developer Advik would like to work over Christmas if he can take his holiday for Diwali. However, for this, he would need support from John in the US, who is determined to have his holiday over Christmas.

Your job: In your meeting with Advik and John, try to be supportive, because you want to keep both developers happy. However, you cannot offer more than the contractually provided holidays, and you have been advised that the agreement you reach might be considered as setting a precedent for other employees in similar situations, i.e., it must be sustainable for Hindu, Christian, Confucian, Buddhist and Jewish employees.

References

Alkharusi, M. J. (2018). Intercultural communication study in the Middle East. In Y. Y. Kim & K. McKay-Semmler (eds.), *The international encyclopedia of intercultural communication* (pp. 1156–1164). Volume 2. Chichester: Wiley-Blackwell.

Ayish, M. I. (1998). Communication research in the Arab world: A new perspective. *The Public*, 15, 33–57.

Byram, M. (1997): *Teaching and assessing intercultural communicative competence*. Clevedon: Multilingual Matters.

Chikudate N. (1995). Communication network liaisons as cultural interpreters for organizational adaptation in Japan–Europe business environments. *Management International Review*, 35(2), 27–38.

de Toro, A. (1997). *Postmodernidad y postcolonialidad: Breves reflexiones sobre la cultura latinoaméricana*. Frankfurt am Main: Vervuert.

de Toro, A. (ed.) (2013). *Translatio: Transmédialité et transculturalité en littérature, peinture, photographie et au cinema: Amériques – Europe – Maghreb*. Paris: L'Harmattan.

de Toro, A. & Tauchnitz, J. (eds.) (2019). *The world in movement: Performative identities and diasporas*. Leiden: Brill.

Dussel, E. (1994). *1492: El encubrimiento del Otro: Hacia el origen del 'mito de la Modernidad'*. La Paz: Plural.

Dussel, E. (2013). *Ethics of liberation: In the age of globalization and exclusion.* Durham, NC: Duke University Press.

Feghali, E. (1997). Arab cultural communication patterns. *International Journal of Intercultural Relations*, 21, 345–378.

García Canclini, N. (1995). *Hybrid cultures: Strategies for entering and leaving modernity.* Translated by Christopher L. Chiappari and Silvia L. Lopez. Minneapolis: University of Minnesota Press.

García Canclini, N. (2001). *Consumers and citizens: Globalization and multicultural conflicts.* Translated by George Yúdice. Minneapolis: University of Minnesota Press.

García Canclini, N. (2014). *Imagined globalization.* Durham, NC: Duke University Press.

GLOBE (2020). An overview of the 2004 study: Understanding the relationship between national culture, societal effectiveness and desirable leadership attributes. Online. https://globeproject.com/study_2004_2007 (last accessed 17 April 2022).

Green, E. (2016). What are the most-cited publications in the social sciences (according to Google Scholar)? *LSE Impact Blog.* 12 May. Online. https://bit.ly/3vgYs9G (last accessed 15 April 2022).

Gültekin, B. (2012). Dialog and mediation education in intercultural communication. *Procedia – Social and Behavioral Sciences*, 55, 1124–1133.

Gumperz, J. (1982). *Discourse strategies.* Cambridge: Cambridge University Press.

Hall, E. T. (1959). *The silent language.* New York: Doubleday.

Hall, E. T. (1966). *The hidden dimension.* New York: Doubleday.

Hall, E. T. (1976). *Beyond culture.* New York: Doubleday.

Halualani, R. T. (2014). Critical intercultural communication. *Key Concepts in Intercultural Dialogue*, 30. Online. https://bit.ly/36j0PjK (last accessed 15 April 2022).

Hofstede, G. (2001). *Culture's consequences* (2nd edition). London: SAGE.

Hofstede, G., Hofstede, G. J. & Minkov, M. (2010). *Cultures and organizations: Software of the mind* (3rd edition). New York: McGraw Hill.

Hu, W. & Grove, C. (1999). *Encountering the Chinese: A guide for Americans.* Yarmouth, ME: Intercultural Press.

Hu, W. (1994). *Culture and communication.* Beijing: Foreign Language and Teaching Press.

Hua, Z. (2014). *Exploring intercultural communication: Language in action.* Abingdon: Routledge.

Ishii, S. (2004). Proposing a Buddhist consciousness-only epistemological model for intrapersonal communication research. *Journal of Intercultural Communication Research*, 33(2), 63–76.

Ito, Y. (1992). Theories on interpersonal communication styles from a Japanese perspective: A sociological approach. In J. G. Blumer, J. M. McLeod & K. E. Rosengren (eds.), *Comparatively speaking: Communication and culture across space and time* (pp. 238–268). Newbury Park, CA: Sage.

Ito, Y. (2000). What causes the similarities and differences among the social sciences in different cultures? Focusing on Japan and the West. *Asian Journal of Communication*, 10(2), 93–123.

Jackson, J. (2014). *Introducing language and intercultural communication.* New York: Routledge.

Jandt, F. E. (2010). *An introduction to intercultural communication: Identities in a global community* (6th edition). Los Angeles: SAGE.

Kitao, K. & Kitao, S. K. (eds.) (1989). *Intercultural communication: Between Japan and the United States.* Tokyo: Eichosha Shinsha.

Leo, C., Bennett, R. & Cierpicki, S. (2005). A comparison of Australian and Singaporean consumer decision-making styles. *Journal of Customer Behavior*, 4(1), 17–45.

Martin, J. & Nakayama, T. (2010). *Intercultural communication in contexts* (5th edition). Boston: McGraw Hill.

Martin, J. N. & Nakayama, T. K. (1999). Thinking about culture dialectically. *Communication Theory*, 9(1), 1–25.

Martin, J., Nakayama, T. K. & Carbaugh, D. (2020). A global look at the history and development of language and intercultural communication studies. In J. Jackson (ed.), *The Routledge handbook of language and intercultural communication* (2nd edition), (pp. 19–38). Abingdon: Routledge.

McConachy, T. & Liddicoat, A. J. (2016). Meta-pragmatic awareness and intercultural competence: The role of reflection and interpretation in intercultural mediation. In F. Dervin & Z. Gross (eds.), *Intercultural competence in education: Alternative approaches for different times* (pp. 13–31). London: Palgrave Macmillan.

Mignolo, W. D. (2002). The geopolitics of knowledge and the colonial difference. *The South Atlantic Quarterly*, 101(1), 57–96.

Mignolo, W. D. (2011). *The darker side of western modernity: Global futures, decolonial options*. Durham, NC and London: Duke University Press.

Miike, Y. (2007). An Asiacentric reflection of Eurocentric bias in communication theory. *Communication Monographs*, 74(2), 272–278.

Nakayama, T. K. & Halualani, R. T. (eds.) (2012). *Handbook of critical intercultural communication*. Malden, MA: Wiley-Blackwell.

Noma, H. (2009). How unique is Japanese culture? A critical review of the discourse in intercultural communication literature. *Journal of International Education in Business*, 2(2), 2–14.

Rehbein, J. (2006). The cultural apparatus: Thoughts on the relationship between language, culture and society. In K. Bührig & J. D. Ten Thije (eds.), *Beyond misunderstanding: The linguistic reconstruction of intercultural discourse* (pp. 43–96). Amsterdam: Benjamins.

Rehbein, J. (2013). Intercultural communication. In C. A. Chapelle (ed.), *The encyclopedia of applied linguistics* (pp. 2758–2765). Oxford: Blackwell.

Rings, G. (2010). *La Conquista desbaratada: Identidad y alteridad en la novela, el cine y el teatro hispánicos contemporáneos*. Madrid: Iberoamericana.

Rings, G. (2018). *The other in contemporary migrant cinema*. New York: Routledge.

Rings, G. (2020). From the American dream to the European dream in 'Buen día, Ramón'. In V. Dolle (ed.), *¿Un sueño europeo? Europa como destino anhelado de migración en la creación cultural latinoamericana (2001–2015)* (pp. 161–182). Madrid: Iberoamericana.

Rogers, E. M., Hart, W. B. & Miike, Y. (2002). Edward T. Hall and the history of intercultural communication: The United States and Japan. *Keio Communication Review*, 24(3), 3–26.

Salo-Lee, L. (2020). Towards integrative intercultural communication. In G. Rings & S. M. Rasinger (eds.), *The Cambridge handbook of intercultural communication* (pp. 120–135). Cambridge: Cambridge University Press.

Schutte, P. (2009). Revisiting Hofstede among South African students: Some intercultural communication guidelines for the workplace. *Communitas*, 14, 1–16.

Scollon, R. & Scollon, S.W. (2007). Nexus analysis: Refocusing ethnography on action. *Journal of Sociolinguistics*, 11, 608–625.

Smirl, L. (2015). *Spaces of aid: How cars, compounds and hotels shape humanitarianism*. London: Zed Books.

Standing, G. (2011). *The precariat: The new dangerous class*. London: Bloomsbury Academic.

Standing, G. (2016). What is the precariat? *TEDxPrague*. 30 October. www.youtube.com/watch?v=nnYhZCUYOxs (last accessed 15 April 2022).

Ten Thije, J. D. (2020). What is intercultural communication? In G. Rings & S. M. Rasinger (eds.), *The Cambridge handbook of intercultural communication* (pp. 35–55). Cambridge: Cambridge University Press.

Trompenaars, F. & Hampden-Turner, C. (1997). *Riding the waves of culture* (2nd edition). London: Nicholas Brealey.

Walker, S., Eketone, A. & Gibbs, A. (2006). An exploration of kaupapa Maori research, its principles, processes and applications. *International Journal of Social Research Methodology*, 9(4), 331–344.

Yoshino, K. (1992). *Cultural nationalism in contemporary Japan: A sociological enquiry*. London: Routledge.

Yu, X., Weiler, B. & Ham, S. (2002). Intercultural communication and mediation: A framework for analysing the intercultural competence of Chinese tour guides. *Journal of Vacation Marketing*, 8(1), 75–87.

Zhang, D. & Wu, S. J. (2014). Achieving successful business in China: Assessing the changing Chinese culture. *Journal of Asia-Pacific Business*, 15(4), 307–323.

3 Rethinking Intercultural Competence

Based on our working definition of intercultural communication in Chapter 2, we would now like to examine how we can improve that communication. This brings us to intercultural competence as a developmental aim of the field and especially to its structural and process-oriented aspects, which we want to explore in detail.

AIMS
By the end of this chapter, you should be able to:
1. define intercultural competence;
2. distinguish between two key approaches to intercultural competence;
3. explain the extent to which these constructs are connected to questions of power.

> **KEY TERMS**
> intercultural competence – Global North – Global South – ubuntu – whānau – alli kawsay – kizuna – silaturahmi – zhong dao – vishwa roopa darshanam

3.1 Key Ideas

> **TASK**
>
> What in your opinion is key to becoming interculturally competent? Please consider for your response the discussion of concepts of culture and intercultural communication in Chapters 1 and 2 as well as Figure 3.1.

Figure 3.1 *Intercultural Competence* by Alíz Kovács-Zöldi

3.1.1   Popular Definitions

We looked at different cultural identity concepts in Chapter 1, including interculturality, and while doing this, we also referred to **intercultural competence**.
Jackson offers a good introductory summary when she defines intercultural competence as 'the ability to communicate *effectively* and *appropriately* in intercultural
situations based on one's intercultural knowledge, skills and attitudes' (2014,
p. 373, our emphasis).

As such, the concept could be described as a key aim of intercultural communication studies, which must be examined from more than one perspective,

hence '*effectiveness* being determined by the individual and *appropriateness* being determined by the other person(s) in the interaction' (Deardorff, 2020, p. 495; our emphasis). Finally, *knowledge, skills* and *attitudes*, that is, the cognitive, conative and affective domains, refer to a basic *structural model* of intercultural competence that deserves to be elaborated in greater detail.

3.1.2 Byram's Structural Model

Michael Byram, who took a leading role in the development and wider dissemination of this model, stresses in a key publication for the Council of Europe the crucial role of *knowledge* [or '*savoirs*'] of 'social groups and their products and practices in one's own and in one's interlocutor's country, and of the general processes of societal and individual interaction' (Byram et al., 2002, p. 12). That includes culture-specific insights, but also knowledge about common ground and differences in communication, self-awareness and the contexts that shape the interaction. Potential factors worth considering are different communication patterns (e.g. regarding politeness, frequency of words like 'please' and 'thank you' in comparable statements) and the influence of cultural programming on individual worldviews (e.g. US American nationalist and protestant perspectives, or Turkish nationalist and Islamic views?), but also questions of power, which have been marginalised by Byram and other groundbreaking scholars of intercultural competence. *Power* might manifest itself directly through the *role of participants* involved in negotiation (e.g. employer–employee, doctor–patient, teacher–student, aid giver–aid receiver) and more indirectly, for example through their *nationality, ethnicity, race, language, class, age, gender, physical or mental abilities* and other aspects in a given context (see Section 2.1).

TASK

Think of your own experiences in negotiations: In which situation(s) did you notice the impact of economic, social or political power particularly well? What exactly was key for the power hierarchy between you and the other person(s) involved? How did this influence the outcome of the negotiation?

Skills could be defined as 'the abilities one possesses', such as 'perspective-taking, observation, flexibility, interaction, trust-building, empathizing, helping mindfulness, reflection and self-efficacy' (Deardorff, 2020, p. 495). Byram subdivides these and other skills into three main categories, which are key for every intercultural mediator: *interpreting and relating* ('*savoir comprendre*'), the *discovery and interaction* ('*savoir apprendre/faire*') and *critical awareness* ('*savoir s'engager*') (Byram et al., 2002, p. 13). In *interpreting and relating*, intercultural mediators are asked to compare and evaluate texts from two or more cultures in order to explore other perspectives. Abilities like observation, perspective-taking and empathising, but also self-efficacy might be important for this. *Discovery and interaction* summarise

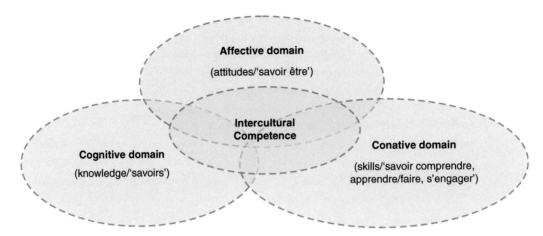

Figure 3.2 Basic structural model of intercultural competence with Byram's 'savoirs'
© Guido Rings

abilities to acquire new knowledge and involve people from other cultures in it, for example ask them for their reasons for particular patterns of behaviour that might lead to often unconscious beliefs and values. Interaction, trust-building and flexibility could be essential in this context. Finally, *critical awareness* refers to abilities to evaluate a person's own and other people's values critically. Helping mindfulness and reflection might be key for this.

However, the 'foundation' role for the development of intercultural competence rests for Byram and colleagues with efficient and appropriate *attitudes* (*'savoir être'*), especially 'curiosity and openness' and 'readiness to suspend disbelief about other cultures and belief about one's own' (2002, pp. 11–12). These attitudes could be linked to feelings, positions and ways of thinking, but the key is ultimately the willingness to decentre, that is, to question one's own behaviours, beliefs and values. Deardorff adds 'respect for others' as an important attitude, for which she asks intercultural mediators to demonstrate 'that they are valued', for example by 'showing interest in them and listening attentively to them' (Deardorff, 2020, p. 495).

Above all, we should consider that knowledge, skills and attitudes are linked and that intercultural competence stays and falls with their connection. For example, knowledge depends on related skills and attitudes to be implemented, while skills and attitudes without the related knowledge are unlikely to go far. Hence, we suggest presenting the basic *structural model of intercultural competence* as shown in Figure 3.2 (with overlap and blurred boundaries between the key dimensions).

3.1.3   Comparable Approaches

It is worth stressing that comparable knowledge, skills and attitudes are being discussed under a wide variety of terminology: while publications from the United Nations Educational, Scientific and Cultural Organization (UNESCO, 2013) and the Council of Europe (2011) tend to draw on 'intercultural competence', the Organisation for Economic Co-operation and Development (OECD, 2017) and Asia Society (2018) prefer *global competence*. Healthcare professions and social work focus on *cultural competence* (Anand & Lahiri, 2009), and in business studies we find predominantly discussions of *cultural intelligence* (Earley & Ang, 2003).

Competing notions are *global citizenship* and *world citizenship* (Oxfam, 2020, World Service, 2020), which tend to show particular concern for questions of power in the development of international relations and the assessment of intercultural competence. Deardorff indicates the importance of economic and sociopolitical power when she argues that we have to ask 'competence according to whom, influenced by what and to what degree' (2020, p. 497). To start with, it should be stressed that especially due to major inequalities in resources, most intercultural training programmes are still designed on the basis of conceptual research and teaching material developed in the **Global North**. Also, participants are predominantly students, sales representatives, healthcare managers and other professionals from institutions in that part of the world who want to negotiate more effectively and appropriately with people from other cultures, including the **Global South** (for the North–South divide see Sajed, 2020).

If, for example, managers and sales representatives of US American companies receive intercultural training to enhance their business negotiation competence in Mexico, Kenya, Lebanon and other countries of the Global South, as many case studies in Ferraro's course book help to prepare for (Ferraro, 2010), then there is a risk of othering. That risk is particularly high if training success is measured by chief executive officers with increasing sales figures as key criteria, because that could lead to a reduction of potential partners and customers in target cultures for objects of US American company aims and policies. While power hierarchies go well beyond dynamic North–South divides, this example might help to understand why it is extremely important to integrate conceptual perspectives from the Global South into discussions of what exactly intercultural competence might be, and how it can be developed and assessed. We find that such perspectives are particularly helpful in the development of process-oriented ideas of intercultural competence, which are key for contemporary discussions of the concept and will, therefore, be the topic of the next chapter.

TASK

Before we start Section 3.2, let us briefly look beyond the Global North–South divide: Can you think of an example, in which economic, social or political power had an impact on the negotiation either between people from two comparable countries (e.g. both from the Global North) or between two people with the same cultural background? How did the power hierarchy shape that negotiation?

3.2 Linking Structural and Process-Oriented Models

3.2.1 Process-Oriented Models

Next to structural approaches, which aim to describe in a rather fixed manner what exactly intercultural competence might be (see Figure 3.2), we can find *process-oriented models* that focus on ways of achieving that competence, which tend to consider contextual aspects much more than their predecessors. One of the most popular process-oriented approaches is still the *Developmental Model of Intercultural Sensitivity* (DMIS) proposed by Bennett (1993, 2009), which examines the growth in individual sensitivity from ethnocentrism to ethnorelativism. Within these two stages, individuals can develop from denial, defence and minimisation of difference in ethnocentrism to acceptance, adaptation and integration in ethnorelativism, and the latter is important for the development of intercultural knowledge, skills and attitudes. However, culture shock, discrimination and numerous other challenging experiences could easily block or reverse such developments, that is, we cannot assume linear progress.

3.2.2 Linking Up Key Ideas

Process-oriented models have also been proposed by Mezirow (2000) and Deardorff (2008). However, one of the most recent contributions to knowledge comes from Bolten's (2020) connection of structural and process-oriented models, which is summarised in Figure 3.3.

Bolten's discussion of intercultural competence as *transfer competence* starts from the assumption that there is only a gradual difference between general action competence in familiar situations, that is, within a relatively well-known cultural context, and intercultural competence in predominantly unfamiliar situations.

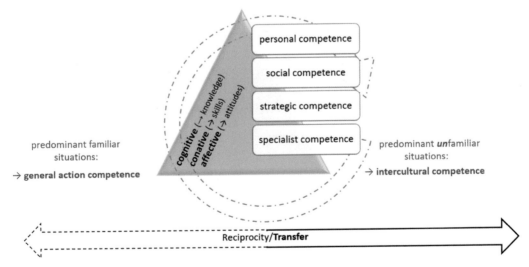

Figure 3.3 Intercultural competence as transfer competence
Source: Bolten (2020, p. 61); © J. Bolten.

In both situations, people have to draw on particular knowledge, abilities (skills) and attitudes, as highlighted in the basic structural model of intercultural competence. However, it is essential to bring these dimensions together to enhance that competence, which has been broken down into the four basic dimensions characteristic for process-oriented models, that is, *personal, social, strategic and specialist competencies* (Erpenbeck & Heyse, 2007).

Furthermore, Bolten (2020, p. 59) outlines how structural and process-oriented dimensions complement each other: for example, relevant knowledge (*cognitive dimension*) might be visible in the familiarity with one's own strengths and weaknesses (personal competence) and the rules of communication in a particular context (social competence), but it should also include problem-solving strategies (strategic competence) and specialist expertise (specialist competence). Similarly, suitable skills (*conative dimension*) might be self-criticism (personal) and empathy (social), but also the ability to manage time (strategic) and communicate relevant (specialist) knowledge. Finally, relevant attitudes (*affective dimension*) might include the motivation to show initiative (personal) and tolerance (social), but of similar importance might be goal-orientation (strategic) and the willingness to use particular (specialist) knowledge.

TASK

How do you tend to solve problems with your closest friends? Think of one successful example, which involves particular knowledge, skills and/or attitudes. To what extent were you able to transfer these competencies to negotiations with less familiar people, that is, new fellow students or colleagues at a workplace?

Considering that the ability to communicate effectively and appropriately with others remains key for intercultural competence, further conceptual development could be expected from notions of interconnectedness and oneness as starting points. Such notions are now increasingly brought into international discussions, but they still tend to receive more attention outside – rather than within – the United States or Europe, and that could lead to a shift in pioneering roles in the development of intercultural competence research.

Concepts that advocate interconnectedness beyond monocultural boundaries are for example South African *ubuntu*, Māori *whānau*, Kichwa *alli kawsay*, Japanese *kizuna* and Malayan *silaturahmi*. Ogude et al. (2019) summarises the communitarian ethos behind **ubuntu** as follows: 'It is about coming together as a community, building a consensus around what affects the community. And once you have debated, then it is understood what is best for the community, and then you have to buy into that' (Ogude et al., 2019). **Whānau** is a Māori concept that is based on worldviews that had traditionally strong monocultural orientations with focus on family and/or tribe. However, it increasingly now includes friends, associates and even unrelated people who support each other, for example in whānau rooms in hospitals (Walker, 2017). A comparable relationship enhancing concept is **alli kawsay**, which is key for the indigenous Kichwa people of Ecuador (Ferrer et al., 2019). It promotes 'good life' ideas in practice and in philosophical orientation that aim to develop sustainable societies whose interest in social equality and connection with nature stands in critical distance to the capitalist accumulation principles advanced in colonial and neo-colonial discourses. The desire to establish and maintain social connections is also essential for **kizuna**, a Japanese concept that became kanji of the year after the Fukushima nuclear power plant disaster and has been increasingly commodified ever since (Miller, 2017). Similarly, Malayan **silaturahmi** is not limited to kinship or beliefs, but focuses on the need to establish mutual respect and trust between hosts and visitors, for which a highly symbolic context is key (Wiryomartono, 2014, p. 22).

Chinese *zhong dao* and Hindu *vishwa roopa darshanam* are concepts that can support the development of intercultural competence through a focus on individual and collective oneness. Chen and An elaborate on **zhong dao** as 'guidepost for the action to achieve the equilibrium state of communication or leadership competence', for which *cheng*, that is, a 'sincere and honest mind' of the individual, is crucial (Chen & An, 2009, p. 200). Manian and Naidu discuss **vishwa roopa darshanam**, that is, the vision of the universe as one, with particular focus on the need to show respect for man, animals and plants, ancestors and holy scriptures (Manian & Naidu, 2009, p. 245). All this should be guided by conscious, whole and undivided individuals who have to 'look beyond external differences' (2009, p. 246).

GROUP TASK

Please explore one of the above outlined concepts that you are less familiar with in greater detail (e.g. *whānau*): What does that concept now stand for? If you want to fall in line with it, which behaviour do you have to change and why? Do you think that it can help to develop our understanding of intercultural competence and, if so, why (or why not)?

3.2.3   In Summary

In all concepts discussed in this chapter, be it intercultural competence as proposed by Bolten (2020) or *zhong dao* as discussed by Chen & An (2009), the boundaries between intracultural and intercultural situations appear blurred. After all, for Bolten, relevant personal, social, strategic and specialist competencies are key for all forms of negotiation. Similarly, *zhong dao* and *cheng* are dimensions that managers are expected to show, irrespective of their own or their employees' origin. In other words, each perspective highlights in its own cultural framework that effective and appropriate communication rests ultimately on comparable key competencies and the ability to transfer what has been learned in theory and practice, for example from more familiar to less familiar contexts and vice versa. Consequently …

> Intercultural competence has to be imagined – just like general action competence – as an open, highly dynamic and lifelong process, and the same applies to *ubuntu, whānau, alli kawsay, kizuna, silaturahmi, zhong dao* and *vishwa roopa darshanam*.

3.3 In Summary

While working definitions of intercultural competence continue to draw heavily on structural models, it is essential to understand the concept as open, highly dynamic and always depending on context. In particular, there seems to be at best a gradual difference between people's action competence in their own culture and their intercultural competence in less familiar terrains. Both so called *intracultural* and *intercultural* competence depend on knowledge, skills and attitudes relevant for a particular context and, consequently, experiences can be transferred, for example from more to less familiar situations and vice versa.

Considering the need to imagine intercultural competence – just like general action competence – as a lifelong process, ideas for further development should include perspectives and practical experiences from related concepts and applications that have already managed to blur cultural boundaries, such as *ubuntu, whānau, alli kawsay, kizuna, silaturahmi, zhong dao* and *vishwa roopa darshanam*.

However, in all cases, we have to consider power hierarchies that might show up very explicitly – through the role of participants in negotiation processes (e.g. employer–employee), or more implicitly through, for example, their nationality, race or class. Quite apart from the immediate context, there are international inequalities to be taken into account, which might have a strong impact on numerous negotiations. This includes inequalities between the so-called Global North and the Global South, with the former still leading relevant conceptual discussions, producing most teaching material and implementing most intercultural training programmes, all of which tends to facilitate the marketing and sales of 'Northern' goods and ideas in 'Southern' cultures more than in the other direction.

DISCUSSION QUESTIONS

Which of the above-outlined aspects of structural and process-oriented intercultural competence would you consider to be part of your strengths and which seem weaknesses? Which country would you like to travel to next, and what could you do to improve your intercultural competence in preparation for that trip?

CASE STUDY – ROLE PLAY

You are a friend of Michael, a professor of Film Studies at a British university, who has received a visiting professorship at a university in Seoul. After a bad week in Seoul, he Skypes you to share some of his problems, because they might have something to do with intercultural competence. Try to help him.

After receiving two teaching project awards for student engagement at his university, Michael is keen to apply his knowledge of student-centred methodologies in his seminars on European cinema at the Korean university. However, things are not working out. Neither the well-prepared brainstorming and concept-mapping sessions, nor the detailed interactive design of the seminars with post-ups and storyboarding, in which he repeatedly asks students for their opinions on selected film scenes, lead to the engagement he is used to. Only a handful of participants (of around thirty) contributes well, while the others appear to be busy making notes.

Michael emphasises that all texts for his sessions are available to download, so that nobody has to make notes. He also stresses that he does not want students to make notes, but to participate instead. Temporarily, most stop note-taking for now, but they do not contribute any more than before, except in some group work sessions when he is not nearby.

In a break, Michael learns that the active students all had a year abroad, mostly in the United States, and he asks them for their opinion regarding the lack of participation. Some mention that it might be the others' weakness in English, because they have not been abroad. That makes a lot of sense to Michael, so he starts speaking more slowly, and uses shorter sentences and easier vocabulary. He also addresses the less active students more directly and speaks particularly slowly on those occasions, but that seems to alienate them even more.

References

Anand, R. & Lahiri, I. (2009). Intercultural competence in health care – developing skills for interculturally competent care. In D. K. Deardorff (ed.), *The Sage handbook of intercultural competence* (pp. 387–402). Thousand Oaks, CA: Sage.

Asia Society. (2018). *Teaching for global competence in a rapidly changing world.* New York: Asia Society. https://doi.org/10.1787/9789264289024-en

Bennett, M. J. (1993). Towards ethnorelativism: A developmental model of intercultural sensitivity. In R. M. Paige (ed.), *Education for the intercultural experience* (pp. 21–71). Yarmouth: Intercultural Press.

Bennett, M. J. (2009). Cultivating intercultural competence: A process perspective. In D. Deardorff (ed.), *The Sage handbook of intercultural competence* (pp. 121–140). Thousand Oaks, CA: Sage.

Bolten, J. (2020). Rethinking intercultural competence. In G. Rings & S. M. Rasinger (eds.), *The Cambridge handbook of intercultural communication* (pp. 56–67). Cambridge: Cambridge University Press.

Byram, M., Gribkova, B. & Starkey, H. (2002). *Developing the intercultural dimension in language teaching*. Strasbourg: Council of Europe.

Chen, G.-M. & An, R. (2009). A Chinese model of intercultural leadership competence. In D. Deardorff (ed.), *The Sage handbook of intercultural competence* (pp. 196–208). Thousand Oaks, CA: Sage.

Council of Europe. (2011). *Developing intercultural competence through education*. Strasbourg: Council of Europe.

Deardorff, D. (2008). Intercultural competence: A definition, model, and implications for education abroad. In V. Savicki (ed.), *Developing intercultural competence and transformation: Theory, research, and application in international education* (pp. 32–52). Sterling, VA: Stylus.

Deardorff. D. K. (2020). Defining, developing and assessing intercultural competence. In G. Rings & S. M. Rasinger (eds.), *The Cambridge handbook of intercultural communication* (pp. 493–503). Cambridge: Cambridge University Press.

Earley, P. C. & Ang, S. (2003). *Cultural intelligence: Individual interactions across cultures*. Stanford, CA: Stanford Business Books.

Erpenbeck, J. & Heyse, V. (2007). *Die Kompetenzbiographie: Wege der Kompetenzentwicklung* (2nd edition). Münster: Waxmann.

Ferraro, G. P. (2010). *The cultural dimension of international business* (6th edition). Upper Saddle River, NJ: Prentice Hall.

Ferrer, A. M. A., Astudillo Banegas, J. E. & Martines Tola, J. S. (2019). La práctica del alli kawsay desde la resistencia: Caso de Zhiña, Ecuador. *Universum*, 34(2), 81–104.

Jackson, J. (2014). *Introducing language and intercultural communication*. New York: Routledge.

Manian, R. & Naidu, S. (2009). India: A cross-cultural overview of intercultural competence. In D. K. Deardorff (ed.), *The Sage handbook of intercultural competence* (pp. 233–248). Thousand Oaks, CA: SAGE.

Mezirow, J. (2000). Learning to think like an adult. In J. Mezirow & Associates (eds.), *Learning as transformation: Critical perspectives on a theory in progress* (pp. 3–33). San Francisco: Jossey-Bass.

Miller, L. (2017). Japan's trendy word grand prix and kanji of the year: Commodified language forms in multiple contexts. In J. R. Cavanaugh & S. Shankar (eds.), *Language and materiality: Ethnographic and theoretical explorations* (pp. 43–62). Cambridge: Cambridge University Press.

OECD. (2017). *Preparing our youth for an inclusive and sustainable world: The OECD PISA global competence framework*. Paris: OECD.

Ogude, J., Paulson, S. & Strainchamps, A. (2019). I am because you are: An interview with James Ogude. Consortium of Humanities Centers and Institutes (CHCI). Online. https://bit.ly/3xNcxP5 (last accessed 15 April 2022).

Oxfam. 2020. What is global citizenship? Oxfam. Online. https://bit.ly/3KQv5kO (last accessed 15 April 2022).

Sajed, A. (2020). From the third world to the global south. E-International Relations. Online. https://bit.ly/3uKsYJY (last accessed 15 April 2022).

UNESCO. (2013). *Intercultural competences*. Paris: UNESCO.

Walker, T. (2017). Whānau – Māori and family. Te Ara – the Encyclopedia of New Zealand. Online. https://teara.govt.nz/en/whanau-maori-and-family

Wiryomartono, B. (2014). *Perspectives on traditional settlements and communities. Home, form and culture in Indonesia*. Singapore: Springer.

World Service. (2020). World government of world citizens. Online. https://worldservice.org/gov.html (last accessed 15 April 2022).

PART II

THEORIES, KEY CONCEPTS AND APPROACHES

4 Critical Intercultural Communication and Postcolonial Studies

In Chapter 2, we mentioned critical intercultural communication as a more recent approach that explores the extent to which intercultural relations and their portrayals are shaped by media, national governments and other stakeholders. In this chapter, we want to examine how far critical intercultural communication links up to postcolonial studies, which have focused on power structures and their impact for decades, and we would like to analyse its potential to serve as an umbrella concept for other approaches.

AIMS
By the end of this chapter, you should be able to:

1. **define critical intercultural communication and postcolonial studies;**
2. **describe how far and how exactly critical intercultural research could draw on postcolonial studies;**
3. **explain the extent to which critical intercultural communication could integrate other intercultural approaches.**

> ### KEY TERMS
> **critical intercultural communication – cross-cultural management – fake news – colonialism – postcolonialism – internal colonialism – precariat – gig economy – rhizome – essentialism**

4.1 Defining Critical Intercultural Communication in Context

We defined *intercultural communication* in Chapter 2 as mediation aimed at creating mutual understanding between individuals or groups of different cultural backgrounds. We also said that this mediation includes an exchange and negotiation of common ground and differences with a particular focus on the cultural frames that shape interpretations of verbal and non-verbal behaviour as well as the results of that behaviour, for example particular norms, beliefs, products, systems and institutions. **Critical intercultural communication** is all of that, but it goes one important step further by considering how *far* and how *exactly* that mediation is shaped by power hierarchies.

4.1.1   Power Hierarchies

If we just think of employer–employee, doctor–patient and professor–student relations, we know that power can have a significant impact on interactions, and potentially in both directions – top down and bottom up. On the one hand, employers have the power to employ and sack employees, doctors give patients medication or referrals to a specialist (or not), and lecturers give students marks; on the other hand, many employees can rely on unions to defend their interests, while patients and students have complaint procedures at their disposal. How strong the power of the former is and how effective the defence mechanisms of the latter are depends on individual contexts. There are, however, numerous examples of misuses of power in cultural encounters. This includes ongoing ethnic and religious discrimination, for example against Black Africans and Arabs (especially Arab males) in job applications in Europe (Di Stasio & Heath, 2019; Arai et al., 2016).

TASKS

Can you think of other cultural encounters that are affected by unequal power relations, including one that involves you? Try to explain the impact of power in that context, and compare your examples with the illustration of critical intercultural communication below, which is inspired by the Black Lives Matter movement's fights for equality and power.

4.1.2   Functionalist Tendencies in Early Research

In early intercultural communication research and teaching, power hierarchies were often marginalised, partly because of a focus on cultural differences when approaching key functions, rather than internal constitutions, of communicative behaviour and related attitudes and values. There is now wider scholarly agreement about such a *functionalist* tendency in intercultural studies in the twentieth century (Bjerregaard et al., 2009), and it is worth highlighting that contemporary teaching material and related training is still often shaped by that tendency. Critical intercultural communication scholar Thomas Nakayama argues that functionalist tendencies are often connected to an understanding of culture as static and homogeneous, e.g. in images of a 'unified national culture' (Nakayama, 2020, p. 86).

Figure 4.1 *Critical Intercultural Communication* by Alíz Kovács-Zöldi

All this links up to our elaboration of monoculturality in Chapter 1, within which especially national culture is frequently framed as homogeneous, separatist and essentialist. In such a context, culture tends to be reduced to *the* key variable for understanding differences in behaviour. Applications based on Edward Hall's and Geert Hofstede's work, as well as the work itself, have been often criticised for such functionalism (Bjerregaard et al., 2009). However, it would be wrong to limit this tendency to contrastive approaches, as generalisations in all approaches can follow very similar patterns, for example in image studies (see Chapter 6) if the selected texts stabilise stereotypes of a country or an entire content. Examples are the ongoing portrayal of Africa as a poor, unstable and inferior continent in the still powerful 'colonial library' (Matthews, 2018) in different genres, but also the presentation of Europe as idyllic romantic-medieval Other in Mexican tourist websites (Rings, 2020).

TASKS

Can you think of stereotypical presentations of your country (or continent)? Who would benefit from those?

With focus on **cross-cultural management**, Bjerregaard, Lauring and Klit-møller stress related challenges:

> The functionalist perspective has led to an unproductive understanding of culture and acculturation where potential for disagreement, antagonism, power relations and conflict are never dealt with, where social and political overtones are squelched, and where sensitivities relating to hierarchical positioning and power differentials across partisan interests are habitually overlooked.
> (Bjerregaard et al., 2009, p. 208).

4.1.3   Race and Power

Since the end of the twentieth century, critical intercultural communication scholars like Tom Nakayama, Rona Tamiko Halualani and Judith N. Martin have focused on cultural, sociopolitical and economic power-related dynamics (Altman & Nakayama, 1992, Martin & Nakayama, 1999, Nakayama & Halualani, 2012, Halualani, 2017). Their aim is to understand cultural encounters 'in the context of social relations, such as race, class, gender, sexuality and nationality' (Nakayama, 2020, p. 85).

Recent examples include the use of powerful **fake news** in the digital environment to destabilise governments with intercultural orientation and support instead monocultural leadership in the United States (Molina, et al., 2021). For example, Nakayama discusses how the generation of content by users, pseudo-anonymity and status-levelling in social media helped to question the legitimacy of Barack Obama's presidency through completely fabricated but popular claims that Obama was not born in the US (Nakayama, 2020, p. 85), which would have excluded him from the presidency. These claims were further disseminated by Donald Trump (Applebaum, 2015; Ortiz, 2016) and helped him to come to power in 2016 (Nakayama, 2020, p. 88).

On the other hand, Trump weaponised his Twitter account and other media to construct and spread unsubstantiated and often dehumanising claims himself (Ott & Dickinson, 2019). For example, by demonising Mexican immigrants as criminals, drug dealers and rapists, he helped justify his immigration policies and the building of a wall on the Mexican border (Lengel & Newsom, 2020, p. 61; Forster, 2020, p. 29; Wax-Edwards, 2020, p. 112). The culmination of this was when, after losing his presidency in 2020, he used Twitter to make repeated claims about 'rigged elections' in a desperate attempt to overturn the results, which was in line with the way he had been using his account: to 'attack someone or something in more than half of his tweets', often with 'brute repetition' (Shear et al., 2019).

However, the digital environment can also be used to resist domination and enhance intercultural relations. A well-known example is the Black Lives Matter movement, which has since its foundation in 2013 denounced the brutality of the police against Black citizens in the US, and has received mass support by people from all ethnicities. For example, the hashtag #ferguson was used to report the killing of African American Michael Brown in Ferguson, Missouri, and to organise mass protests against contemporary racism (Nakayama, 2020, p. 91).

All these examples highlight that the digital environment remains a tool, just like the printed press, television and other forms of mass media, that can be used for very different kinds of intervention, including monocultural and intercultural aims. It is essential to recognise and question such use, for example through contextualisation and multi-perspective interrogation of fake news and other misleading portrayals, which is where critical intercultural communication scholars come in with questions like: 'Why is that fake idea being disseminated? Who does it help?'

TASK

Explore an example of fake news that portrays migrants in your country in a stereotypical way. Where exactly was it presented, for whom, and who benefits from it? What might a critical intercultural intervention against it look like?

4.2 From Postcolonial Studies to Critical Intercultural Communication

When critical intercultural communication scholars outline the beginnings of their field (e.g. Nakayama, 2020), they sometimes tend to forget that social, political and economic contexts in cultural encounters, including racial boundaries and hierarchies, were critically explored well before the arrival of that field, for example in postcolonial studies. If **colonialism** can be defined as the form of cultural and socio-economic 'exploitation that developed with the expansion of Europe over the last 400 years', that is, post-Renaissance forms of imperialism (Ashcroft et al., 2007, p. 40), then **postcolonialism** examines the impact of that imperialism. In particular, it explores 'how Western forms of knowledge and power marginalise the non-Western world' and, well beyond that, 'the disparities in global power and wealth accumulation' (Nair, 2017, p. 69), especially in their link to traces of colonialism.

4.2.1   Impact of Colonialism

Frantz Fanon prepares important ground for such a critical approach when he examines from a psychological perspective the internalisation of 'white' colonial power hierarchies in colonised 'black' groups in *Black skin, white masks* (1999). The resulting tension in colonised subjects is still quoted as a starting point in understanding assimilation (and resistance) tendencies during and after colonisation (Faulkner, 2013), as well as skin bleaching or 'whitening' in formerly colonised territories in Asia, Africa, but also in the US (Norwood, 2015).

TASK

Search the Internet for skin bleaching practices and write a short report on who continues to do this and why. Discuss the dangers linked to such practices.

With a focus on an imagined Orient as a theatrical stage affixed to Europe, Edward Said examines in his pathbreaking *Orientalism* (1978) these hierarchies as fictional constructs that frame people. For example, he highlights how the imagined boundaries to the Orient, that is, the inferior 'rest', tend to shift depending on contexts. Finally, among the first leading postcolonial scholars, Homi Bhabha highlights the construction of cultural difference, very much in line with critical interculturalists, as a consequence of 'the attempt to dominate in the name of a cultural supremacy which is itself produced only in the moment of differentiation' (Bhabha, 2004, p. 51). This leads directly to paradigms of assimilation and exclusion in monocultural groups, for which the racist abuse Obama received when opening his Twitter account (Davis, 2015; Nakayama, 2020, p. 89) and the frequent insults of 'Others' in Trump's tweets (Shear et al., 2019) are contemporary examples.

Clearly, the 'boundaries of culture where meanings and values are (mis)-read or signs are misappropriated' (Bhabha, 2004, p. 50) do not have to be determined by *colonial* or *neo-colonial* hierarchies in the narrow sense. However, related monocultural tendencies continue through power hierarchies and exploitation tendencies that have been explored by numerous scholars. Worth stressing in particular are post-colonialist Neil Lazarus (2012), who outlines developments towards internal colonialism in post-industrial societies since the 1970s, and migration researcher Joe Turner (2018), who explores the link between internal and traditional colonialism with a focus on nations with a strong colonial legacy like the UK. Of particular interest is also British economist Guy Standing's analysis of the **_precariat_**, that is, the new and fast growing 'class-in-the-making' of people in extremely insecure and low paid employment (Standing, 2011, p. 8), because the precariat could be discussed as a new colonised workforce in a high-capitalist direction of globalisation in the twenty-first century. We discuss this in more detail in Section 4.2.3.

4.2.2 Internal Colonialism

The concept of **internal colonialism**, which originally focused on the working classes in the nineteenth and early twentieth century, has been theoretically underpinned by French philosopher Michel Foucault (Stole, 1995, p. 75), further elaborated by Turner (2018) and applied to documentary film intervention by Rings (2021). It can be understood – just like traditional 'external' colonialism – as 'epistemic violence' and, more precisely, 'exploitation' and 'regulation of hierarchised populations' (Turner, 2018, pp. 771–772). Already in colonial times, 'knowledge and practices of colonial governmentality were constantly fed back through internal colonisation' as ultimately both constituted 'imperial terrain' (2018, pp. 771–772). Later, the loss of manpower during WWII and the disintegration of the British colonial empire after WWII led to a very substantial demand for new cheap labour, which led British companies to push for mass immigration to the UK from the 1950s. This meant that the political elite had to reconsider 'how colonial entailments can be recalibrated in more or less visible ways in contemporary liberal rule' (Turner, 2018, p. 772). A very similar phenomenon could be observed in other former colonial powers, such as France, Belgium and the Netherlands, which led Foucault to summarise the global shift since the post-WWII decolonisation as follows:

> Colonization [...] transported European models to other continents, but [...it also] had a return effect on the mechanism of power in the Occident [...] There had been a whole series of colonial models that had been brought back to the Occident and that made it so that the Occident could traffic in something like a colonization, an internal colonialism.
>
> (Foucault cited in Stole, 1995, p. 75)

Very similarly, Bhabha criticises an 'ongoing colonial present' (2004, p. 128). This includes imagined hierarchies, within which colonisers tend to portray themselves as more rational and civilised representatives of a superior order vis-à-vis the more instinctive and barbarian hence inferior Other (Rings, 2018, p. 14). Abbas (2019) has explored convincingly the extent to which such constructs can be linked to essentialist portrayals of the Self and the Other, for example in frequent characterisations of Muslim refugees as terror suspects in Brexit Britain.

4.2.3 Precarisation

Focusing on the **precariat** as a new colonised 'class', the impact of contemporary outsourcing tendencies is of particular interest, for example, that of cleaning staff and other manual labour as presented in films from Loach's *Bread and Roses* to Mitjáns's *Limpiadores*. In his TED talk 'What is the precariat?', Standing highlights three main characteristics of a concept that brings notions of 'precarious' existence and 'proletariat' together: 'unstable labour and unstable living', 'uncertainty' due to dependence on money wages, and lack of (civil, cultural, social and/or political) rights (Standing, 2016). He also indicates its diversity, which he discusses in detail in his monograph *The Precariat* (Standing, 2011). While the 'fragmentation of national class structures' is characteristic for any society shaped by globalisation, the precariat itself is as a '"class-in-the-making" particularly diverse' (Standing, 2011, p. 8). For example, the precariat can include people with low-paid temporary jobs, so-called part-timers and hourly-paid staff, but dependent contractors and interns might also form part of it, with migrants being disproportionately over-represented in these groups (2011, pp. 13–16). The common denominator is extreme uncertainty, which is a result of the loss of labour-related security, such as employment security, job security, work security and income security, and an extremely low household income that does not allow for significant savings. For the UK, Savage and colleagues estimated the average household income of the precariat at below 40 per cent median UK income with 'negligible savings' assumed (Savage et al., 2013, p. 243), which is well reflected through the poor working and living conditions of cleaners with Latino background in *Bread and Roses* and *Limpiadores*.

A significant part of the precariat works in the so-called **gig economy**, i.e. an economy in which organisations hire people – often through app-based platforms – for short-term commitments under self-employment schemes, with work given out in individual pieces or 'gigs' (Kobie, 2018). Deliveroo, Uber and Hermes are leading examples of the gig economy, and all three have been widely criticised for exploiting their workers through contractor schemes that exclude them from entitlements to the national minimum wage, sick pay and holiday pay. Another example is the 'increasingly competitive and globalised' British Higher Education environment, which Locke highlights as 'in need of reinvigoration and renewal' (Locke, 2017, p. 4), because it is also characterised by mass outsourcing in both its teaching and manual labour. All these examples highlight in their exploitation of uncertain living conditions at the edge of (or below) poverty lines continuities with 'older colonial governmentalities' and reflect the remobilisation, refashioning and creation of 'new colonial distributions' (Turner, 2018, p. 772). As such, they are worth further exploration by critical intercommunication scholars, because they shed light on the link between old and new power structures both between and within nations. However, separatist and neo-colonial tendencies within the field of intercultural communication also deserve our attention, and that leads us to Section 4.3.

TASK

Do you personally know someone who might belong to the precariat, and could you imagine being in it yourself one day? Explore common routes into the precariat and potential ways out of it. What could be done to reduce its size?

4.3   Critical Intercultural Communication as Umbrella Concept?

Considering tendencies towards *populist ultranationalism* and *precarisation*, as well as – partly related – conceptual and methodological challenges in the field (see Chapters 1 and 2), intercultural scholars should probably focus on common ground and interdisciplinary work, rather than academic coexistence. Salo-Lee has therefore recently argued for more intercultural dialogue with a view to enhancing 'integrative intercultural communication' as a means for 'unifying [...] complementary approaches within this multidisciplinary field' (Salo-Lee, 2020, p. 120). In particular, she suggests bringing comparative and interactional approaches closer together, because 'comparative studies can provide culture-interactional studies with valuable baselines for interpretation purposes' (Salo-Lee, 2020, p. 125). After all, culture shows both *permanence*, which is key for comparative scholars like Hofstede, and *variability*, which attracts the attention of interaction scholars like Salo-Lee more. In this sense, Salo-Lee argues for a *rhizomatic approach* inspired by the Finnish discourse studies scholar Sari Pietikäinen (2015) and Canadian linguistic anthropologist Monica Heller (Heller et al., 2018), because the **rhizome** reflects both stability and variety, including multiple non-hierarchical conceptions of knowledge and, above all, the openness and dynamics that every culture shows.

TASK

Run an internet image search for 'rhizome' as plant stem to get a better idea of the metaphor scholars like Pietikäinen tend to draw on. By drawing on such images, could you explain the extent to which the rhizome could represent both permanence and variability, and why it might be better than traditional presentations of cultures as trees?

We fully support such an integrative direction based on a rhizomatic approach, but for precisely that reason we argue for interdisciplinarity beyond hierarchisations of approaches well beyond comparative and interactional work, and propose critical intercultural communication as a potential umbrella concept, within which such an enhanced interdisciplinary re-orientation can take place.

To start with, if culture shows both permanence and variability, then the link between comparative and interactional approaches should probably be imagined more reciprocally than in the one-way direction mentioned above. Just like comparative studies could inform interaction research, interactional studies could support more open and dynamic comparative research like the World Values Survey, which explores global shifts in values and beliefs, such as support for (or opposition to) democracy and gender equality. The key point here is to accept cultural continuities as well as discontinuities with a focus on culture as being under construction by human agents and other factors. However, clearly not all people have the same impact on cultural dynamics, and power has often shifted back to elites with homogeneous, separatist and essentialist visions of culture, which leads us to discuss the tasks of critical intercultural communication in greater detail.

4.3.1   De-essentialising and De-colonising as Key Tasks

Lengel, Atay and Kluch are critical of the fact that 'much intercultural communication research […] essentializes culture' and highlight that even critical scholars continue to 'remain US- and Western European-centric' (Lengel et al., 2020, p. 207). Of particular interest is their assessment of early intercultural communication research as 'developed with colonial and imperialistic tendencies', which indexes Edward Hall's (and other scholars') training of US Foreign Service officers for posts abroad (2020, p. 206). From there it is only a small step to see colonial continuities in intercultural inquiries shaped by white Euro-American academics studying other cultures (Leeds-Hurwitz, 2010).

'De-essentializing and decolonizing intercultural communication' (Lengel et al., 2020, p. 207) is consequently a key task for contemporary and future critical intercultural communication scholars. That task starts with the acceptance of an overarching postcolonial aim underpinned by postcolonial theory, that is, 'to take a critical, feminist, postcolonial approach to challenge traditional hierarchies of knowledge and incorporate the scholarship and perspectives of non-Western scholars, problematizing the traditional self-other distinction' (Shah & Kurshid, 2018, p. 257).

TASK

To what extent could feminist perspectives (elaborated in Chapter 9) help to explore and destabilise essentialist binary constructs in colonial texts?

The following list of the most common binaries might help you to answer the question: coloniser–colonised imagined as white–black, civilised–primitive, advanced–retarded, good–evil, teacher–pupil, adult–child, male–female, rational–irrational (Ashcroft et al., 2007, p. 19; Rings, 2010, pp. 46–50).

At this stage, Lengel and colleagues follow recent tendencies in trying to distinguish between postcolonial and decolonial work by arguing that postcolonialism interrogates how the colonial condition can be undone, while that 'undoing' is a 'decolonizing mission' (Lengel et al., 2020, pp. 208–209). The authors leave open how productive the erection of this new boundary really is. However, the push for such a boundary implies a desire to erect and defend a strict demarcation of comparative and interactive research, which Salo-Lee and others now question as both too simplistic and a major challenge for interdisciplinary and *integrative intercultural research*. In this context, such boundary demarcation processes should themselves be explored with academic power structures and career opportunities in mind. After all, the value of academic research tends to be linked to 'a significant contribution to the field of study', which is already a key requirement for doctoral degrees (University of Cambridge, 2020), that is, the basic qualification for most lectureships, and becomes even more important later on. The development of new concepts, which tends to imply boundary demarcation against established concepts, could consequently help to boost careers and international recognition.

4.3.2   How to Undo Essentialism within and beyond Colonialism

An important question for our discussion of critical intercultural communication is how exactly colonial and neo-colonial power structures and their essentialist framing of the world can be questioned most effectively with a view to 'undoing' the colonial condition. There seems to be wider scholarly agreement that postcolonial theory, feminism, queer theory and contributions from decolonial scholars can all help to 'locate individual actions within relations of dominance and subordination that [...] characterize the world' (Markula & Silk, 2011, p. 39). This implies a 'micro' focus on interpersonal conflicts and a 'macro' focus on the role of power structures (Halualani & Nakayama, 2013), for which a variety of methodological tools should be considered.

The starting point is that knowledge production through academic research is always shaped by individual researchers and their contexts (Braun et al., 2014), including theoretical and methodological backgrounds, research time given at particular universities and/or external funding. To address such factors and decolonise the methodologies themselves, Lengel and colleagues propose collaborative knowledge production, which should consider *collaborative, reflexive, ethical, feminist* and *queer, intersectional* and *indigenous methodologies* (Lengel et al., 2020, p. 210). Collaboration should be key for academics, for example in interdisciplinary research, but also for the link between academics and stakeholders (Simpson & Ake, 2010, p. 86).

TASKS

If you want to write a new study on the reasons for migration from Mexico to the United States, which academic disciplines would you like to draw on, and why? Also, who would be the stakeholders that you want to consider, and why?

Researchers should throughout their project reflect consequently not only on their own viewpoints, but on the perspectives of the stakeholders involved (Patton, 2002, p. 65). This includes the development of an 'ethics of care' towards those stakeholders, for example by promoting equity through unstructured interview protocols (Lengel et al., 2020, pp. 212–213, Seidman, 2006, p. 109). Feminist and queer methodologies can contribute to all of this due to their successful questioning of unequal, hierarchical and patriarchal power structures that are characteristic of (neo-)colonial perspectives, yet intercultural scholars have so far marginalised feminist and queer studies (Chávez, 2013, p. 84). Their full integration into critical intercultural communication research is particularly important because the construction of an inferior Other in colonial texts tends to work at the intersection of race, gender and other identity markers.

For example, Rings elaborates how Spanish colonial texts tend to frame colonised indigenous people as female creatures through a selective focus on their appearance (having long hair, skirts, facial colours), adapted stereotypes (being more emotional/instinct-led) and by retrospectively applying the impact of successful conquest (being weaker, more enclosed) (Rings, 2010, pp. 46–50). This facilitates mutual reinforcement of racial and gender stereotypes culminating in the claim that the more instinct-led weak Others need rational patriarchal guidance, which only the Spanish colonisers can provide, and that helps to justify Spanish colonisation itself (2010, pp. 46–50). With a focus on the portrayal of black men as instinct-led, albeit usually with an additional emphasis on violence and hypersexuality, Jackson & Dangerfield (2002) highlight a comparable intersection of race and gender stereotypes, which should be approached with intersectional methodology.

Finally, and precisely in the context of such findings, indigenous methodologies deserve much more attention. Indigenous education scholar Linda Tuhiwai Smith (2012, p. 198) lists a wider spectrum of different approaches, which might inspire researchers to dig deeper into methodologies that might be relevant for their projects. For postcolonial projects related to cultures in the Andes, Florencio Molina Mamani directs our attention to fundamentally different indigenous perspectives of the cosmos imagined as '*pacha*', within which so called natural, human and sacred communities are in constant dialogue and exchange (Molina Mamani, 2013, pp. 17–19). Such a highly dynamic concept of the cosmos and, especially, '*pachakuti*' as time to remake the world by restoring the mythological balance through exchange and solidarity, has been used by indigenous politicians and novelists to question linear visions of colonialism and neo-colonial directions in globalisation, and also to propose decolonial alternatives. Examples are former Bolivian president Evo Morales (2015) and novelists Óscar Colchado Lucio (*Rosa Cuchillo*, 1997) and Alison Spedding (*De cuando en cuando Saturnina*,

2010). From there, it is only a small step to imagining direct contributions of such an indigenist approach to ongoing discussions in the United Nations about sustainability, the need to reduce global warming and ways of actually achieving it, and the fight against populist ultranationalism as well as other forms of ethnocentricity.

4.4 In Summary

We started this chapter by defining critical intercultural communication as a relatively new direction in research, which explores the extent to which and how exactly intercultural mediation is shaped by power hierarchies. We then looked at different scenarios, in which power plays a significant role. They include stereotypical categorisation and discrimination of people in top-down contexts, for example in Trump's misuse of Twitter to present migrants as criminals, and in bottom-up encounters, such as when white supremacists question the legitimacy of Obama's presidency on the same platform through fake news arguing that he is not US-American.

Contemporary critical intercultural work distances itself from functionalist tendencies in early intercultural communication research and related teaching, but it also rejects the traces of colonialism within contemporary power structures. Especially in this regard, the discipline can draw on postcolonial theory, which has through the work of Edward Said, Homi Bhabha, Neil Lazarus and numerous other scholars laid the foundation for de-colonisation and, in a wider sense, de-essentialisation. This includes a critical interrogation of ongoing internal colonialism, for example through the creation and exploitation of a new class-in-the-making, the precariat, which has replaced cheap colonial labour in most post-industrial nations today.

Finally, we have proposed that critical intercultural communication should be an umbrella concept for other directions in intercultural research since all related scholars have to work towards de-essentialisation and de-colonisation to qualify as interculturalists (as defined in Chapter 2). In this context, a key question has been how to undo essentialism within and beyond colonialism, for which numerous ideas have been presented.

DISCUSSION QUESTIONS

1. If we consider the principles of critical intercultural communication, could we draw up lists of what to do and what not to do for each culture, as used to be common in older intercultural textbooks?
2. How could we reduce racism in the digital environment more effectively?
3. Since ethnic and religious discrimination is known to persist in employment and recruitment, at both job applications and interview stages, what could we do to reduce that?

CASE STUDY

Please analyse the following excerpt from Dave's *Black* by drawing on critical intercultural communication concepts in the context of contemporary events. How does the rap text present the life of black people in the UK? Which aspects are transferable to other parts of the world, and where are the limits of this presentation?

> Look, black is beautiful, black is excellent
> Black is pain, black is joy, black is evident
> It's workin' twice as hard as the people you know you're better than
> 'Cause you need to do double what they do so you can level them
> Black is so much deeper than just African-American
> Our heritage been severed, you never got to experiment
> With family trees, 'cause they teach you 'bout famine and greed
> And show you pictures of our fam on their knees
> Tell us we used to be barbaric, we had actual queens
> [...] A kid dies, the blacker the killer, the sweeter the news
> And if he's white you give him a chance, he's ill and confused
> If he's black he's probably armed, you see him and shoot.
>
> (Dave, 2020)

References

Abbas, M.-S. (2019). Conflating the Muslim refugee and the terror suspect: Responses to the Syrian refugee 'crisis' in Brexit Britain. *Ethnic and Racial Studies*, 42(14), 2450–2469.

Altman, K. E. & Nakayama, T. K. (1992). The fallacy of the assumption of a unitary culture. Conference paper. Speech Communication Association convention, Chicago.

Applebaum, A. (2015). Donald Trump: Spokesman for birthers, truthers and internet trolls. *Washington Post*. 21 August. https://wapo.st/37x4dIc (last accessed 17 April 2022).

Arai, M., Bursell, M. & Nekby, L. (2016). The reverse gender gap in ethnic discrimination: Employer stereotypes of men and women with Arabic names. *International Migration Review*, 50(2), 385–412.

Ashcroft, B., Griffiths, G. & Tiffin, H. (2007). *Post-colonial studies: The key concepts*. Abingdon: Routledge.

Bhabha, H. K. (2004 [1994]). *The location of culture*. Abingdon: Routledge

Bjerregaard, T., Lauring, J. & Klitmøller, A. (2009). A critical analysis of intercultural communication research in cross-cultural management: Introducing newer developments in anthropology. *Critical Perspectives on International Business*, 5(3), pp. 207–228.

Braun, K. L., Browne, C. V., Ka'Opua, L. S., Kim, B. J. & Mokuau, N. (2014). Research on indigenous elders: From positivistic to decolonizing methodologies. *The Gerontologist*, 54(1), 117–126.

Chávez, K. R. (2013). Pushing boundaries: Queer intercultural communication. *Journal of International and Intercultural Communication*, 6(2), 83–95.

Colchado Lucio, Ó. (1997). *Rosa Cuchillo*. Lima: Editorial Universitaria.

Dave, S. (2020). Black. The BRIT Awards 2020. 18 February. www.youtube.com/ watch?v=mXLS2IzZSdg (last accessed 17 April 2022).

Davis, J. H. (2015). Obama's Twitter debut, @POTUS attracts hate-filled posts. *New York Times*, 22 May. A19.

Di Stasio, V. & Heath, A. (2019). Are employers in Britain discriminating against ethnic minorities? GEMM Briefing Note. Online. https://bit.ly/3xyOgvG (last accessed 17 April 2022).

Fanon, F. (1999 [1952]). *Black skin, white masks*. Translated by Charles Lam Markmann. London: Pluto Press.

Faulkner, M. F. (2013). *Belonging-in-difference: Negotiating identity in Anglophone Caribbean literature*. Cambridge: ARRCIMS.

Forster, D. E. (2020). Narcos television and Trump's politics of fear. *iMex*, 9(18), 28–48. DOI:10.23692/iMex.18

González Mitjáns, F. L. (2015). *Limpiadores*. United Kingdom: Vimeo. https://vimeo .com/154155933 (last accessed 17 April 2022).

Halualani, R. T. (2017). *Intercultural communication: A critical perspective*. San Diego, CA: Cognella Academic Publishing.

Halualani, R. T. & Nakayama, T. K. (2013). Critical intercultural communication studies: At a crossroads. In T. K. Nakayama & R. T. Halualani (eds.), *The handbook of critical intercultural communication* (pp. 1–16). Malden, MA: Wiley-Blackwell.

Heller, M., Pietikäinen, S. & Pujolar, J. (2018). *Critical sociolinguistic research methods: Studying language issues that matter*. New York: Routledge.

Jackson, R. & Dangerfield, C. (2002). Defining black masculinity as cultural property: An identity negotiation paradigm. In L. Samovar & R. Porter (eds.), *Intercultural communication: A reader* (pp. 120–130). Belmont, CA: Wadsworth.

Kobie, N. (2018). What is the gig economy and why is it so controversial? *WIRED*. 14 September. Online. https://bit.ly/3OhAELl (last accessed 17 April 2022).

Lazarus, N. (2012). *Postcolonial unconsciousness*. Cambridge: Cambridge University Press.

Leeds-Hurwitz, W. (2010). Writing the intercultural history of intercultural communication. In T. K. Nakayama & R. T. Halualani (eds.), *The handbook of critical intercultural communication* (pp. 21–33). Malden, MA: Wiley-Blackwell.

Lengel, L. & Newsom, V. A. (2020). Contested border crossings in shifting political landscapes: Anti-invasion discourses and human trafficking representations in US film and politics. *iMex*, 9(18), 61–82. DOI:10.23692/iMex.18

Lengel, L., Atay, A. & Kluch, Y. (2020). Decolonising gender and intercultural communication in transnational contexts. In G. Rings & S. M. Rasinger (eds.), *The Cambridge handbook of intercultural communication* (pp. 205–226). Cambridge: Cambridge University Press.

Loach, K. (2000). *Bread and roses*. United Kingdom: Parallax Pictures.

Locke, W. D. (2017). *The changing dynamics of UK higher education institutions in an increasingly marketised environment: Academic work and rankings*. London: UCL Institute of Education.

Markula, P. & Silk, M. (2011). *Qualitative research for physical culture*. New York: Palgrave Macmillan.

Martin, J. N. & Nakayama, T. K. (1999). Thinking about culture dialectically. *Communication Theory*, 9(1), 1–25.

Matthews, S. (2018). Confronting the colonial library: Teaching political studies amidst calls for a decolonized curriculum. *Politikon*, 45(1), 48–65.

Molina, M. D., Sundar, S. S., Le, T. & Lee, D. (2021). 'Fake news' is not simply false information: A concept explication and taxonomy of online content. *American Behavioral Scientist*, 65(2), 180–212.

Molina Mamani, F. (2013). *Cosmovisión andina*. Oruro: Latinas Editores.

Morales, E. (2015). Ceremonia en Tiwanaku. 21 January. Evo Morales. www.youtube .com/watch?v=qyMN ysHyFMg (last accessed 17 April 2022).

Nair, Sheila (2017). Postcolonialism. In S. McGlinchey, R. Walters & C. Scheinpflug (eds.), *International Relations Theory* (pp. 69–75). Bristol: E-International Relations Publishing.

Nakayama, T. K. (2020). Critical intercultural communication and the digital environment. In G. Rings & S. M. Rasinger (eds.), *The Cambridge handbook of intercultural communication* (pp. 85–95). Cambridge: Cambridge University Press.

Nakayama, T. K. & Halualani, R. T. (eds.) (2012). *Handbook of critical intercultural communication*. Malden, MA: Wiley-Blackwell.

Norwood, K. J. (2015). 'If you is white, you's alright.' Stories about colorism in America. *Global Studies Law Review*, 14(4), 585–607.

Ortiz, E. (2016). Trump kept 'Birther' beliefs going long after Obama's birth certificate was released. NBC News. 16 September. https://nbcnews.to/3K2771A (last accessed 17 April 2022).

Ott, B. L. & Dickinson, G. (2019). *The Twitter presidency. Donald J. Trump and the politics of white rage*. New York: Routledge.

Patton, M. Q. (2002). *Qualitative evaluation and research methods* (3rd edition). Thousand Oaks, CA: Sage.

Pietikäinen, S. (2015). Multilingual dynamics in Sámiland: Rhizomatic discourses on changing language. *International Journal of Bilingualism*, 19(2), 206–225. https://doi .org/10.1177/1367006913489199

Rings, G. (2010). *La Conquista desbaratada: Identidad y alteridad en la novela, el cine y el teatro hispánicos contemporáneos*. Madrid: Iberoamericana.

Rings, G. (2018). *The other in contemporary migrant cinema: Imagining a new Europe?* New York: Routledge.

Rings, G. (2020). From the American dream to the European dream in 'Buen día, Ramón'. In V. Dolle (ed.), *¿Un sueño europeo? Europa como destino anhelado de migración en la creación cultural latinoamericana (2001–2015)* (pp. 161–182). Madrid: Iberoamericana.

Rings, G. (2021). The superdiverse precariat of British Higher Education? 'Limpiadores' revisited. *Current Sociology*, 70(2), 291–307. https://doi .org/10.1177/0011392120983345

Said, E. W. (1978). *Orientalism*. London: Penguin.

Salo-Lee, L. (2020). Towards integrative intercultural communication. In G. Rings & S. M. Rasinger (eds.), *The Cambridge handbook of intercultural communication* (pp. 120–135). Cambridge: Cambridge University Press.

Savage, M., Devine, F., Cunningham, N., et al. (2013). A new model of social class? Findings from the BBC's Great British Class Survey Experiment. *Sociology*, 47(2), 219–250.

Seidman, I. (2006). *Interviewing as qualitative research* (3rd edition). New York: Teachers College Press.

Shah, P. P. & Khurshid, A. (2018). Writing against culture: Unveiling education and modernity for Hindu Indian and Muslim Pakistani women through an 'ethnography of the particular'. *International Journal of Qualitative Studies in Education*, 31(4), 257–271.

Shear, M. D., Haberman, M. Confessore, N., Yourish, K., Buchanan, L. & Collins, K. (2019). How Trump reshaped the presidency in over 11,000 tweets. *New York Times*. 2 November. https://nyti.ms/3uMx58m

Simpson, M. & Ake, T. (2010). Whitiwhiti korero: Exploring the researchers' relationship in cross-cultural research. *Journal of Intercultural Communication Research*, 39(3), 185–205.

Spedding, A. (2010[2004]). *De cuando en cuando Saturnina. Saturnina from time to time: Una historia oral del futuro*. La Paz: Mama Huaco.

Standing, G. (2011). *The precariat: The new dangerous class*. London: Bloomsbury Academic.

Standing, G. (2016). What is the precariat? *TEDxPrague*. 30 October. www.youtube.com/watch?v=nnYhZCUYOxs (last accessed 17 April 2022).

Stole, A. L. (1995) *Race and the education of desire: Foucault's history of sexuality and the colonial order of things*. Durham, NC: Duke University Press.

Tuhiwai Smith, L. (2012). *Decolonizing methodologies: Research and indigenous peoples*. London: Zed.

Turner, J. (2018). Internal colonisation: The intimate circulations of empire, race and liberal government. *European Journal of International Relations*, 24(4), 765–790.

University of Cambridge (2020). Requirements for research degrees. https://bit.ly/3OgORYS (last accessed 17 April 2022).

Wax-Edwards, J. (2020). Re-animating mexicanidad: Mexican cultural representations in 'The Book of Life' (2014) and 'Coco' (2017). *iMex*, 9(18), 112–129. DOI:10.23692/iMex.18

5 Contrastive Theories

In our historical discussion of intercultural communication scholarship in Section 2.2, we mentioned Geert Hofstede as a popular representative of contrastive research and elaborated on the global impact he has had. Following a brief discussion of the national cross-cultural values approach itself, we would now like to examine the extent to which and under what circumstances the work from Hofstede, Fons Trompenaars, Charles Hampden-Turner, Ronald Inglehart and Christian Welzel could be applied within critical intercultural communication (see also Chapter 4).

AIMS

By the end of this chapter, you should be able to:

1. explain the origin and application of contrastive theories;
2. describe continuities and discontinuities between selected contrastive approaches;
3. explain the extent to which they are connected to questions of power.

> **KEY TERMS**
> 6D model – 7D model – World Cultural Map

5.1 Setting the Context for National Cultural Approaches in the Twenty-First Century

The extensively referenced 'contrastive' or 'cross-cultural' studies from Hofstede to Trompenaars and Hampden-Turner and then to Inglehart and Welzel share above all the following features: they examine national cultural core values through mass questionnaires, express those values through cultural dimensions like individualism or self-expression, and contrast national tendencies through the scores linked to survey responses, for example, the existence of higher individualism and more self-expression in the United States than in China. However, that is precisely what they have been repeatedly criticised for in recent decades, and it is helpful to discuss and question fundamental critiques before we explain three particularly popular contrastive approaches in detail in Sections 5.2, 5.3 and 5.4.

Sixteen years after the first edition of Hofstede's *Culture's consequences* (Hofstede, 2001) and three years after the first edition of Trompenaars's *Riding the waves of culture* (Trompenaars, 1993), both now major classics in the field, leading network society analyst Manuel Castells elaborated on the crisis of the nation state, and continued to make this claim in later editions of his key publication, *The rise of the network society* (Castells, 1996, p. 24; 2010, p. xviii). Other critics have included Baskerville, who argues that a nation is 'not the proper unit for studying culture' (Baskerville, 2003, p. 8), and McSweeney and colleagues, who are even 'sceptical about the existence of [an] enduring [...] shared national culture' (McSweeney et al., 2016, p. 49).

However, this criticism has to be questioned in the context of the worldwide rise of neo-nationalism since the end of the twentieth century, which has been examined in depth in social anthropological and political research (Gingrich & Banks, 2006; Becker, 2019). It shows in the destabilisation of supranational organisations like the European Union and the United Nations: the former through populist ultranationalist parties in all EU states, sometimes in governments, which also led to Brexit; the latter for example through the failure to establish UN sanctions against Israel's settler colonialism in the occupied Palestinian territories due to repeated US-American vetoes. Even reactions to the global COVID-19 pandemic in 2020/2021 were shaped considerably more by constantly changing nationalist initiatives than by global intervention from, for example, the World Health Organization, which might help to explain the enormous dissemination and long-lasting impact of the pandemic and confirms evolutionary psychology research on the continuity of national tribalism (see Chapters 1 & 4).

Considering the impact of international mass migration, which has significantly shaped the demographics of most nation states, the strength of these nationalist movements might at first glance be surprising. However, on the one hand, growing neo-nationalism has often been explored as a reaction to precisely those migration trends, for example, white supremacy movements returning to the mainstream as anti-immigration movements in the United States under the Trump administration (Clark, 2020). On the other hand, national and even nationalist values are increasingly shared by former immigrants too. Mazanec et al. (2015) explain this convincingly with homogenisation tendencies in immigration: in the context of enhanced sociocultural programming, for example in pre-school, school and other environments, the values of the host culture tend to be assimilated significantly more by the second generation of immigrants onwards than by the first generation.

While all this should not lead us to ignore or tolerate the influence of new global players, including the monopoly power of companies like Facebook or Amazon, it helps to understand why Magala's hypothesis that the 'nation state remains the basic organisational form of contemporary societies' (Magala, 2005, p. 2) is still valid, and it is not surprising that in this context the support for national cultural values research like Hofstede's 6D model remains strong (Magala, 2005; Paulson, 2005; Tuleja & Schachner, 2020).

TASKS

- Access one of your online social network accounts, e.g. Facebook. With whom do you exchange messages most frequently? Do you know most of these people from personal encounters?
- If your online and offline social networks are largely identical, then what change from offline to online networks would you expect from people whose family and friends are overwhelmingly of the same national background?
- If your online and offline social networks are fundamentally different, examine the reasons for that. Compare your findings with the findings of others.
- Figure 5.1 represents *contrast* as a dominant concept. Compare this with the illustration of culture in Figure 1.1 and link this to your comments above.

Figure 5.1 *Contrast* by Alíz Kovács-Zöldi

5.2 Hofstede's 6D model

In the first edition of his *Culture's Consequences* in 1980, Hofstede elaborated on four cultural dimensions – *individualism, uncertainty avoidance, power distance* and *masculinity* – and developed related scores for forty countries, based on large-scale surveys at IBM (more than 116,000 between 1967 and 1973; Hofstede, 2001). In the second and last edition of the book, he adds *long-term orientation* as a fifth dimension (Hofstede, 2001), and in *Cultures and Organisations* (Hofstede et al., 2010) he completes the **6D model** by adding *indulgence versus restraint* and the scores for what now totals seventy-six countries, with surveys going well into the twenty-first century. According to Green's calculation (2016), *Culture's Consequences* remains among the fifteen most cited books in the social sciences, and this brief outline indicates that Hofstede's work cannot be altogether rejected on the grounds that it is outdated and/or does not explain a particular sociopolitical phenomenon, as McSweeney et al. (2016) suggest. We follow here in particular Taras et al.'s (2012) meta-analysis of Hofstede's dimensions, which confirms through an analysis of more than 400 Hofstede-based applications that the 6D scores continue to show high validity, especially in the rankings of countries relative to each other (see also Eringa et al., 2015).

Hofstede's six dimensions have now been applied widely on all continents, which is confirmed by a Google Scholar (2021) search for Hofstede's cultural dimensions that leads to tens of thousands of results. The six dimensions have also inspired integrative and competitive research. The most popular example of an integrative approach is probably the attempt of the GLOBE project (2020) to bring key ideas from Hofstede, Trompenaars and Hampden-Turner together, while competitive research confirms overlaps in individual dimensions. For example, *individualism*, defined as 'a preference for a loosely-knit social framework in which individuals are expected to take care of only themselves and their immediate families' (Hofstede Insights, 2021), has been highlighted by Triandis as 'the most significant difference among cultures' (Triandis, 2001, p. 907), which reappears in the dimensions of Trompenaars and Hampden-Turner. *Uncertainty avoidance*, which explores the 'extent to which the members of a culture feel threatened by ambiguous or unknown situations' (Hofstede Insights, 2021), recalls Schwartz's discussion of 'conservative' and 'open' cultures (Schwartz, 2006) and Triandis and Suh's 'tight' and 'loose' cultures (Triandis & Suh, 2002, p. 39). In particular, groups that score high in *uncertainty avoidance* tend to focus on established rules for everyday behaviour, which is reflected in 'conservative' and 'tight' cultures. *Power distance* focuses on 'the extent to which the less powerful members of institutions and organisations [...] accept that power is distributed unequally' (Hofstede Insights, 2021), while *masculinity* measures competitiveness, which tends to relate to job satisfaction, in contrast to life satisfaction mirrored in relationship enhancement (Hofstede, 2001, p. 292).

Finally, *long-term orientation* (LTO) explores the emphasis on long-term gains, rather than short-term benefits, while *indulgence versus restraint* (IvR) examines differences between the focus on 'desires and impulses' and the tendency to suppress or regulate gratification (Hofstede Insights, 2021). The former is often reflected in savings (potentially high LTO) and credit card debts (low LTO), although purchasing power and other factors have to be taken into account, while the latter shows in advertising campaigns like Red's 'Me time' and L'Oreal's 'Because you're worth it!' (high IvR focus). It might be worth stressing that the 6D model has been applied particularly frequently to advertising, for example by Albers (1994), Albers-Miller and Gelb (1996) and De Mooij (1998), and it is very likely that Hofstede's and other contrastive research continue to play an important role in advertising development and analysis in the context of enhanced cross-cultural marketing (Lazović, 2012; Retnowati, 2015). On the other hand, there has been criticism that goes well beyond the nation state approach (see Section 5.1), which will be elaborated at the end of Section 5.3 because it addresses Hofstede's as much as Trompenaars and Hampden-Turner's work.

TASKS

There are plenty of McDonald's adverts on YouTube: please compare McDonald's advertising in China and the United States on the basis of Hofstede's 6D model (Hofstede Insights, 2021). Which features relate to his dimensions (e.g. *individualism* in adverts and cultural scores), which don't, and why?

5.3 Trompenaars and Hampden-Turner's 7D model

Trompenaars and Hampden-Turner's seven dimensions are *individualism versus communitarianism, universalism versus particularism, specific versus diffuse, affective versus neutral, achievement versus ascription, sequential versus synchronic time*, and *inner versus outer directed*. While there is some overlap with Hofstede's work, especially regarding *individualism*, other aspects of the **7D model** show significant differences, such as *universalism versus particularism*. According to Trompenaars and Hampden-Turner, people in universalist cultures like Switzerland, Canada or the United States tend to prefer one definition for 'what is good and right' that should be applied worldwide, while in the particularist cultures of Venezuela, Korea and Russia, there is a tendency to put more weight on relationships and related obligations (Trompenaars & Hampden-Turner, 1997, p. 8). One popular example is what exactly friends can expect from you, even if they break the law: in a particularist culture, they can expect a relatively high degree of loyalty, which might include false statements, for example if the police want to penalise them for breaking the speed limit and you intervene on their behalf by testifying that they were driving at a lower speed than you know they were (Trompenaars, 2013).

Through their analysis of *specific and diffuse* cultures, Trompenaars and Hampden-Turner attempt to capture the difference between people who tend to separate public and private spheres quite strictly (e.g. in the United States) vis-à-vis people who tend to engage others diffusely in numerous – public and private – areas of their lives (e.g. Greece), because this might be 'necessary before business can proceed' (Trompenaars & Hampden-Turner, 1997, p. 9; Trompenaars, 2013). The *affective versus neutral* dimension explores how acceptable or even desirable the expression of feelings is (e.g. loud laughter), while *achievement versus ascription* examines how people tend to be judged: whether predominantly on the basis of accomplishments or related to status, including your role in a company, academic title, age and/or gender (1997, pp. 72–80, 104–119). *Sequential versus synchronic time orientation* elaborates on the difference exemplified through ancient Greek gods Chronos and Kairos: Chronos stands for the sequence of clock time, which encourages people to do one thing at a time, while Kairos – the god of opportunity – inspires to break with such sequences if that opens up new possibilities. In Chapter 8, we will see that the notion of time also plays an important role in anthropological approaches to intercultural communication. Finally, *inner versus outer direction* addresses differences shaped by the focus on the self as a point of departure for the right action (e.g. in the United States) vis-à-vis a focus on the environment, from other people to nature (e.g. in Norway; 1997, p. 232).

While Hofstede criticises Trompenaars and Hampden-Turner predominantly for 'the lack of content validity' (Hofstede, 1996, p. 197), most scholars highlight *cultural determinism* and/or *essentialism* as risks associated with contrastive approaches (Croucher, 2017, p. 88; Ten Thije, 2020, p. 42). This can in our opinion be observed in the work of all three authors, but even more in simplified applications of these approaches (as in Macdonald, 2013). These risks seem even greater if cultural features are categorised into binary oppositions, which is particularly explicit in Hofstede's sixth dimension, *indulgence versus restraint*, and in summaries of his work (as in Tuleja & Schachner, 2020), but also in Trompenaars and Hampden-Turner's wording of their seven dimensions. Key to reducing essentialist tendencies is in our opinion the consideration of individual differences and the wider spectrum of other cultural factors, including class, age, gender and educational background, but also tensions between the local, regional, national and supranational identity constructs discussed in Chapters 1 and 2.

It is worth highlighting that the authors acknowledge the importance of such variables within and beyond national culture: Hofstede elaborates for example on the individual level of human programming when he presents his pyramid of mental programming (Hofstede, 2001, pp. 3, 4), and he discusses an impressive number of studies that consider gender, religion, health and other variables, including Inglehart and Welzel's work (2001, p. 33). However, his key publications focus on national culture, and the potential impact of these other variables, for example, on national culture scores if differentiated according to gender, age, and so on, are rarely discussed in detail. Similarly, Trompenaars and Hampden-Turner highlight the importance of individual personality as mediator (Trompenaars & Hampden-Turner, 1997, p. 26) and distinguish between national, corporate and professional cultures (1997, p. 7), but then they focus on national culture without closer scrutiny of individual mediation and the tension between these different cultures.

GROUP TASK

Work together, ideally with people from two different cultures, and analyse Coca Cola adverts for these cultures by drawing on Trompenaars and Hampden-Turner's seven-dimensional model. If the adverts are different, to what extent does the model help you understand these differences, and what are the limitations? If they are the same ('global advertising'), which values are disseminated, and how far do they relate to the seven dimensions?

5.4   Inglehart and Welzel's World Cultural Map

The **World Cultural Map** is dynamic, because the World Values Survey (WVS) Association, founded by Ronald Inglehart and Chris Welzel, organises regular surveys to measure values and beliefs (WVS, 2021; Tuleja & Schachner, 2020, p. 108). So far, that team has completed seven major surveys, from 'Wave' 1 (1981–1984) to Wave 7 (2017–2021), the latter in cooperation with the European Values Study (EVS) team, and it aims to run more every five years to examine

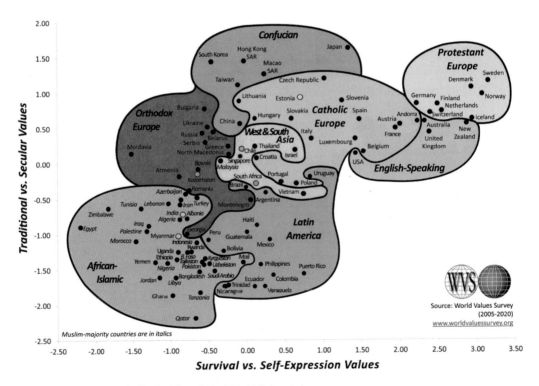

Figure 5.2 *The Inglehart-Welzel World Cultural Map*
Source: World Values Survey 7 (2020)

developments (WVS, 2021). Since 1981, the coverage has been expanded to include seventy-eight countries, with sample sizes ranging from 1,000 to 3,200 responses per country covering fourteen themes, including 'social values attitudes and stereotypes', 'religious values', 'ethical values and norms' and 'societal well-being' (2021). A set of questions has been identical over time, but new questions have been added to capture new developments, for example in social media use, while less relevant questions have been phased out (Besova, 2015). The map in Figure 5.2 is based on Wave 7 data.

The map shows significant differences between 'African-Islamic' countries scoring high on *traditional* and *survival* values like Jordan, Zimbabwe and Ghana in the lower left corner, and protestant European countries scoring high on *secular* and *self-expression* values like Sweden, Norway and Germany. According to WVS (2021), this means an emphasis on 'the importance of religion, parent–child ties, deference to authority and traditional family values' (traditional values) and 'economic and physical security' (survival) in the former, but more emancipation from traditional values (secularism) and more tolerance of foreigners and homosexuals, interest in gender equality and 'participation in decision-making' (self-expression) in the latter.

GROUP TASK

Work together again, ideally with people from two different cultures. Locate your cultures on the map and examine the extent to which the people you know from those cultures seem to be good examples of the WVS categorisation. If your cultures are not shown, work from two cultures that are and which you are familiar with.

A comparison with previous WVS data shows diagonal movement of countries from traditional-survival to more secular-rational and self-expression orientations (e.g. Mexico, India and China), which has partially been interpreted as a result of increased standards of living measured in GDP per capita (Matei & Abrudan, 2018, p. 662). This is in line with Tang and Koveos's observation that 'changes in economic conditions are the source of cultural dynamics' (Tang & Koveos, 2008, p. 1045), and Hofstede's findings that better economic conditions for 'the entire population' tend to reduce *power distance* and enhance *individualism* (Hofstede et al., 2010, pp. 87, 134), which reflects higher self-expression in the WVS data. Finally, economically advanced countries appear to have changed more rapidly, which might help to explain the growing gap between the traditional-survival focus in lower-income countries and the secular-rational and self-expression focus in higher-income countries (WVS, 2021).

However, the country clusters remain in relation to each other relatively stable in the forty years observed, in that African-Islamic countries have kept traditional-survival orientations vis-à-vis more secular-rational and self-expressionist values in protestant European countries, with West and South Asian but also catholic European countries between these poles. This supports the claim that core values show strong continuities (Hofstede Insights, 2021; Beugelsdijk et al., 2015, p. 224), and Hofstede draws on WVS data to support the validity of his dimensions: in particular, he identifies a correlation between traditional orientation and high *power distance*, and the development of the *indulgence versus restraint* dimension starts from the observation of higher well-being outside survival-focused countries and its link to high *individualism*, low masculinity and *indulgence* (e.g. in Finland and Denmark; Hofstede et al., 2010, pp. 44–45, 94; Helliwell et al., 2020, p. 24).

TASK

Compare the WVS model with Hofstede's and Trompenaars and Hampden-Turner's models: what are the advantages and disadvantages? To what extent can all three models help you to understand cultural differences and similarities? What are the risks and limitations of using these models?

Critics highlight that the WVS has become 'a pivotal source of data to explain secularization, gender equality, interpersonal trust, post-modernization and democratization' (Alemán & Woods, 2016, p. 1040; see also Ciftci, 2010 and Coffé & Dilli, 2015). Also, through regular mass surveys, it enables insights into developments in values and beliefs that Hofstede, Trompenaars and Hampden-Turner, and also other contrastive approaches, such as Schwartz (2006) and Minkov et al. (2018), do not provide. However, Alemán & Woods argue that WVS data 'are not configural, metric, and scalar invariant and hence comparable cross-nationally, except among a small number of Western post-industrial societies' (Alemán & Woods, 2016, p. 1060), which raises questions regarding the success in decolonising agency, methodological approaches and conceptual basis of the surveys (see Chapter 4). Considering fast growing economic inequality in income and household wealth *within* nations, for example in the United States and most OECD countries since the 1970s (Inglehart, 2016), the extent to which the differentiation between low and high-income 'countries' continues to explain shifts in values as suggested on the WVS website (WVS, 2021) also remains questionable. Certainly, GDP growth is neither on its own nor per capita (as argued in Matei & Abrudan, 2018, p. 662) a convincing measurement, since highly uneven distribution might ultimately reduce *individualism* and enhance *power distance*, especially due to the links between economic and legal inequality, for example 'the super-rich can lobby with legislators and pay lawyers who earn a multiple of the salaries of judges' (Hofstede et al., 2010, p. 87).

5.5 In Summary

Considering our discussion of critical intercultural communication as a potential umbrella concept for the field (Chapter 4), contrastive approaches deserve more postcolonial scrutiny and further revision. However, *if* national cultural 'programming' is genuinely considered as only one variable in interaction and *if* the dimensions and themes are in a transcultural sense applied to different overlapping but also conflictive collectives, from local to supranational level including other variables from personality traits to class, education and gender (Chapters 1 & 2), then they can provide very useful contributions to the development of the field. Avoiding or at least reducing essentialising tendencies in national cultural profiling is a task for authors of contrastive research, but also for scholars and teachers who discuss and apply these studies, because far too often monocultural essentialising (Chapter 1) is particularly strong at application level.

DISCUSSION QUESTIONS

Return to the McDonald's adverts that you examined with Hofstede's dimension before (Section 5.2) and now explore them with reference to the other two models (Trompenaars and Hampden-Turner, WVS). To what extent does that help you to examine these adverts in greater depth? What are the limits? Which other dimensions do you know and how can they help you?

CASE STUDY

Please analyse the following case study by drawing on Hofstede Insights' dimensions (Hofstede Insights, 2021), and comment on the potential and limits of your approach.

> Ralph K., a US American owner of a successful book distributor in Nairobi, saw that his Kenyan employees were behind schedule in their preparations of an important proposal for a major government contract. Meeting the deadline was essential, and he therefore decided to work closely with his staff to help them deliver the goods on time. When that deadline was only a few hours away, he even started helping junior administrators make copies and collate them in the right order. However, he noticed that his employees did not seem to appreciate that. They withdrew as much as they could and often stared at him coldly. Ralph was surprised to see that he was so unwelcome.
>
> Adapted from Ferraro (2010).

References

Albers, N. D. (1994). Relating Hofstede's dimensions of culture to international variations in print advertisements: A comparison of appeals. PhD. University of Houston.

Albers-Miller, N. D. & Gelb, B. D. (1996). Business advertising appeals as a mirror of cultural dimensions: A study of eleven countries. *Journal of Advertising*, 25(4), 57–70. https://doi.org/10.1080/00913367.1996.10673512 (last accessed 17 April 2022).

Alemán, J. & Woods, D. (2016). Value orientations from the world values survey: How comparable are they cross-nationally? *Comparative Political Studies*, 49(8), 1039–1067. https://doi.org/10.1177/0010414015600458

Baskerville, R. F. (2003). Hofstede never studied culture. *Accounting, Organizations and Society*, 28(1), 1–14. https://doi.org/10.1016/S0361-3682(01)00048-4

Becker, J. (2019). *Neo-nationalism in the EU: Social and economic policy platforms and actions*. Brussels: AK Europa.

Besova, M. (2015). How are world values changing? Higher School of Economics. 20 November. Online. www.hse.ru/en/news/research/166381530.html (last accessed 21 January 2021).

Beugelsdijk, S., Maseland, R., & Van Hoorn, A. (2015). Are scores on Hofstede's dimensions of national culture stable over time? A cohort analysis. *Global Strategy Journal*, 5(3), 223–240. https://doi.org/10.1002/gsj.1098

Castells, M. (1996). *The rise of the network society* (1st edition). Malden, MA: Blackwell.

Castells, M. (2010). *The rise of the network society* (2nd edition). Chichester: Wiley-Blackwell.

Ciftci, S. (2010). Modernization, Islam, or social capital: What explains attitudes toward democracy in the Muslim world? *Comparative Political Studies*, 43(11), 1442–1470. https://doi.org/10.1177/0010414010371903

Clark, S. (2020). How white supremacy returned to mainstream politics. Center for American Progress. 1 July. Online. https://ampr.gs/3rwbqze (last accessed 17 April 2022).

Coffé, H. & Dilli, S. (2015). The gender gap in political participation in Muslim-majority countries. *International Political Science Review*, 36(5), 526–544. https://doi.org/10.1177/0192512114528228

Croucher, S. M. (2017). *Global perspectives on intercultural communication*. New York: Routledge.

De Mooij, M. K. (1998). *Global marketing and advertising: Understanding cultural paradoxes*. Thousand Oaks, CA: Sage.

Eringa, K., Caudron, L. N., Rieck, K., Xie, F. & Gerhardt, T. (2015). How relevant are Hofstede's dimensions for inter-cultural studies? A replication of Hofstede's research among current international business students. *Research in Hospitality Management*, 5(2), 187–198. https://doi.org/10.1080/22243534.2015.11828344

Ferraro, G. (2010). *The cultural dimension of international business* (6th edition). Upper Saddle River, NJ: Prentice Hall.

Gingrich, A. & Banks, M. (2006). *Neo-nationalism in Europe and beyond: Perspectives from social anthropology*. New York: Berghahn Books.

GLOBE (2020). An overview of the 2004 study: Understanding the relationship between national culture, societal effectiveness and desirable leadership attributes. Online. https://globeproject.com/study_2004_2007 (last accessed 17 April 2022).

Google Scholar (2021). Hofstede cultural dimensions. https://bit.ly/3jK9EX1

Green, E. (2016, May 12). What are the most-cited publications in the social sciences (according to Google Scholar)? *LSE Impact Blog*. https://bit.ly/3vgYs9G (last accessed 15 April 2022).

Haerpfer, C., Inglehart, R., Moreno, A., Welzel, C., Kizilova, K., Diez-Medrano J., Lagos, M., Norris, P., Ponarin, E. & Puranen, B. et al. (eds.) (2020). *World values survey: Round seven – country-pooled datafile.* Madrid and Vienna: JD Systems Institute & WVSA Secretariat. https://doi.org/10.14281/18241.1

Helliwell, J. F., Layard, R., Sachs, J. D. & De Neve, J.-E. (2020). *World happiness report* (8th edition). New York: Sustainable Development Solutions Network.

Hofstede, G. (1996). Riding the waves of commerce: A test of Trompenaars' 'model' of national culture differences. *International Journal of Intercultural Relations*, 20(2), 189–198. https://doi.org/10.1016/0147-1767(96)00003-x

Hofstede, G. (2001). *Culture's consequences* (2nd edition). London: SAGE.

Hofstede, G., Hofstede, G. J. & Minkov, M. (2010). *Cultures and organizations: Software of the mind* (3rd edition). New York: McGraw Hill.

Hofstede Insights (2021). Country comparison. Online. https://bit.ly/3vvDSCC (last accessed 17 April 2022).

Inglehart, R. (2016). Inequality and modernization. Why equality is likely to make a comeback. *Foreign Affairs*, 95(1), 2–10.

Lazović, V. (2012). Content analysis of advertisements in different cultures. *ELOPE*, 9(2) 39–51. https://doi.org/10.4312/elope.9.2.39-51

Macdonald, S. (2013). The psychology of effective conversion rate optimization. Searchenginepeople. 11 September. Online. https://bit.ly/3MbcsZj (last accessed 17 April 2022).

Magala, S. (2005). *Cross-cultural competence.* Abingdon: Routledge.

Matei, M. C. & Abrudan, M.-M. (2018). Are national cultures changing? Evidence from the World Values Survey. *Procedia – Social and Behavioral Sciences*, 238, 657–664.

Mazanec, J. A., Crotts, J. C., Gursov, D. & Lu, L. (2015): Homogeneity versus heterogeneity of cultural values: An item-response theoretical approach applying Hofstede's cultural dimensions in a single nation. *Tourism Management*, 48, 299–304.

McSweeney, B., Brown, D. & Iliopoulou, S. (2016). Claiming too much, delivering too little: Testing some of Hofstede's dimensions. *Irish Journal of Management*, 35(1), 34–57. https://doi.org/10.1515/ijm-2016-0003

Minkov, M., Bond, M. H., Dutt, P., Schachner, M., Morales, O., Sanchez, C., Jandosova, J., Khassenbekov, Y. & Mudd, B. (2018). A reconsideration of Hofstede's fifth dimension: New flexibility versus monumentalism data from 54 countries. *Cross-Cultural Research*, 52(3), 309–333. https://doi.org/10.1177/1069397117727488

Paulson, S. K. (2005). An integrated social science perspective on global business ethics. *International Journal of Commerce and Management*, 15 (3/4), 178–186. https://doi.org/10.1108/10569210580000195

Retnowati, Y. (2015). Challenges in cross cultural advertising. *Humaniora*, 27(3), 340–349. https://doi.org/10.22146/jh.v27i3.10594

Schwartz, S. H. (2006). A theory of cultural value orientations: Explication and applications. *Comparative Sociology*, 5(2–3), 137–182. https://doi.org/10.1163/156913306778667357

Tang, L. & Koveos, P. E. (2008). A framework to update Hofstede's cultural value indices: Economic dynamics and institutional stability. *Journal of International Business Studies*, 39(6), 1045–1063. https://doi.org/10.1057/palgrave.jibs.8400399

Taras, V., Steel, P. & Kirkman, B. L. (2012). Improving national cultural indices using a longitudinal meta-analysis of Hofstede's dimensions. *Journal of World Business*, 47, 329–341.

Ten Thije, J. D. (2020). What is intercultural communication? In G. Rings & S. M. Rasinger (eds.), *The Cambridge handbook of intercultural communication* (pp. 35–55). Cambridge: Cambridge University Press.

Triandis, H. C. (2001). Individualism-collectivism and personality. *Journal of Personality*, 69(6), 907–924. https://doi.org/10.1111/1467-6494.696169

Triandis, H. C. & Suh, E. M. (2002). Cultural influence on personality. *Annual Review of Psychology*, 53, 133–160.

Trompenaars, F. & Hampden-Turner, C. (1997). *Riding the waves of culture* (2nd edition). London: Nicholas Brealey.

Trompenaars, F. (2013). Riding the waves of culture. TEDxAmsterdam. 6 November. www.youtube.com/watch?v=hmyfjKjcbm0 (last accessed 17 April 2022).

Tuleja, E. A. & Schachner, M. (2020). From shared values to cultural dimensions. In G. Rings & S. M. Rasinger (eds.), *The Cambridge handbook of intercultural communication* (pp. 96–119). Cambridge: Cambridge University Press.

WVS (2021). World Values Survey. WVS Wave 7. www.worldvaluessurvey.org (last accessed 17 April 2022).

6 Imagological Perspectives in Literature and Film

We highlighted in Chapter 2 that contributions to the development of intercultural communication increasingly tend to come from literature and film; this reflects their portrayal and often critical discussion of power hierarchies in cultural encounters. The latter is key for critical intercultural communication, which we have explored as a new umbrella concept for the field. In this chapter, we want to examine the importance of literature and film in greater detail. Of particular interest are cultural stereotypes, which tend to be reconstructed in intercultural fiction in order to question them, as well as the hierarchies and mechanisms of exclusion, suppression and discrimination behind them. Such a study of stereotypical images can be categorised as '**imagology**', that is, an image studies approach originally developed in comparative literature.

AIMS
By the end of this chapter, you should be able to:
1. explain the extent to which and how exactly literature and film can contribute to critical intercultural competence;
2. demonstrate how fictional narratives can be used to support monocultural worldviews;
3. describe the relation between fictional narratives and power.

> **KEY TERMS**
> imagology – tribalism – Third Space

6.1 Critical Intercultural Intervention through Fictional Narratives

6.1.1 The Power of Fictional Narratives

Literature and *film* can both be explored as fictional narratives (Chatman, 1990; Fludernik, 2008, p. 15) that are 'told', that is, they are events that 'come to us mediated through an organizing consciousness' (Hawthorn, 2017, p. 6) and expressed through words and/or images. A good starting point is the discussion of imaginative works of prose, poetry and film as cultural stories, which have the power to explain 'the world' from different perspectives. Highly influential

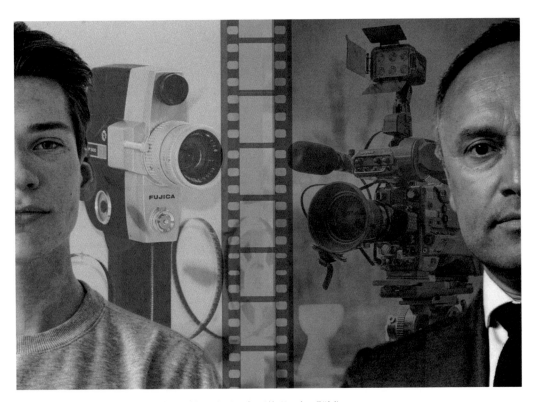

Figure 6.1 *Imagological Perspectives* by Alíz Kovács-Zöldi

philosopher and former Harvard professor Nelson Goodman elaborates how such stories contribute to 'worldmaking' through the creation of 'multiple alternative world-versions' (Goodman, 1995, p. 107), which can fight the simplistic mono-cultural binary portrayals that we have discussed as particularly frequent in populist political and tabloid messages in Chapter 1. German film studies scholar Joanne Leal confirms that potential, when she argues that films 'can actively promote intercultural communication [...] by offering representational alternatives to conservative notions of national belonging and exclusionary constructions of what social cohesion should mean' (Leal, 2020, p. 288).

The multiple meanings (*'polyvalence'*) of fictional narratives helps to enhance readers and viewers' critical distance from the established knowledge portrayed: on the one hand, fictional narratives are always connected to the directly experienced (*'empirical'*) world, because they embody 'widespread cultural norms and modes of behaviour' (Attridge, 2004, p. 21) of that world. On the other hand, the creative potential of the fictional realm helps to 'put the represented knowledge playfully under erasure and create a sense of ambiguity that invites readers to enter into an open dialogue with the text' (Neumann, 2020, p. 139), and – for example – question exclusionary knowledge and related feelings, such as populist stereotypes of migrants as threats. All this is key for the enhancement of intercultural competence.

The power of literature and film does not stop at cognitive levels. Through the wide spectrum of rhetorical means, from repetitions to allegories and metaphors, their stories can have a measurable impact on the affective and pragmatic competences of readers and viewers. It could be argued that film has the additional advantage of image and sound, which provide a multimedia experience that can strengthen the impact on intercultural competence. Literature, however, allows for a much greater flexibility in individual reception, such as reading at a personal pace with the option of easily skipping backwards and forwards within the text, which is more difficult in film viewing and not possible at all in cinemas. Rather than deciding for one medium, it might therefore be recommendable to get inspiration from both, as literature and film can in all their forms – from short stories and novels to animated and non-animated films – enhance cognitive, affective and pragmatic competences, which are essential for intercultural competence development (Antor, 2020, p. 78; Lüsebrink, 2008, p. 9; Erll & Gymnich, 2015, pp. 11–13).

6.1.2 *Bandhobi* – Intercultural Intervention through Film

For example, *Bandhobi* (2009), an award-winning film by Korean director Shin Dong-il, at first glance presents two very different protagonists in South Korea, Karim and Min-soe: Karim is a migrant worker from Bangladesh, whose illegal status is abused by Korean employers; Min-soe is a Korean, who rebels against any form of authority, be it in school or in her broken family at home, while paying her college fees through prostitution. However, the film also explores the similarities of both protagonists as outsiders within a capitalist South Korean society, and argues that it is important for them to unite against the oppression that both of them suffer: Karim as exploited worker and Min-soe as exploited prostitute. Frequent close-ups and a level angle camera focus on Karim and Min-soe help viewers identify with the suffering and angry rebellion of the protagonists, who belong to the precariat of post-industrial Korea, that is, a very diverse class whose employment and life are extremely insecure (see the discussion in Chapter 4). Led by the protagonists, viewers are therefore invited to develop an informed stance against internal colonialism in neoliberal societies (Chapter 4), which is also a focus in contemporary European film – from renowned British director Ken Loach's *Bread and Roses* (2000) to postgraduate student Fernando Mitjáns's *Limpiadores* (2015) (see Rings, 2021). In all these cases, films demonstrate their potential to evoke different but also comparable categorisations of experiences, beliefs, values, fears and hopes, which Neumann (2020) discusses with a focus on literature.

6.1.3 *The Harp and the Shadow* – Literary Intervention

Colonialism can also be questioned far more explicitly. For example, in the celebrated historical novel *The harp and the shadow* (1979), famous Cuban author Alejo Carpentier presents a Columbus with many features of the well-known discoverer, from his famous voyages to America to Pope Pius XI's proposition to make him a saint. However, in parallel, he constructs him as a '*pícaro*', that is, a roguish character who constantly misleads everybody – his crew, the Spanish kings, indigenous people and ultimately himself – to justify more voyages and get as much gold as possible from the New World (Rings, 2010, pp. 99–111). Given the scarcity of reliable first-hand accounts of Columbus's voyages, the picaresque character cannot be fully backed up by historical sources, but it is also difficult to reject all of its aspects. In this sense, Carpentier fills a gap in historical knowledge with a construct that invites us to laugh about the still celebrated discoverer and above all see human characteristics in him, especially the desire of a poor tradesman to make his fortune and a name for himself.

Through this portrayal, Carpentier's Columbus questions the binary construct and logic of colonial and neo-colonial European imperialism (Ashcroft et al., 2007, p. 19), within which morally superior colonisers seem to focus above all on a Christianising and civilising mission to help the morally inferior, pagan and primitive Other in the new world. In presenting Columbus as a failed discoverer, conqueror and coloniser, *The harp and the shadow* also destabilises the strict separation in contemporary schoolbooks between (glorious) discoverers and (usually less glorious) conquerors that keeps colonial binaries alive. All this helps to shift the focus on some historical facts that have been marginalised for centuries, including Columbus's desperate reconstruction (or invention) of America as the fictional Asia known from Marco Polo's travels, which correlates with his inability to understand that he had not found an alternative route to India (Rings, 2010, p. 117).

TASK

Search for contemporary portrayals of Columbus in your culture, e.g. your schoolbooks, a leading newspaper, literature or film, and compare these images. To what extent are they similar to or different from colonial glorification and/or the critical portrayal in *The harp and the shadow*?

6.1.4 *Bandhobi* and *The Harp and the Shadow* – Potential and Limits

To conclude our exploration of a filmic and a literary example, it could be argued that the ambivalent portrayal of the protagonists in each text helps receivers to question binary images. In particular, *Bandhobi* wants viewers to examine the rigorous separation of migrants (like Karim) from non-migrants (like Min-soe) in a neoliberal society, and consider that this might help to cover up wider inequalities and maintain existing power hierarchies through a principle of 'divide and rule' (*divide et impera*). *The harp and the shadow* challenges the artificial separation of discoverers from conquerors, but also of conquerors from conquered through its portrayal of Columbus as 'discovered discoverer' and 'conquered conqueror', who ultimately dies impoverished in his illusion that he had discovered prosperous India (Rings, 2010, p. 251).

Overall, the presentation of images between these binaries, or *'border thinking'* – as Mignolo (2000, p. xxv) puts it, is in both texts essential to question ongoing colonial difference. Comparable is also the structural approach: both texts start their critical intervention with a reconstruction of the imagined need for a strict separation of people to then destabilise that construct, because 'the colonial difference creates the conditions for dialogic situations in which a fractured enunciation is enacted from the subaltern perspective as a response to the hegemonic discourse and perspective' (2000, p. xxv). This is particularly obvious in the camera focus on social outsiders Karim and Min-soe, but also in the narrative focus on the feelings and thoughts of a roguish Columbus, who admits proudly on his deathbed that he – a man of humble origins – had managed to mislead even the Catholic kings. Finally, the critical intercultural intervention in *Bandhobi*, *The harp and the shadow* and numerous other postcolonial narratives helps to understand the values, norms and customs of people categorised as Others better, from migrant Karim to indigenous Diego. Neumann elaborates on such an intercultural potential for literature (Neumann, 2020, p. 137).

It is worth stressing that no fictional narrative can be categorised as a homogeneous construct, because – due to the polyvalence – there is always some room for interpretation depending on the questions asked and methodologies used, and it is common to find alternative – if not contradictory – images within a story. For example, both *Bandhobi* and *The harp and the shadow* could be questioned for their portrayal of historical agency of the colonised, since neither Bangladeshi

Karim nor indigenous Diego are ultimately able to break with the colonial exploitation principle. In particular, it could be argued that such a presentation is in line with the portrayal of the colonised in (neo-)colonial discourses as people who suffer history, while the coloniser appears as a 'maker of history' (Blaut, 1993, pp. 1, 96). However, precisely that image has been convincingly questioned by contemporary historical and anthropological studies arguing that colonised people had through their behaviour, for example assimilation, integration or rebellion, a substantial impact on the development of the colonial project (for an overview see Rings, 2010, pp. 66–71). All this should, however, not distract from the postcolonial orientation and intercultural aims of the two very different fictional texts outlined so far, and numerous other postcolonial, decolonial, intercultural and transcultural texts (see the conceptual discussions in Chapters 1 and 4, and the analysis of comparable literature and film in Rings, 2010 & 2018).

Unfortunately, not all authors and directors make such substantial use of the potential of fictional narratives to advance intercultural communication, which brings us to the next section.

6.2 Monocultural Continuities in Literature and Cinema

In their discussion of the film *Rambo: Last blood* (Grünberg, 2019), critical intercultural communication scholars Lengel and Newsom elaborate on the construction of Rambo as an Anglo-American anti-hero and saviour, who is 'being pushed to kill' in order to protect 'his own' (Lengel & Newsom, 2020, p. 66). They also highlight how far his actions are 'rooted in assumptions of white male victimisation due to increases in immigration, feminisms, and multicultural concerns' (2020, p. 62), which reflect the populist ultranationalist ideas discussed in Chapter 1. In this sense, *Rambo: Last blood* is an example of predominantly monocultural film production that focuses on the reconstruction of traditional cultural hierarchies: on the one hand, viewers are confronted with the brutality of Mexican sex trafficking cartels; on the other hand, they can expect redemption from Rambo – the morally superior white US-American working-class victim played over nearly four decades by Hollywood star Sylvester Stallone in the *Rocky* and *Rambo* series. In the supposedly final *Rambo* film in 2019, Stallone defends US civilisation once again against immoral Others on screen, in this case savage Mexicans.

In this context, Rambo exemplifies, however, above all nationalist '**tribalism**' (Rings, in Trinder, 2021; Hobfoll, 2018), which Leal highlights as a pattern in Hollywood cinema's attempt 'to spread widely the message of the "American way of life" [...] promoting US economic and political interests at the expense of, amongst other things, cultural heterogeneity' (2018, p. 287). Instead of the '**Third Space**' (Bhabha, 2004, p. 92) construction in *Bandhobi* and *The harp and the shadow*, *Rambo: Last blood* focuses – like most Stallone action movies – on the confirmation and enhancement of traditional binaries. What is problematic in that *Rambo* movie in particular is the reduction of Mexico to a savage nation. This is in line with Hollywood cinematic traditions, in which the portrayal of Mexicans as criminals has had a long history (Pressler, 2019, pp. 32–42) that gained momentum in the decade preceding *Rambo: Last blood* through films like *Savages* (Stone, 2012), *Sicario* (Villeneuve, 2015), *Sicario 2*: *Soldado* (Sollima, 2018), and the Netflix series *Narcos* (Bernard et al., 2015–2017).

Finally, *Rambo: Last blood* can also build on ex-president Trump's propaganda as expressed in his tweets, in which he has repeatedly reduced Mexico to a 'crime nation', against which the United States has to build a wall (Trump, 2017). He has furthermore labelled illegal migration from Mexico as an 'invasion' (Trump, 2018a) and 'assault on our country' due to 'Criminal elements and DRUGS pouring in' (Trump, 2018b, capital letters in original). All this highlights a conservative reinforcement between media and political discourses through the re-creation, confirmation and enhancement of traditional monocultural binaries, which serve different aims – from enhanced box office sales to individual political success – and remain a major challenge for the advancement of critical intercultural communication. The 'Dangers of "a single story"', which Nigerian novelist Adichie explores in her famous TED talk (Adichie, 2009), and against which she writes, are therefore very widely disseminated – not only beyond, but also within fictional narratives.

However, just like the intercultural literature and film explored in Section 6.1, monocultural fiction also tends to include cracks in the images they present. You can easily see that in the wider scholarly discussion around Defoe's *Robinson Crusoe*, which has been categorised as an outstanding example of British colonialism (Joyce, 1964; Said, 1991), but is now increasingly examined for the alternative images it also presents, including aspects of a fearful and self-contradictory protagonist with a psychotic fear of cannibals and a fundamental rejection of exploitative-unproductive modern stock exchange style capitalism (Hulme, 1986; Rings, 2011). Similarly, you can see cracks in the cultural hierarchy that *Rambo: Last blood* confirms, for example through the presence of a very few marginalised 'good' Mexicans who help Rambo survive.

TASK

Which fictional texts that you have read and/or seen would you now classify predominantly as monocultural? Why? To revisit the definition of monoculturality, you might want to go back to Chapter 1.

6.3 In Summary

Despite monocultural tendencies in many popular stories, from Defoe's *Robinson Crusoe* to Grünberg's *Rambo: Last blood*, literature and film remain very important tools for the (re-)construction and dissemination of alternative cultural stories. These alternative stories provided by novels like *The harp and the shadow* and films like *Bandhobi* invite readers and viewers to virtual journeys (Noujaim, 2006) on which established 'truths' – including the artificial monocultural separation of migrants and non-migrants, discoverers and conquerors, or conquerors and conquered – can and should be questioned. In particular, these narratives contribute to a dense and ambivalent form of 'worldmaking', which facilitates the destabilisation of stereotypical images of Self and Other that are particularly frequent in populist ultranationalist political and media discourses. They may also help to imagine more developed intercultural 'worlds', which can inspire readers and viewers to take appropriate action, for example by further disseminating these stories, developing petitions, supporting appropriate movements or founding such movements themselves. All this has been made easier by social media, albeit for both monocultural and intercultural intervention.

It might be worth adding that there is no need to leave the production of such stories to established authors and directors, because there is artistic potential in everyone (Kim, 2010), and the shared economy facilitates a wider and freer dissemination of personal literary and filmic outputs, for example via platforms like *FictionPress* and *YouTube*. We will address the growing media dimension of intercultural communication through the latter (see Lüsebrink, 2008; Nakayama, 2020) in Chapter 12.

DISCUSSION QUESTIONS

Drawing on the intercultural stories presented above and those that you remember from your personal experience, which themes could you easily develop into narratives? Which genre would you prefer to use for this purpose (e.g. short story, novel, (non-)animated film), and why?

RELATED TASKS

Write an intercultural short story (e.g. three pages) and upload it to a platform like *FictionPress* for easy access and wider dissemination. Then prepare a short presentation on that short story, in which you discuss its intercultural potential and modes of further development, e.g. through a novel or a film.

CASE STUDY

Please analyse the following excerpt from Héctor Tobar's *Barbarian nurseries* (2012). How does the novel present Araceli's life in the United States, and to what extent does it question the American Dream?

> Now there was only Araceli, alone with el *señor* Scott, la *señora* Maureen, and their three children, in this house on a hill high above the ocean, on a cul-de-sac absent of pedestrians, absent of the banter of vendors and policemen. It was a street of long silences. When the Torres-Thompson and their children left on their daily excursions, Araceli would commune alone with the home and its sounds, with the kick and purr of the refrigerator motor, and the faint whistle of the fans hidden in the ceiling. It was a home of steel washbasins and exotic bathroom perfumes, and a kitchen that Araceli had come to think of as her office, her command centre, where she prepared several meals each day: breakfast, lunch, dinner and assorted snacks and baby 'feedings'.
>
> A single row of Talavera tiles ran along the peach-colored walls, daisies with blue petals and bronze centres. [...] Her fingertips transported her, fleetingly, to Mexico City, where these porcelain squares would be weather-beaten and cracked, decorating gazebos and doorways. She remembered her long walks through the old seventeenth-, eighteenth-, and nineteenth-century streets, a city built of ancient lava stone and mirrored glass, a colonial city and an Art Deco city and a Modernist city all at once. [...] Now she lived in an American neighbourhood where everything was new, a landscape vacant of the meanings and shadings of time, each home painted eggshell-white by association rule, like featureless architect models plopped down by human hands on a stretch of empty savanna.

References

Adichie, C. N. (2009). The danger of a single story. *TEDGlobal*, July. https://bit.ly/3uQxIxK (last accessed 18 April 2022).

Antor, H. (2020). Interculturality or transculturality? In G. Rings & S. M. Rasinger (eds.), *The Cambridge handbook of intercultural communication* (pp. 68–82). Cambridge: Cambridge University Press.

Ashcroft, B., Griffiths, G. & Tiffin, H. (2007). *Post-colonial studies: The key concepts*. Abingdon: Routledge.

Attridge, D. (2004). *The singularity of literature*. Abingdon and New York: Routledge.

Bernard, C. et al. (2015–17). *Narcos*. United States: Dynamo, Gaumont International Television, Netflix.

Bhabha, H. K. (2004 [1994]). *The location of culture*. Abingdon: Routledge.

Blaut, J. M. (1993): *The coloniser's model of the world: Geographical diffusionism and Euro-centric history*. New York: Guilford Press.

Carpentier, A. (1979). *The harp and the shadow* [El arpa y la sombra]. London: Mercury House.

Chatman, S. (1990). *Coming to terms: The rhetoric of narrative in fiction and films*. Ithaca, NY: Cornell University Press.

Erll, A. & Gymnich, M. (2015). *Uniwissen: Interkulturelle Kompetenzen: Erfolgreich kommunizieren zwischen den Kulturen*. Stuttgart: Klett.

Fludernik, M. (2008). *Erzähltheorie: Eine Einführung* (2nd edition). Darmstadt: Wissenschaftliche Buchgesellschaft.

Goodman, N. (1995). *Ways of worldmaking*. Indianapolis: Hackett Publishing.

Grünberg, A. (2019). *Rambo: Last blood*. United States: Lionsgate, Millennium Films, Campbell Grobman Films.

Hawthorn, J. (2017). *Studying the novel* (7th edition). London: Bloomsbury.

Hobfoll, S. E. (2018). *Tribalism: The evolutionary origins of fear politics*. London: Palgrave Macmillan.

Hulme, P. (1986). *Colonial encounters: Europe and the native Caribbean 1492–1797*. London: Methuen.

Joyce, J. (1964). *Daniel Defoe*. Buffalo, NY: State University of New York.

Kim, Y. (2010): Be an artist, right now. *TEDxSeoul*, July. https://bit.ly/3MfrtcK (last accessed 18 April 2021).

Leal, J. (2020). Cinema as intercultural communication. In G. Rings & S. M. Rasinger (eds.), *The Cambridge handbook of intercultural communication* (pp. 286–301). Cambridge: Cambridge University Press.

Lengel, L. & Newsom, V. A. (2020). Contested border crossings in shifting political landscapes: Anti-invasion discourses and human trafficking representations in US film and politics. *iMex*, 9(18), 61–82. www.imex-revista.com/xviii-contested-border-crossings DOI:10.23692/iMex.18.5

Loach, K. (2000). *Bread and roses*. United Kingdom: Parallax Pictures.

Lüsebrink, H. J. (2008). *Interkulturelle Kommunikation: Interaktion – Fremdwahrnehmung – Kulturtransfer*. Stuttgart: Metzler.

Mignolo, W. (2000). *Local histories/global designs*. Princeton, NJ: Princeton University Press.

Mitjáns, F. (2015). *Limpiadores*. United Kingdom: Vimeo. https://vimeo.com/154155933 (last accessed 17 April 2022).

Nakayama, T. K. (2020). Critical intercultural communication and the digital environment. In G. Rings & S. M. Rasinger (eds.), *The Cambridge handbook of intercultural communication* (pp. 85–89). Cambridge: Cambridge University Press.

Neumann, B. (2020). The power of literature in intercultural communication. In G. Rings & S. M. Rasinger (eds.), *The Cambridge handbook of intercultural communication* (pp. 136–154). Cambridge: Cambridge University Press.

Noujaim, J. (2006). My wish: A global day of film. *TED2006*, February. https://bit.ly/3xzzrsQ (last accessed 18 April 2022).

Pressler, E. M. (2019). Hispanic stereotypes in contemporary film. Georgia Southern University Honors College. Thesis. https://digitalcommons.georgiasouthern.edu/honors-theses/425 (last accessed 22 April 2022).

Rings, G. (2010). *La Conquista desbaratada: Identidad y alteridad en la novela, el cine y el teatro hispánicos contemporáneos*. Madrid: Iberoamericana.

Rings, G. (2011). Robinson Crusoe today: Continuities and discontinuities from Daniel Defoe's literary work to Robert Zemeckis' 'Cast Away'. *Anglistik*, 22(2), 119–136.

Rings, G. (2018). *The other in contemporary migrant cinema: Imagining a new Europe?* New York: Routledge.

Rings, G. (2021). The superdiverse precariat of British higher education? 'Limpiadores' revisited. *Current Sociology*, 70(2), 291–307. https://doi.org/10.1177/0011392120983345

Said, E. (1991). *The world, the text and the critic*. London: Vintage.

Shin, D. (2009). 반두비 *[Bandhobi]*. South Korea: Cinema Dal.

Sollima, S. (2018). *Sicario 2: Soldado*. United States: Columbia Pictures, Black Label Media, Thunder Road Pictures.

Stone, O. (2012). *Savages*. United States: Ixtlan, Onda Entertainment, Relativity Media.

Tobar, H. (2012): *Barbarian nurseries*. London: Hodder & Stoughton.

Trinder, S. (2021). Interview with Guido Rings: 'We need intercultural solidarity if we want to survive and prosper in a world hit by ultranationalism'. *Disjuntiva*, 2(1), 74–80.

Trump, D. (2017). Mexico – one of the highest crime nations. 27 August. https://twitter.com/realDonaldTrump/status/901802524981817344 (last accessed 24 August 2021).

Trump, D. (2018a). Invasion. 18 November. https://twitter.com/realDonaldTrump/status/1064227483187318784 (last accessed 24 August 2021).

Trump, D. (2018b). Assault. 18 October. https://twitter.com/realDonaldTrump/status/1052888451199262725 (last accessed 24 August 2021).

Villeneuve, D. (2015). *Sicario*. United States: Lionsgate, Black Label Media, Thunder Road Pictures.

7 Linguistic Approaches to Intercultural Communication

Over the next few chapters, we want to take a closer at the different methodological approaches to studying intercultural communication, drawing upon the various disciplines that contribute to the field in order to reflect its diversity. We begin by looking at how the study of language can help us understand intercultural communication. The fact that language and culture are closely linked is easy to see, and there is an immense body of research to evidence this. For example, different ethnic groups often have their own language (in reality, a lot of groups are multilingual!), and this is closely linked to their cultural identity and heritage.

But even within a language and amongst its native-speakers (i.e., those for whom a language is the first language), there can be considerable variation in the way it is being used: for example, one of the most seminal works in sociolinguistics is William Labov's study of English in New York (Labov, 2006), which has shown how accent is linked to socioeconomic group. Preece's handbook (Preece, 2016) brings together recent work on language and identity, and cultural issues in their various forms play a major role in many of the chapters. The edited volume by Angouri & Baxter (2021) provides a state-of-the-art overview of how language and gender are linked; in Chapter 9, we will look at the role of gender in culture and intercultural communication, and, by proxy, language. We will also look at some aspects pertaining to language in Chapter 8, when we introduce anthropological approaches. In the current chapter, after a quick review of what communication actually is, we will introduce two particular aspects of language and intercultural communication: intercultural politeness and translation.

AIMS
By the end of the chapter, you should be able to:

1. identify some of the ways in which linguistics can contribute to the study of intercultural communication;
2. describe some of the key aspects of intercultural politeness;
3. understand the link between translation and intercultural communication.

Figure 7.1 *Linguistic Approaches* by Alíz Kovács-Zöldi

KEY TERMS
code – intercultural rapport – politeness – face – translation

WARM-UP TASK

Looking at Figure 7.1, what aspects can you identify that link language with culture?

7.1 Language and Communication – Some Basics

In a book on intercultural communication, and especially in a chapter dealing with the role that language plays in it, we need to remind ourselves of some of the basics of what communication actually consists of, and go back in time a bit. Roman Jakobson (1960) divides a speech event into six components (Figure 7.2): a speaker sends a message to a listener; for that there needs to be some sort of physical contact between them – like being in the same room so the sound waves the speaker makes reach the ears of the listener, radio waves to

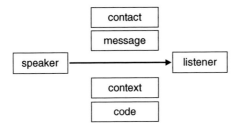

Figure 7.2 A basic communication model
Adapted from Jakobson (1960).

transmit information between our mobile phones, or being connected by fibre-optic cables for videoconferencing.

At this point in the book, it is clear that in the world today, the likelihood of speaker and listener being from different cultural backgrounds is quite considerable, and we will look into the nuances a little more over the subsequent chapters. Later on, in Chapter 12, we will also look at how different communication channels (i.e., the *contact*), especially digital ones, influence communication, and in particular intercultural communication. For our discussion here, we will focus primarily on the **code** and the *context*, and, by extension, the *speaker* and *listener*.

At a basic level, according to the Oxford English Dictionary, we can define a *code* as a 'system of signs or symbols' (Oxford English Dictionary, 2020), and while this might sound a bit abstract, a language is exactly that: a system of verbal or written signs we use to communicate with each other. For this communication to work successfully, the speaker (or writer) and the listener (or reader) need to share the same code, that is, use a language that they are both able to produce and comprehend. Going back to our photograph in Figure 7.1, this extends to the visual representation of language: only very few of you (if any) will have been able to understand what is being written in the picture, because we do not have the requisite knowledge to decode the symbols.

As we will see in this chapter, it is not quite that simple: using the same words and the same grammar is only half the story; there is a lot more encoded in language than just the content: *how* we say it is just as important as *what* we say, and a lot of the *how* is influenced by our cultural background. Language as a code also allows us to use language to talk about language; Jakobson calls this the 'meta function'. For example, we can rephrase or repeat utterances to avoid miscommunication or conflict. Code also becomes interesting when speaker and listener use different codes (that is, speak different languages), so for the message to be conveyed successfully, it needs to be translated from the speaker's language to the listener's language – we will discuss this in more detail below in Section 7.3. Moreover, Anna Wierzbicka's work suggests that the study of language, and especially vocabulary and semantics, can help us to identify cultural patterns (Wierzbicka, 1997). *Context* refers – broadly speaking – to the environment in which the utterance takes place.

This can complicate matters even more: *what* and *how* something is said may differ from context to context, and from culture to culture.

Now that we have outlined some of the basic aspects, the chapter will address two issues: we will start by looking at (intercultural) politeness, and the challenges that come with it. We will then discuss issues around translation.

7.2 Being (Im)polite

TASK

Throughout the book so far, we have asked you to reflect critically on an intercultural encounter you have had, and the issues you have observed. For this task, we would like you to do the same, but this time, focus specifically on the role that language has played. What were the key challenges? Maybe you communicated in a second language, or a language you were not fully proficient in? Or maybe you misinterpreted the 'real' meaning of something that was said?

One of the issues you have probably come up with are 'pure' or 'core' linguistic problems: you have met someone whose first language is different from your own, and while they have some element of proficiency in your language (or you in theirs), communication is impaired simply on these core linguistic grounds. Maybe you did not share enough vocabulary to make the exchange flow smoothly, or you have problems decoding grammatical structures (i.e., some gap in the shared code). We will look at these issues in Section 7.3. We start by focusing on those instances where, although there are no problems with comprehension, something doesn't seem quite right. Maybe what the other person has said is a little odd, or maybe it was a little – or even downright – rude. Helen Spencer-Oatey identified five domains of language use that are relevant in the building and management of **intercultural rapport**, that is, harmonious relationships between people from different cultural backgrounds:

1. the *Illocutionary Domain* refers to how speech acts such as requests and apologies are performed in order to create and maintain harmonious relations;
2. the *Discourse Domain* is about the topics that are selected and how ideas are structured;
3. the *Participation Domain* relates to 'the procedural aspects of an interchange', that is, behaviour like turn-taking;
4. the *Stylistic Domain* is about the stylistic aspects, such as the degree of formality, or appropriate use of syntax and lexis;
5. the *Non-Verbal Domain*, which includes the use of gestures, eye contact, and so on (Spencer-Oatey, 2000, pp. 19–20)

In any of these domains, behaviour that is unexpected or unfamiliar can negatively affect the exchange. For example, in the *participation domain*, the way we take turns in conversation is often said to be culturally specific: Tannen explains that we grow accustomed to the turn-taking conventions of the speech community we are used to, so '[j]ust because one person feels interrupted does not mean that the other intended to interrupt' (Tannen, 2012, p. 135). Such supposed (but unintentional) non-compliance with turn-taking rules can easily lead to a speaker being perceived to be impolite.

7.2.1   Politeness

Most of us will have some pre-existing concept when it comes to politeness. We think about it in terms of polite behaviour, or etiquette, but also what we should or should not do or, important for communication, *say* in a particular context. Watts et al. (2005) refer to this as *first-order politeness*, or *politeness1*. It is 'the various ways in which polite behaviour is perceived and talked about by members of sociocultural groups' (2005, p. 3), so it is the way in which laypeople understand the term. Interesting, we more often seem to recognise *im*polite than polite behaviour: as soon as someone says something rude to us, for example, a little red flag will go up in our mind, but unless someone is exceptionally polite, we probably do not notice this but take it for granted.

Second-order politeness, or *politeness2*, refers to the more theoretical or 'scientific' construct. Penelope Brown and Stephen Levinson were some of the first to provide a theoretical approach to linguistic politeness (Brown & Levinson, 1987). In the more than thirty years since then, much more than we could ever cover in this section has been written about the topic. However, a key term that comes up repeatedly is that of **face**. George Yule provides us with a straightforward definition: '[face] is your public self-image. This is the emotional and social sense of self that everyone has and expects everyone else to recognise' (Yule, 2006, p. 110). Politeness, then, 'can be defined as showing awareness of and consideration for another person's face' (2006, p. 110). We can maybe best understand this when we think about 'losing face': 'notions of being embarrassed or humiliated' (Brown & Levinson, 1987, p. 61). In terms of Jakobson's model, both types of politeness relate to the meta-function of language: we use the code to talk about the code, and, we will see, to make judgements based on this code.

7.2.2   Intercultural Politeness

TASK

Based on your own culture(s) and language(s), make a list of what counts as *im*polite. Why is it impolite?

What is perceived to be polite or impolite varies across cultures. Even Brown and Levinson acknowledge that 'the content of face will differ in different cultures' (Brown & Levinson, 1987, p. 61). Richard Watts reminds us that 'social activities are culturally relative' (Watts, 2003, p. 28), and gives the example of queuing:

people in Britain are well known for forming orderly queues, be it at bus stops, service counters and so on, and queue-jumping is a serious social faux pas; in Britain, queuing is an internalised and institutionalised convention. In other parts of the world, this is not the case. So what is perceived as impolite behaviour in one culture may not be perceived that way in another and consequently would not have the same impact.

Culpeper and his colleagues used the Oxford English Corpus (a two-billion-word collection of contemporary English taken mainly from the Internet) and Twitter data to compare British and North American politeness. By looking at how the term 'politeness' occurs in the two corpora, and the words that co-occur with it, they found a lot of overlaps between British and North American notions of politeness; but their analysis also provided evidence for the British politeness stereotype: 'British data is [...] in harmony with the stereotype of politeness articulated by lay people, especially the famed emotional reserve of the British' (Culpeper et al., 2019, p. 109). In other words, the way politeness is reflected in the language is culturally distinct.

When it comes to politeness in an intercultural setting, Claus Erhardt provides a good summary of some of the main issues, at least a few of which we assume you will have come up with too:

> Everyone who is engaged in [intercultural] communication will find difficulties to interpret the behaviour of the partners; they might seem to speak too much or too little, too loudly, might get too close to their partners while speaking, or not pay enough attention to them. On the other hand, it is a quite normal experience that it is not always clear which form of address can be used, if it would be appropriate to thank for something, to apologize, to give compliments (and how), or if it is acceptable to cheek-kiss the business partner's wife.
>
> (Ehrhardt, 2020, p. 243)

The study of intercultural politeness is still a relatively young field (Haugh & Kádár, 2017); yet there are interesting themes emerging. Traditionally, pragmatics – the study of language in use, under which politeness theory also falls – is based on an assumption of commonality. Groups of speakers develop particular conventions for interacting with each other: how to give compliments, what volume to speak at, and so on. In the context of intercultural communication, however, the focus moves from the social to the individual: conventions and norms that apply in monocultural/monolingual situations 'need to be co-constructed usually from scratch' in intercultural settings (Kecskes, 2016, p. 66), as there are no immediate, shared underlying norms and conventions. In a conversation between two speakers where the language used is the first language of one of the speakers, it is clear that the power balance will implicitly shift towards that speaker: if an English speaker and a Spanish speaker communicate in English, it is the English speaker with their assumptions about what is 'polite' or 'impolite' who has a distinct advantage. So a Spanish speaker of

English might be perceived as impolite because their behaviour does not match the English norms and assumptions, even though this behaviour might be perfectly acceptable based on Spanish norms.

The issue is exacerbated when we consider a situation where two speakers of different languages communicate using a third language, or *lingua franca*; for example, an Arabic and a Chinese speaker use English as a shared third language – not unusual in the world today. In this case, István Kecskes argues, there is little common ground between the two speakers, who, as a consequence, may tend to fall back on to the politeness strategies they know from their first language (Kecskes, 2017).

The interpretation of situational context – usually a key piece of information in the interpretation of utterances – can also be problematic, especially if there are underlying linguistic problems. Kecskes illustrates this with an example of an exchange between an American professor and a Japanese student:

NORITAKA: Hi Professor Brown.
PROFESSOR: Hi Noritaka. How are you? Why don't you sit down?
NORITAKA: Because you did not tell me to.
PROFESSOR: OK, I am telling you now.

(Kecskes, 2017, p. 21)

In the example, the student misinterprets 'How are you? Why don't you sit down?' by failing to recognise it as a formulaic expression of invitation. On the linguistic surface, 'Why don't you sit down?' is a question that requires a response in the form of an explanation, and the student interprets it as such. But in fact, it is an invitation: what is required is not an explanation, but action (Kecskes, 2017, p. 21) – please do sit down. Kecskes concludes that when communicating in a language other than their own, 'interpretation generally depends on what the utterance says rather than on what it actually communicates' (Kecskes, 2017, p. 27). In the example here, the student interprets what the utterance says (a question) when it actually communicates an invitation. In terms of Jakobson's model, the student decodes the message as he shares the same code with the professor, but the meaning of the message is distorted because of a lack of relevant contextual knowledge.

In Chapter 3, where we introduced the concept of intercultural competence, we defined it as open, highly dynamic and always depending on context, and suggested that there is a gradual difference between people's action competence in their own culture and their intercultural competence in less familiar terrains. We can argue that politeness, then, would also fall under the broad category of intercultural competence. Moving the focus beyond politeness, Kecskes et al. introduce the concept of *basic interactional competence* (BIC) and argue that BIC forms the basis of interpreting and contributing to conversations between native and non-native speakers. They argue that 'BIC is the foundation for the formation of the culture-specific procedures and practices of interaction in one's native culture and those of other cultures one may move into' (Kecskes et al., 2018, p. 17).

7.3 Communicating across Codes: Translation and Intercultural Communication

In this chapter so far, we have looked at intercultural interactions where both speakers use the same language – even if it is not their own. There is, of course, another constellation: when speaker and listener do not use the same language, and communication takes place via the medium of **translation**.

TASK

Think of a word in a language you speak well. Then translate it into another language you speak well. Are the meanings for these two words really identical? Are there differences or nuances? What are they?

On the most simplistic level, we could argue that translation serves as the vehicle that enables communication between two different languages and cultures. Indeed, Alíz Kovács-Zöldi, the photographer who has provided the images for this book, states in her rationale for the design of the image for this chapter:

> I used images of ancient languages overlapping behind a figure who represents the linguist or the interpreter. I wanted him to take a central position with the corners of the texts overlap behind him to indicate he can see how these seemingly very different texts can connect.[1]

However, as Davies points out, linguistic and cultural boundaries are not always clear cut (Davies, 2012). We have seen in our example of British and American politeness in Section 7.2.2 that there are differences even within a language; in contexts with more than one language and culture involved, this becomes even more complex. Davies identifies two approaches to conceptualising translation in the context of intercultural communication. On the one hand, it may serve as a medium for intercultural exchange. Within this approach, we can distinguish between two manifestations: translation can serve as a bridge between cultures, facilitating the exchange of ideas, but it can also be a barrier. As Davies points out, the use of a translator in interaction between two groups may deliberately highlight their separateness from each other (Davies, 2012, pp. 370–372). For example, in fraught political negotiations between two groups with different linguistic backgrounds, the parties may choose to communicate via a translator even if they speak each other's language so as not to be seen as 'giving ground'. Language, in this case, becomes a tool of power and identity.

On the other hand, translation is also about the agency of the translator or interpreter. Davies (2012) highlights that to that end, translators and interpreters may serve as both facilitators but also manipulators of intercultural exchanges. Juliane House showed how English–German/German–English translators applied a 'cultural filter' between the original and the translated text in order to 'compensate' for cultural differences: 'with the use of this filter, the translator can take account of culture specificity accommodating differences in sociocultural norms and differences' (House, 2012, p. 503). For example, Riabtseva looked at Russian idioms and the problems when translating them into English, and concluded that 'many emotional components of a Russian original cannot and even should not be transferred into its translation into English' because this would result in a clash with English conventions and mentality (Riabtseva, 2001, p. 376) – the target text in English would be overly emotional. Suffice to say then, that a successful translator needs to have a good understanding of the target culture in order to produce an appropriate translation – a skill that goes far beyond simply matching words and syntactic structure from one to the other language (Olk, 2009). This, in turn, opens the door for pedagogic application: used in an education context, translation can tell us a lot about (inter)cultural understanding and attitudes, and can be used to assess – and promote – intercultural competence (Elorza, 2008). We will explore the development and assessment of intercultural competence in more detail in Chapter 17.

Lastly, looking at translation between Arabic and English, Bahameed (2008) highlights situations where translation from one language to another is nearly impossible, as the cultural concept does not exist in the target language. He uses the examples of the Arabic terms *saHuur* (a meal eaten before the dawn for fasting); *khalwah* (unmarried man and woman found in a place where there is nobody else there); and *qaTii'at al-arHaam* (to be on bad terms with one's relatives) which are difficult to translate into English: not only are there lexical gaps in English (i.e., there are no equivalent words), but the entire concepts are unknown.

7.4 Sign Language, Culture and Intercultural Communication

When laying the foundations of the chapter in Section 7.1, we presented language in a way that implied that it only occurs either in spoken or written form. This is neither accurate nor sufficient as a definition, for there exists a third form: sign languages. It would be negligent not to at least introduce the topic here. A common misconception is that sign languages are merely gestures. As R. L. Trask reminds us with reference to American Sign Language (ASL), 'sign language is not just a crude approximation to language, [...] nor is it merely a coded version of English' (Trask, 1995, p. 20). Sign languages are fully developed languages with their own systematic structures (Crystal, 1987). And just like there is not just one spoken language, there exist various different sign languages, including American Sign Language, British Sign Language (BSL), Chinese Sign Language, Khmer Sign Language and several African sign languages (Baker et al., 2016). Baker et al.'s *The linguistics of sign languages* (2016) provides an excellent introduction to the topic.

What is of interest for us here are the cultural aspects that go hand in hand with the use of sign languages. Sign languages are commonly (although not exclusively) used by people who are deaf, and traditionally, deafness was considered a disability. From around the 1980s onwards, though, deaf people increasingly started to consider themselves a cultural minority, using their local sign language as their first language (Baker et al., 2016, p. 330), just like an ethnic minority would consider their heritage language their first language. Alongside, we have seen the development of a deaf identity – deaf people identifying as deaf (as opposed to disabled), in the same way we have seen people identify along other characteristics (Chen, 2014). As a result, medical interventions to 'cure' people from deafness, such as cochlear implants, are often looked at with dismay by people from the deaf community and considered a threat to their culture (Sparrow, 2005).

With the deaf community having a distinct culture and identity of its own, communication between the deaf and the hearing communities is at least to some extent intercultural, with similar themes and challenges to communication between other cultures we discuss in this book. In a study of communication between hearing and deaf students at a South African university, Ntsongelwa & Rivera-Sánchez (2018) observed limited interaction between the two cultures outside classes, with linguistic barrier – the lack of hearing students' proficiency in using South African Sign Language – being one key factor in preventing communication and access to deaf culture. However, the authors also identified other, culture-focused factors, too, including deaf students' preference for using dedicated facilities, as well as limited opportunities for deaf and hearing students to interact.

7.5 In Summary

In this chapter, we have looked at what the study of language can contribute to the study of intercultural communication. We have seen that language is not merely a tool for conveying information, but also for creating mutual understanding (Çalişkan et al., 2016). As the main medium which we use to communicate with each other, it plays an integral part not only in intracultural and monolingual, but also intercultural and multilingual exchanges. Using Jakobson's communication model as a guide, we have explored how language is used to create identities, and how language and identity intersect in intercultural scenarios. We then turned to a discussion of politeness, and saw that politeness has both a linguistic and a conceptual level and how these levels interrelate: neither linguistic competence nor cultural competence alone can account for a successful intercultural exchange. Finally, we touched on the role translation. Translation, we have argued, is not merely the one-to-one mapping of words from one language to another, but needs to take into account cultural considerations too, with translators and interpreters having a key role as 'cultural filters' to ensure that the target text is culturally appropriate.

DISCUSSION QUESTIONS

a. Based on what you have learned in this chapter, what are potential implications for learning a second/foreign language?
b. How would you explain verbal aggression? Which of the elements that we have raised in this chapter come into it, and how?

CASE STUDY

Look at the following short vignette. What issues can you identify, and how do they relate to the topics discussed in this chapter?

Halfway through a semester, a tutor at a British university gets the following complaints from students on a course with a multicultural and multilingual group of students:
'The Spanish girl always hogs the floor, she never stops talking.'
'The Chinese students never say anything. They are lazy and don't contribute to discussions.'
'We can't understand the English speakers when they speak so fast.'
'Sir, we mustn't call you by your first name, it's very rude.'

Note

1   Personal communication, September 2021.

References

Angouri, J., & Baxter, J. (eds.) (2021). *The Routledge handbook of language, gender, and sexuality*. Abingdon: Routledge.

Bahameed, A. (2008). Hindrances in Arabic–English intercultural translation. *Translation Journal*, 12(1), 1–16.

Baker, A. E., van den Bogaerde, B., Pfau, R., & Schermer, T. (2016). *The linguistics of sign languages: An introduction*. Amsterdam: John Benjamins.

Brown, P., & Levinson, S. C. (1987). *Politeness: Some universals in language usage*. Cambridge: Cambridge University Press.

Çalişkan, H., Pikhart, M., Önder, I., Masal, E., & Beşoluk, Ş. (2016). Intercultural linguistics as a new academic approach to communication. SHS Web of Conferences, 26, 01005. DOI:10.1051/shsconf/20162601005

Chen, G. (2014). Influential factors of deaf identity development. *Electronic Journal for Inclusive Education*, 3(2).

Crystal, D. (1987). *The Cambridge encyclopaedia of language*. Cambridge: Cambridge University Press.

Culpeper, J., O'Driscoll, J. & Hardaker, C. (2019). Notions of politeness in Britain and North America. In E. Ogiermann & P. Garcés-Conejos Blitvich (eds.), *From speech acts to lay understandings of politeness: Multilingual and multicultural perspectives* (pp. 177–200). Cambridge: Cambridge University Press.

Davies, E. E. (2012). Translation and intercultural communication: Bridges and barriers. In C. B. Paulston, S. F. Kiesling, & E. S. Rangel (eds.), *The handbook of intercultural discourse and communication* (pp. 367–388). Oxford: Wiley Blackwell.

Ehrhardt, C. (2020). Linguistic politeness. In G. Rings & S. M. Rasinger (eds.), *The Cambridge handbook of intercultural communication* (pp. 243–260). Cambridge: Cambridge University Press.

Elorza, I. (2008). Promoting intercultural competence in the FL/SL classroom: Translations as sources of data. *Language and Intercultural Communication*, 8(4), 261–277. DOI:10.1080/14708470802303090

Haugh, M., & Kádár, D. Z. (2017). Intercultural (im)politeness. In J. Culpeper, M. Haugh, & D. Z. Kádár (eds.), *The Palgrave handbook of linguistic (im)politeness* (pp. 601–632). London: Palgrave Macmillan.

House, J. (2012). Translation, interpreting and intercultural communication. In J. Jackson (ed.), *The Routledge handbook of language and intercultural communication* (pp. 495–509). Abingdon: Routledge.

Jakobson, R. (1960). Linguistics and poetics. In T. Sebeok (ed.), *Styles in language* (pp. 350–377). Cambridge, MA: MIT Press.

Kecskes, I. (2016). Can intercultural pragmatics bring some new insight into pragmatic theories? In A. Capone & J. L. Mey (eds.), *Interdisciplinary studies in pragmatics, culture and society* (pp. 43–69). Heidelberg: Springer.

Kecskes, I. (2017). Context-dependency and impoliteness in intercultural communication. *Journal of Politeness Research*, 13(1), 7–31. DOI:10.1515/pr-2015-0019

Kecskes, I., Sanders, R. E., & Pomerantz, A. (2018). The basic interactional competence of language learners. *Journal of Pragmatics*, 124, 88–105. DOI:10.1016/j.pragma.2017.10.019

Labov, W. (2006). *The social stratification of English in New York City* (2nd edition). Cambridge: Cambridge University Press.

Ntsongelwa, A., & Rivera-Sánchez, M. (2018). Intercultural communication between deaf and hearing students at a South African university. *Communitas*, 23, 165–177.

Olk, H. M. (2009). Translation, cultural knowledge and intercultural competence. *Journal of Intercultural Communication*, 20. Online. www.immi.se/intercultural/nr20/olk.htm

Oxford English Dictionary. (2020). 'code, n.' Oxford: Oxford University Press.

Preece, S. (ed.) (2016). *The Routledge handbook of language and identity*. Abingdon: Routledge.

Riabtseva, N. (2001). Contrastive phraseology in a cross-cultural and cognitive perspective. In M. Thelen & B. Lewandowska-Tomaszczyk (eds.), *Translation and meaning*. (Vol. 5, pp. 365–378). Maastricht: Hogeschool Zuyd Maastricht School of Translation and Interpreting.

Sparrow, R. (2005). Defending deaf culture: The case of cochlear implants. *The Journal of Political Philosophy*, 13(2), 135–152.

Spencer-Oatey, H. (2000). Rapport management: A framework for analysis. In H. Spencer-Oatey (ed.), *Culturally speaking. Managing rapport through talk across cultures* (pp. 11–46). London: Continuum.

Tannen, D. (2012). Turn-taking and intercultural discourse and communication. In C. Bratt Paulston, S. F. Kiesling, & E. S. Rangel (eds.), *The handbook of intercultural discourse and communication* (pp. 135–157). Oxford: Wiley-Blackwell.

Trask, R. L. (1995). *Language: The basics.* London: Routledge.

Watts, R. J. (2003). *Politeness.* Cambridge: Cambridge University Press.

Watts, R. J., Ide, S., & Ehlich, K. (2005). Introduction. In R. J. Watts, S. Ide, & K. Ehlich (eds.), *Politeness in language: Studies in its history, theory and practice* (2nd edition), (pp. 1–20). Berlin and New York: Mouton de Gruyter.

Wierzbicka, A. (1997). *Understanding cultures through their key words: English, Russian, Polish, German, and Japanese.* Oxford: Oxford University Press.

Yule, G. (2006). *The study of language* (3rd edition). Cambridge: Cambridge University Press.

8 Anthropological Perspectives

We looked at how the study of language can help us explain intercultural phenomena in Chapter 7 and saw that there is a close link between language and culture. In the current chapter, we will explore how the discipline of anthropology approaches intercultural communication. With intercultural communication as an academic field having emerged from the work of anthropologists more than fifty years ago, we will start with a brief historic overview of some of the key anthropological frameworks that underlie the field. We will then turn towards a closer focus on communication, and explore how anthropology can help us explore communication between people of different cultures.

AIMS
By the end of this chapter, you should be able to:

1. describe the key anthropological frameworks intercultural communication is based on;
2. explain the role that ethnographic fieldwork plays in the study of culture;
3. identify some of the key issues pertaining to language, communication and culture in the context of intercultural communication.

> **KEY TERMS**
> proxemics – monochronism – polychronism – high-context culture – low-context culture – value orientations – linguistic relativity – ethnography – ethnography of speaking – speech community – communicative competence

8.1 Anthropology: A Brief Definition

We looked at the concept of 'culture' and its development over time in some detail in Chapter 1 (if you are still a little unsure about certain aspects, you may want to go back to it briefly). Anthropology is concerned with the study of cultures. It first appeared at the end of the sixteenth century as 'the study of man', and, from the nineteenth century onwards, split into two broad branches: physical anthropology, and social and cultural anthropology (Williams, 1985). The former, sometimes also known as biological anthropology or paleoanthropology, is primarily

Figure 8.1 *Anthropological Perspectives* by Alíz Kovács-Zöldi

concerned with human (physical) evolution and adaptation (Crevecoeur & Van Dyck, 2013). More important for us here, however, are social and cultural anthropology: the study of human culture and society, and its differences. As Thomas Hylland Eriksen puts it:

> [a]nthropology tries to account for the social and cultural variation in the world [...] anthropology is about how different people can be, but it also tries to find out in what sense it can be said that all humans have something in common.
>
> (Eriksen, 2001, p. 1)

In the following sections, we want to look at how anthropologists have approached culture, with a particular focus on those elements that are important for the study of intercultural communication. For more general overviews of how the concept has evolved in the field of anthropology, Erickson (2011) and Gonzáles (2010) provide good introductions.

8.2 Anthropology and Intercultural Communication: The Work of Edward T. Hall

We mentioned in Chapter 2 that intercultural communication first emerged from the work of anthropologists, for example Edward T. Hall's work for the United States of America Foreign Service Institute. In research spanning several decades, Hall proposed a framework that comprised three *dimensions of culture*: *space*, *time*, and *context*.

8.2.1 Space

In *The silent language* (Hall, 1959), Hall first discussed *space* as a cultural concept. The way we perceive and act within space, Hall argues, is culturally specific. In *The hidden dimension* (Hall, 1966), in what he calls **proxemics**, he differentiates between four types of personal space: *intimate distance* refers to two people being really close together – 'the distance of love-making and wrestling, comforting and protecting' (1966, p. 117). *Personal distance*, while still close, surrounds people with 'a small protective sphere or bubble' (1966, p.119); Hall estimates this at between 60 and 120 centimetres. Social distance, at around 1.2–3.5 metres, moves interlocutors yet further apart, and is associated with more formal contexts – maybe a business meeting, a transaction in a shop, or a meeting between acquaintances. Finally, *public distance*, beyond 3.5 metres, is what is used in formal occasions. Space, however, is also culturally significant: aspects such as how close we stand to one another during conversations, for example, are culturally specific, with different cultures having different notions of what an 'appropriate' distance for each context is. Even how we arrange furniture in a room may vary across cultures (Hua, 2014).

8.2.2 Monochronic and Polychronic Time

When we think about time, it would be fair to assume that most of us think about it in terms of days, weeks, hours or minutes – all of which are measurable units. In many cases, these units relate to duration, and this duration is fixed. As a result, two minutes are exactly twice as long as one minute, an hour consists of sixty minutes, which in turn are units of sixty-second duration, and so on. And even though sometimes 'time flies' or 'the day never ends', we still have some sense of time as a series of units of duration, which in turn means it can be planned: I currently have thirty minutes 'left' to write on this chapter before I need to go to my next meeting. This duration-based concept of time, however, is a 'Western' concept, though it has since spread across the globe. As Hall explains, some cultures perceive time very differently: the Hopi, a Native American people, perceive time as a series of events: 'It is what happens when the corn matures or a sheep grows up [...] It is the natural process that takes place while living substance acts out its life drama' (Hall, 1959, p. 171). This in turn means that time is not the same collection of static units' duration: if corn takes longer to mature, maybe because of adverse weather condition, time does not 'move on' as the event has not yet occurred. So, we can say that the perception of time is a culture-specific concept.

That difference does not need to be as extreme as the Hopi example where the entire concept of time differs. Hall also introduced the distinction between **monochronism** and **polychronism**. In monochronic societies, people tend to do one thing at a time (Hall, 1959, p. 178). In polychronic cultures, people tend to do several things at the same time. Spencer-Oatey and Franklin summarise the difference as follows: in monochronism the 'emphasis is on schedules and promptness; activities are compartmentalized and treated in a linear fashion', while polychronism emphasizes 'involvement with people and completion of transaction rather than adherences to preset schedules' (Spencer-Oatey & Franklin, 2009, p. 23).

8.2.3 Low-Context, High-Context

The last of Hall's dimensions are **low-context** versus **high-context** cultures. It relates to how much information in a communicative exchange is explicitly verbalised. In our discussion of Jakobson's communication model in Chapter 7, we saw that a *message* is transmitted from a speaker to a hearer via a *code* – a shared language. In low-context cultures, the vast majority of the information is encoded in the code: it is explicitly verbalised, and can hence be understood without (much) contextual information. But, as per Jakobson's model, communication also takes place in a *context*. In high-context cultures, most of the information is located in the context – either the physical context, or shared cultural knowledge and experiences – and does not need to be explicitly verbalised (Hall, 1976, p. 91; Spencer-Oatey & Franklin, 2009, p. 23). Traditionally, cultures such as the German or Scandinavian are said to be low-context, the Chinese high-context (Hall, 1976), and most others located on a spectrum between those two poles.

This categorisation into high-/low-context cultures is not unproblematic: in a meta-analysis of studies on high- and low-context cultures, Kittler and colleagues found several shortcomings, first and foremost a lack of adequate empirical evidence and reliance on anecdotal data (Kittler et al., 2011).

8.2.4 Cultural Dimensions in an Intercultural Context

Hall's framework still plays a role in the field of intercultural development 'perhaps, because it is straightforward and plausible, resonating as it does with many people's experiences of cultural difference' (Spencer-Oatey & Franklin, 2009, p. 24). In an often-quoted example, Hall states: 'If you are a Latin American, talking to a North American at the distance he insists on maintaining is like trying to talk across a room' (Hall, 1955, p. 86); and while this might be somewhat outdated and stereotypical, many of us can relate to similar experiences: someone who stands 'too close for comfort' while they see nothing wrong with it, is a common example. Or maybe we have interacted in a situation where we missed that the context, for example social hierarchies, carried a lot more information than was apparent from the verbal interaction alone; or maybe we had to spell out explicitly what we thought was clear from the context.

Hall was also one of the first to move beyond the traditional anthropological approach of focusing on a single culture to comparing different cultures (Rogers et al., 2002). Human culture, Hall argues, is inseparably linked to communication, and vice versa (Hall, 1992, p. 212). From there, it is only a small step to moving on to exploring what happens if people from different cultures communicate, and the field of intercultural communication.

TASK

Using Hall's three dimensions and specific examples, where do you see potential challenges in intercultural communication?

8.3 From Dimensions to Orientations: Cultural Value Orientations

A second major anthropological influence on the field of intercultural communication is the work of Florence R. Kluckhohn and Fred L. Strodtbeck, which they reported in *Variations in value orientations* (Kluckhohn & Strodtbeck, 1961). As with Hall's cultural dimensions, their framework allows for a classification and comparison of cultures based on a range of criteria. Based on a review of hundreds of ethnographic studies, Kluckhohn and Strodtbeck identified five of what they called '**value orientations**' – areas that pose sites of struggle for all societies (Jackson, 2020, p. 286):

Value orientations are complex but definitely patterned (rank-ordered) principles [...] which give order and direction to the ever-flowing stream of human acts and thoughts as these relate to the solution of 'common human' problems.
(Kluckhohn & Strodtbeck, 1961, p. 4)

The first orientation is the *relationship with the environment*. According to Kluckhohn and Strodtbeck, societies respond to this particular issue on a spectrum that ranges from subjugation to nature, to harmony with nature, to mastery over nature. In simplistic terms: at one end of this spectrum, humans rule over nature; at the other end, nature rules over humans. The second orientation is about the *relationship among people*: cultures tend to prefer one of three types of organisation. They may show a preference for hierarchical organisations ('lineality'), group organisation ('collectivism') or individual autonomy ('individualism'). The third orientation relates to the *mode of human activity*, which Kluckhohn and Strodtbeck divide into three different manifestations: 'being', whereby members of a culture accept the status quo, 'becoming', whereby the focus is on transformation and change, and 'doing', which focuses on active and direct intervention to bring about change. The *belief about basic human nature* – the fourth orientation – divides cultures into those who believe that humans are basically good, those who believe that humans are basically evil, and those in between. The last orientation relates to *orientation to time* – we can see that time is an important element in anthropological work. Cultures fall within one of three orientations towards time: a focus on the past, with a tendency to maintain traditional beliefs; a focus on the present, attempting to accommodate changes; and a focus on the future, with a strong sense of forward planning (Hills, 2002, p. 5; Spencer-Oatey, 2000, p. 5; Spencer-Oatey & Franklin, 2009, p. 25). Thomas, for example, has used this value orientation framework to evaluate citizens of the United States. According to him, US Americans show a tendency towards domination of the environment (relationship to the environment), are individualistic (relationship among people), are a 'doing culture' (mode of human activity) who believe that humans are neither inherently good nor evil (belief about basic human nature), and show a time orientation that is focused on the present (Thomas, 2008, p. 49).

As with Hall's work, Kluckhohn & Strodtbeck's (1961) *cultural value orientation* framework has seen considerable criticism. Fox highlights methodological weaknesses in the definition of the underlying concepts but also criticises the lack of the inclusion of space as an orientation (Fox, 1963), although space had appeared in an earlier version of the framework. Hills, however, found that while Kluckhohn and Strodtbeck's framework had shortcomings, in particular because it is rather general, it was still of value as it allowed for an approach to studying and comparing cultures, even if broad-brush (Hills, 2002). The framework has also been modified and expanded over time. Maznevski and colleagues, for example, used data from Canada, Mexico, the Netherlands, Taiwan and the United States, and identified patterns of convergence for cultures from industrialised countries, resulting in 'low hierarchy, low subjugation, and low being', an 'agreement of priorities [that] facilitates the conduct of global coordination' (Maznevski et al., 2002, p. 288).

Similar approaches that put cultures into a range of 'categories' or 'dimensions' have also been used by later researchers from other disciplines, such as Geert Hofstede's psychological work on cultural value dimensions.

TASK

How would you classify your own culture based on Kluckhohn and Strodtbeck's value orientations?

8.4 Culture, Language and Communication Patterns

The idea of a relationship between language and culture is one that goes back a long way in anthropology. Franz Boas was one of the first to emphasise the relationship between language and culture (Hall, 1966). Boas argued for an inclusion of the study of languages in the study of anthropology:

> If ethnology [anthropology] is understood as the science dealing with the mental phenomena of the life of the peoples of the world, human language, one of the most important manifestations of mental life, would seem to belong naturally to the field of work of ethnology.
>
> (Boas, 1911, p. 63)

Boas's student Edward Sapir and Sapir's student Benjamin Lee Whorf, both also studying Native American peoples and languages, took these ideas further. While Boas was an early proponent of **linguistic relativity** – the idea that the language we speak influences the way we think about the world (Lucy, 1997) – Sapir and especially Whorf went a step further and argued for what is known as *linguistic determinism*: the view that our language determines the way we see the world. Using an analysis of Hopi grammar, Whorf concluded that:

> the background linguistic system (in other words, the grammar) of each language is not merely a reproducing instrument for voicing ideas but rather is itself the shaper of ideas, the program and guide for the individual's mental activity, for his analysis of impressions, for his synthesis of his mental stock in trade.
>
> (Whorf, 1956, p. 212)

As a result, different cultures, using different languages, would perceive the world around them differently. For example, in the Hopi language, the verb form *wíwa* ('he stumbles') becomes *wiwáwata* ('he is hobbling along') by adding a single inflection (*-wata*) at the end. A single action word (to stumble) becomes a prolonged action verb (to hobble). So, in Hopi, 'stumbling' and 'hobbling' along are in essence the same action. In English, however, 'to stumble' and 'to hobble' are two very different verbs, each referring to a different type of action. So if a Hopi and an English speaker communicate, misunderstandings might arise not only on linguistic grounds, but also on a conceptual level: for the Hopi, stumbling and hobbling are the same type of motion, for the English, they are different (Ottenheimer, 2006, pp. 25–26).

A more contemporary example is the Danish word *hygge*, which has become increasingly popular in the UK over the last few years – and even made it on to the 'Word of the year' list of the *Collins Dictionary* in 2016. *Hygge* can be defined as 'the practice of creating cosy and congenial environments that promote emotional well-being' (*Collins English Dictionary*, 2016). The concept is deeply embedded within Danish culture and linked to Scandinavian ideas of egalitarianism (Beltagui & Schmidt, 2015; Linnet, 2011), and while lifestyle magazines and advertising have provided a myriad of information about how to create *hygge*, it is debatable how much of the concept can really be understood outside Danish culture.

Both linguistic relativity and linguistic determinism have been a key point of interest for anthropologists, but, as with most theories, are not uncontroversial. For example, the fact that languages change over time, sometimes quite dramatically, undermines a strong version of linguistic determinism. So rather than constraining our thought processes, language might shape our thought processes but allows us to seek different perspectives too (Ottenheimer, 2006).

TASK

In English, the time 11.15 a.m. is expressed as 'quarter past eleven', while 11.45 a.m. is 'quarter to twelve'. In German, based on region, these can variably be expressed as

– 11.15 *viertel nach elf* ('quarter past eleven') or *viertel zwölf* ('quarter twelve')

– 11.45 *viertel vor zwölf* ('quarter to twelve') or *dreiviertel zwölf* ('three quarters twelve')

A similar pattern exists in Czech. What can this tell us about the perception of time? Can you think of similar examples from other languages?

8.5 Language, Communication and Culture: Methods and Examples

8.5.1 Ethnography of Speaking, Speech Community and Communicative Competence

At the heart of anthropology is the methodological approach of **ethnography.** Ethnography is based on an in-depth description and analysis of a culture or group, based on often extensive observation (Scott & Marshall, 2005). From that, Dell Hymes developed a framework that particularly focuses on communicative practices: **ethnography of speaking**. At the core of this is the assumption that language is an integral part of cultural behaviour, with different cultures using different conventions for linguistic practices (Foley, 1997). This goes beyond the linguistic level but includes the entire communicative exchange. For example, in Britain it would not be unusual if, in a conversation between several people, some of them only take a peripheral role with little active involvement in the form of contributions but act as listeners. Amongst Aboriginal Australians, these practices are markedly different in that a conversational norm is that *all* participants contribute, with conversations where only one or few people actively participate being considered to have 'failed' (Foley, 1997, p. 252). Closely linked to this phenomenon is the concept of **speech community**: groups of people who do not just speak the same language but have agreed on norms and conventions of *how* to use language, and how to communicate. That is, they share not only common usage, but also common evaluations of communicative practices (see, for example, Hymes, 2009; Labov, 2006): there is cultural and social significance not only in *what* is being said, but also *how* it is being said (Duranti, 2009a, p. 153). The ability to use language not only correctly but also appropriately in a given speech community is known as **communicative competence** (Hymes, 1972).

8.5.2 Examples
Greetings

TASK

In your culture, what are the 'rules' for greetings? Is there a particular sequence of events, such as a preference for who initiates and who responds? Have you observed different rules in other cultures?

We will finish the chapter with two brief examples. The first one relates to the communicative practice of greetings: they are often considered universal, are often formulaic and hence easily recognisable, for example 'Hello!' or 'Good morning!'. We have already looked at greetings in Chapter 7 and seen how contextual knowledge is important for the interpretation of greetings: the formulaic nature of greetings means that simply knowing the words does not necessarily ensure a correct interpretation of meaning.

Alessandro Duranti in his study of Samoan greetings argues that in order to understand greetings within a speech community fully, and to compare greetings across different speech communities, we need to move beyond those formulaic units of language and take into account six criteria (Duranti, 2009b, pp. 191–194):

1. They occur near the beginning of the encounter between people.
2. They are followed by immediate mutual recognition or acknowledgement of each other.

3. They are part of a sequence (known as 'adjacency pairs') whereby the initial greeting is followed by some form of response, verbal or otherwise.
4. They are predictable in form and content.
5. They define a distinct interaction. For example, when we meet someone in the morning, we will greet them, but not greet them again in the same meeting. However, if we meet them again later the same day, we will probably exchange some sort of greeting again.
6. They show that the other person is 'worth' greeting, so implies a certain status.

Successfully encoding and decoding these categories can pose considerable challenges for those operating across different languages and cultures. Spencer-Oatey, for example, has shown how international students can face challenges with aspects such as different non-verbal behaviour associated with greetings and the way context influences greeting behaviour (Spencer-Oatey, 2018, p. 311). One of her respondents, a postgraduate student from China, reports that:

> In the first couple months here, I always felt overwhelmed by all the greetings, and was really embarrassed by didn't know how to respond it properly. Among all these 'How are you', 'How's it going', and other phrases, the 'Are you all right' is the one making me most uncomfortable with and felt really confused at first.
>
> (Spencer-Oatey, 2018, p. 309)

Culturally appropriate greeting behaviour, Spencer-Oatey argues, is important in facilitating for friendships and hence social integration. 'How are you?' as a greeting is usually not, as we know, an invitation to receive a detailed account of one's state of mental and physical well-being, but knowing this convention and the appropriate response is important for successful interaction – and repeatedly responding inappropriately will make a speaker look somewhat odd or even impolite (you may want to review Chapter 7 too, where we discuss linguistic politeness). So greetings are not only a linguistic, but also a cultural device.

Language, culture and power

We saw in Chapter 4 that a key component in critical intercultural communication is the notion of power. We can take this a step further: if language, culture and communication are closely linked, it is likely that language can never be truly neutral (Duranti, 2009a, p. 381) but is influenced by certain cultural assumptions, ideologies and power constellations. For example, different speech communities do not all have the same status within their culture, and even within a language, different linguistic features are assigned different ideological values (Morgan, 2004). We can see this most easily by drawing on variational sociolinguistics and dialectology: even within the same language and country, different accents and dialects of the same language carry different levels of prestige (Kerswill, 2007).

But these differences in perception also appear at a wider level. Judith Irvine and Susan Gal show how language ideologies do not assign the same status to all languages (Irvine & Gal, 2009, p. 416): the Macedonian language in south-eastern Europe, for example, has struggled to gain recognition amongst Greeks and Bulgarians as an independent language (as opposed to a variety of Bulgarian or Serbian), mainly because in the nineteenth century both Greece and Bulgaria had territorial claims over parts of Macedonia (Marinov, 2013). The modern dispute with Greece was ultimately settled as part of the Prespa Agreement in 2018 (Vankovska, 2020). What we see here then is that an individual cultural and linguistic group's right of recognition is directly related to issues of political power: linguistically, the language exists (people speak it after all), but the recognition as an individual language is subject to political disputes.

Similarly, as the result of large-scale European colonisation in the past, non-European languages (and, by extension, cultures) have often been seen as 'inferior', resulting in considerable social inequalities (Philips, 2004): in the context of the emergence of pidgin and creole languages on plantations, 'plantation workers were certainly at the periphery of the social order' and 'performance of identity through symbolic expression of the traditions that were left behind was hardly possible' (Jourdan, 2006, p. 149). This links up to our discussion of postcolonial intervention in Chapter 4.

8.6 In Summary

In this chapter, we have looked at the way in which anthropology has contributed to the study of intercultural communication. Following on from Chapter 7, we have further established the close interrelationship between culture, communication and language, looking at different perspectives and approaches. In particular, we have established the strong cultural elements that underlie language and language use, and the impact contextual aspects have on communicative practice.

DISCUSSION QUESTIONS

1. Using Hall's dimensions of culture and Kluckhohn and Strodtbeck's value orientations, critically compare two cultures you are familiar with. In which areas, and why, is the analysis straightforward? Where, and why, are there difficulties?
2. Think of examples of either concepts (such as *hygge*) or communicative practices (such as greetings). To what extent are these culturally specific and significant? If they exist in different cultures, how are they similar or different?

CASE STUDY

A meeting to negotiate an international treaty on climate change includes delegations from France, the USA, China, India and Russia. Each team includes members from a range of specialisations, including lawyers, diplomats and scientists.

- What intercultural communication issues can you foresee?
- There are obvious aspects of culture in this example that have the potential to create friction. Are there also elements that will have a facilitating effect? Think about culture from a slightly wider angle and how different groups of people perceive themselves and others (reviewing Chapters 1 and 7 might also help here).

(based on Avruch, 2009)

References

Avruch, K. (2009). Cross-cultural conflict. *Conflict Resolution, 1,* 45–57.

Beltagui, A., & Schmidt, T. (2015). Why can't we all get along? A study of *hygge* and *janteloven* in a Danish social-casual games community. *Games and Culture, 12*(5), 403–425.

Boas, F. (1911). *Handbook of American Indian languages.* Washington, DC: Government Printing Office.

Collins English Dictionary. (2016). *hygge.*

Crevecoeur, I., & Van Dyck, M. C. (2013). Physical anthropology (paleoanthropology). In A. L. C. Runehov & L. Oviedo (eds.), *Encyclopedia of sciences and religions* (pp. 1706–1709). Dordrecht: Springer.

Duranti, A. (2009a). *Linguistic anthropology: A reader* (2nd edition). Oxford: Wiley-Blackwell.

Duranti, A. (2009b). Universal and culture-specific properties of greetings. In A. Duranti (ed.), *Linguistic anthropology: A reader* (2nd edition), (pp. 188–213). Oxford: Wiley-Blackwell.

Erickson, F. (2011). Culture. In B. A. Levinson & M. Pollock (eds.), *A companion to the anthropology of education* (pp. 25–33). Chichester: Wiley.

Eriksen, T. H. (2001). *Small places, large issues: An introduction to social and cultural anthropology* (2nd edition). London: Pluto.

Foley, W. A. (1997). *Anthropological linguistics: An introduction.* Oxford: Blackwell.

Fox, J. R. (1963). Review of *Variations in value orientations* by Florence Rockwood Kluckhohn and Fred L. Strodtbeck. *The British Journal of Sociology, 14*(3), 281–282.

González, N. (2010). Advocacy anthropology and education. *Current Anthropology, 51*(S2), 249–258. DOI:10.1086/653128

Hall, E. T. (1955). The anthropology of manners. *Scientific American, 192*(4), 84–91.

Hall, E. T. (1959). *The silent language.* New York: Doubleday.

Hall, E. T. (1966). *The hidden dimension.* New York: Doubleday.

Hall, E. T. (1976). *Beyond culture.* New York: Doubleday.

Hall, E. T. (1992). *An anthropology of everyday life: An autobiography.* New York: Doubleday.

Hills, M. D. (2002). Kluckhohn and Strodtbeck's values orientation theory. *Online Readings in Psychology and Culture,* 4(4). https://doi.org/10.9707/2307-0919.1040

Hua, Z. (2014). *Exploring intercultural communication: Language in action.* Abingdon: Routledge.

Hymes, D. (1972). On communicative competence. In J. B. Pride & J. Holmes (eds.), *Sociolinguistics: Selected readings* (pp. 269–293). Harmondsworth: Penguin.

Hymes, D. (2009). Ways of speaking. In A. Duranti (ed.), *Linguistic anthropology: A reader* (2nd edition), (pp. 158–171). Oxford: Wiley-Blackwell.

Irvine, J. T., & Gal, S. (2009). Language ideology and linguistic differentiation. In A. Duranti (ed.), *Linguistic anthropology: A reader* (2nd edition), (pp. 402–434). Oxford: Wiley-Blackwell.

Jackson, J. (2020). *Introducing language and intercultural communication* (2nd edition). Abingdon: Routledge.

Jourdan, C. (2006). Pidgins and creoles genesis: An anthropological offering. In C. Jourdan & K. Tuite (eds.), *Language, culture, and society: Key topics in linguistic anthropology* (pp. 135–155). Cambridge: Cambridge University Press.

Kerswill, P. (2007). Standard and non-standard English. In D. Britain (ed.), *Language in the British Isles* (pp. 34–51). Cambridge: Cambridge University Press.

Kittler, M. G., Rygl, D., & Mackinnon, A. (2011). Special review article: Beyond culture or beyond control? Reviewing the use of Hall's high-/low-context concept. *International Journal of Cross Cultural Management,* 11(1), 63–82.

Kluckhohn, F. R., & Strodtbeck, F. L. (1961). *Variations in value orientations.* New York: Harper and Row.

Labov, W. (2006). *The social stratification of English in New York City* (2nd edition). Cambridge: Cambridge University Press.

Linnet, J. T. (2011). Money can't buy me hygge: Danish middle-class consumption, egalitarianism, and the sanctity of inner space. *Social Analysis,* 55(2), 21–44.

Lucy, J. A. (1997). Linguistic relativity. *Annual Review of Anthropology,* 26, 291–312.

Marinov, T. (2013). Famous Macedonia, the land of Alexander: Macedonian identity at the crossroads of Greek, Bulgarian and Serbian nationalism. In R. Daskalov & T. Marinov (eds.), *Entangled histories of the Balkans* (Vol. 1, pp. 273–332). Leiden: Brill.

Maznevski, M. L., Gomez, C. B., DiStefano, J. J., Noorderhaven, N. G., & Wu, P. C. (2002). Cultural dimensions at the individual level of analysis: The cultural orientations framework. *International Journal of Cross Cultural Management,* 2(3), 275–295.

Morgan, M. (2004). Speech community. In A. Duranti (ed.), *A companion to linguistic anthropology* (pp. 3–22). Maldon, MA: Blackwell.

Ottenheimer, H. (2006). *The anthropology of language: An introduction to linguistic anthropology.* Southbank, Victoria: Thomson, Wadsworth.

Philips, S. U. (2004). Language and social inequality. In A. Duranti (ed.), *A companion to linguistic anthropology* (pp. 474–495). Maldon, MA: Blackwell.

Rogers, E. M., Hart, W. B., & Miike, Y. (2002). Edward T. Hall and the history of intercultural communication: the United States and Japan. *Keio Communication Review,* 24(3), 3–26.

Scott, J., & Marshall, G. (2005). *A dictionary of sociology* (3rd edition). Oxford: Oxford University Press.

Spencer-Oatey, H. (2000). Introduction. In H. Spencer-Oatey (ed.), *Culturally speaking: Managing rapport through talk across cultures* (pp. 1–8). London: Continuum.

Spencer-Oatey, H. (2018). Transformative learning for social integration: Overcoming the challenge of greetings. *Intercultural Education*, 29(2), 301–315.

Spencer-Oatey, H., & Franklin, P. (2009). *Intercultural interaction: A multidisciplinary approach to intercultural communication*. Basingstoke: Palgrave Macmillan.

Thomas, D. C. (2008). *Cross-cultural management: Essential concepts*. London: SAGE.

Vankovska, B. (2020). Geopolitics of the Prespa agreement: Background and after-effects. *Journal of Balkan and Near Eastern Studies*, 22(3), 343–371.

Whorf, B. L. (1956). *Language, thought, and reality: Selected writings of Benjamin Lee Whorf*. Edited by John B. Carroll. Cambridge, MA: MIT Press.

Williams, R. (1985). *Keywords: A vocabulary of culture and society*. London: Fontana.

9 Sociological Approaches

We saw in Chapter 8 that anthropology as a discipline is primarily concerned with the analysis and comparison of cultures. In the current chapter, we want to look in more detail at the range of variation that occurs *within* a culture. In a nutshell, while closely related disciplines, anthropology takes a more holistic approach to looking at cultures, and sociology focuses more on the social structures within a culture. Following on from our discussion of communicative competence in Chapter 8, we will first look at the concept of symbolic (or cultural) capital. We will then move to a discussion of gender and gender identity in the context of intercultural communication. We will conclude by introducing the concept of intersectionality to provide a framework that explains the complexity of modern life.

AIMS
By the end of this chapter, you should be able to:
1. **provide a basic definition of symbolic capital;**
2. **explain the role that capital plays in intercultural communication;**
3. **describe the role of gender and gender identity;**
4. **explain the concept of intersectionality.**

> **KEY TERMS**
> **symbolic capital – queer theory/queer studies –
> heterosexism – intersectionality**

9.1 Sociology and Intercultural Communication: Origins

9.1.1 Meeting the Stranger

Sociological approaches to intercultural communication go back more than eighty years, emerging out of anthropological work and having focused on isolation, conflict and assimilation (Brown, 1939). German sociologist Georg Simmel discussed the phenomenon of the 'stranger', someone who in terms of membership of a particular group is 'both near and far *at the same time*' (Simmel, 1950, p. 407; original emphasis): they are neither a full group member, nor are they complete outsiders. The 'stranger', Simmel argued, shows a lack of full commitment towards a particular group, which provides him with a level of 'objectivity'. Simmel's conceptualisation of a stranger is of one who generally is in a position of power and privilege. In part, the concept is built around the stranger as a traditional trader: someone who acts as the middleman in the exchange of goods not available in a society. The stakes for the trader are limited to the economic transaction, with little involvement in the societies he trades with beyond that. Today, we can think about this in terms of an external consultant coming into a company: someone about whom very little is known, whose behavioural practices are unfamiliar, but who is in a position of privilege, as their advice will impact on how the company operates; yet, there is little at stake for the stranger/consultant beyond that.

However, this idea of a stranger being in a position of privilege does not necessarily hold true today: as Dutta and Martin point out, in an era of mass migration and refugees, privilege is no longer a universal criterion (Dutta & Martin, 2020); being forced from your home in a war-torn country is a long way from the idea of a privileged trading stranger. In particular in migration contexts, Gudykunst argues that in-group members generally have more power as they are part of the majority of society (Gudykunst, 2004, p. 4); we will look at this in more detail in Chapter 13. Migration and mobility can also be a way of life and not purely defined by economic gains (Dutta & Martin, 2020, p. 171): people can make active decisions to live in other countries by choice, be it for the weather, a sense of adventure, or the way of life.

Encounters with – or between – strangers are often associated with uncertainty and, to an extent, anxiety. The lack of shared (cultural) knowledge results in a lack of predictability (Berger & Calabrese, 1974): 'we are unsure about how to behave' (Jandt, 2016, p. 68). William Gudykunst, a sociologist by training, developed this into his *Anxiety/Uncertainty Management Theory* which posits that all interpersonal and intergroup communication is subject to the same processes in which personal and social identities, concepts of self and expectations of others, together with uncertainty and anxiety, play a key role. *Intra*cultural and *intra*ethnic encounters are shown to create lower levels of anxiety and uncertainty than *inter*cultural and *inter*ethnic encounters (Gudykunst & Shapiro, 1996).

Figure 9.1 *Sociological Approaches* by Alíz Kovács-Zöldi

TASK

Think of an example of when you have met a 'stranger' – someone from another culture. How and to what extent did uncertainty and anxiety play a role in this meeting? Provide specific examples.

9.1.2 Symbolic Capital in a Globalised World

We introduced the concept of communicative competence in Chapter 8: the idea that in order to communicate successfully in a given speech community, we need to know not only the words and the sentence structure, but also how to use language appropriately and in line with the prevailing norms. We can expand this idea to include other types of cultural aspects. French sociologist Pierre Bourdieu formulated the concept of a **symbolic capital**: non-monetary assets and resources that are exchanged in day-to-day interaction and which enable access to other resources such as social networks (Moore, 2008). This may, for example, include a job that is regarded as prestigious (like a doctor or a judge), or a degree from a top-ranking university (Mooney & Evans, 2019). It is possession of this symbolic capital that further cements and increases someone's status in society, and likewise, lack of it may prevent someone from achieving social, economic and political success and power. One such cultural asset is language, and in particular the standard and/or official language. Using the development of standard French during the French Revolution as an example, Bourdieu illustrates how the Parisian dialect developed into the standard and official language of France, and how this advantaged the educated and the elite:

> Whereas the lower classes, particularly the peasantry, were limited to the local dialect, the aristocracy, the commercial and business bourgeoisie [...] has access much more frequently to the use of the official language.
> (Bourdieu, 1991, p. 47)

As a result, he concludes:

> the members of these local bourgeoisies of priests, doctors, or teachers, who owed their position to their mastery of the instruments of expression, had everything to gain from the Revolutionary policy of linguistic unification.
> (1991, p. 47)

We can see from the above that language and power go hand in hand, can reinforce each other, and, in turn, also disadvantage those who lack the relevant linguistic-symbolic capital. These power inequalities are also reflected in contemporary multilingual and multicultural societies, in particular where policy and public discourses assume monolinguality or enforce an overlap between territorial and linguistic boundaries (that is, one nation/country/region, one language) in direct contradiction to linguistic realities and diversity, with at times dramatic consequences. For example, the use of language analysis for the determination of origin (LADO) – a system used in the UK to assess where asylum seekers are from – often fails to acknowledge Syrian refugees as Syrian simply because the linguistic diversity of Syria and the heterogeneity of Colloquial Arabic (Albirini, 2016) are not adequately understood; this can result in applications for asylum being rejected on the basis of certain dialects of Arabic being considered 'the wrong type of Arabic' and de facto delegitimating the claim (Ateek & Rasinger, 2018). But there are also less extreme examples. Lee's study on Korean immigrants showed how diverse, multicultural social networks, conceptualised as high social capital, positively contribute to intercultural orientation, with social capital promoting intercultural sensitivity (Lee, 2014, p. 299).

Linked to symbolic capital is the notion of *symbolic violence* (Bourdieu, 1991), reconceptualised by feminist research as 'denying the presence, skills or contributions of the other, calling attention to real and symbolic status downgrading'

(Flam & Beauzamy, 2008, pp. 221–222). This is an issue many migrants are also confronted with on a daily basis, ranging from overt physical avoidance (such as moving to the other side of a room), to verbal aggression, to excessive institutional scrutiny: 'migrants are denied recognition on a daily basis and also barred from access to resources they badly need to make a decent living' (Flam & Beauzamy, 2008, p. 238), for example, in the complex processes of obtaining work or residency permits. With globalisation comes the need for increased *intercultural* capital: intercultural skills, competencies and sensitivities (Pöllmann, 2013, p. 2). We will look at one manifestation of this in Chapter 17, where we discuss intercultural competence.

9.2 Gender and Intercultural Communication

9.2.1 Gender through a Critical Lens

Most textbooks on intercultural communication cover gender as a factor and approach it either through an analysis of gender differences, such as a comparison of women and men in terms of socioeconomic status, educational attainment etc., and in relation to traditional frameworks such as Hofstede's (for example, Jandt, 2016, who dedicates a chapter to 'Culture and Women'), or by exploring the topic through the lens of identity, with gender being part of one's identity (such as Jackson, 2020). For example, a study on corporate elites in Turkey has shown how gender is strategically used as a symbolic capital in line with the country's strong patriarchal ideologies: women in positions of power and influence are shown to seek male allegiances in order to maintain their position (Yamak et al., 2016).

Yet, a lot of intercultural research continues to take an essentialist view of gender identity and is firmly located within Western-centric ideas, as outlined by Lengel et al. (2020). Gender identity is, however, not fixed or static, but in Judith Butler's words, a performance: gender is 'always a doing' (Butler, 1990, p. 34), and is 'socially constructed and culturally mediated' (Lengel & Martin, 2013, p. 338). While societies often have prevailing gender ideologies which strongly influence societal power structures (and vice versa), these are not absolute and must be understood within their historic context. Lengel and Martin (2013) use the wearing of the *hijab* – the traditional head covering of Muslim women – as an example to show how the perception of this cultural practice has changed over time: during the eighteenth and nineteenth centuries, European travellers to Muslim regions 'would most likely have approved of Muslim societies' emphasis on such female modesty' as it aligned with their own beliefs about female modesty at the time (Lengel & Martin, 2013, p. 338). Today, many Europeans and Americans tend to perceive the practice of wearing the *hijab* as female oppression (Sloan, 2011).

9.2.2 Queering Intercultural Communication

Since the 1970s, research across the social sciences and the humanities has explored the experiences of gay, lesbian, bisexual, and, more recently, transgender people, in what is often known as **queer theory** or **queer studies** (Edgar & Sedgwick, 2008). With its focus on difference, queer studies can provide theoretical tools for the study of intercultural communication, too (Yep, 2013). Yep and colleagues propose a multi-level analysis that allows for an integrative approach to intercultural communication that provides a more nuanced and critical understanding (Yep et al., 2019, pp. 2–3): the *macro* level takes into account the political, cultural and historical context (similar to Lengel & Martin, 2013); the *meso* level considers attitudes and relationships between different groups, and the *micro* level focuses on interaction between individuals (Yep et al., 2019, pp. 2–3).

A global economy, of course, means that it is not only gender-normative people who operate in a global marketplace and migrate extensively between different countries and cultures. With homophobia and transphobia still prevalent in parts of the world, LGBT+ people deciding to move to a different culture may face a range of legal, social and cultural obstacles and discrimination, such as the (lack of) recognition of same-sex partnerships, disapproval and marginalisation, and violence and persecution (Gedro et al., 2013). This may result in fewer and less open social relationships with host country/culture members being formed, as well as higher levels of *duplicity*: the adoption of external characteristics of the new culture, with behaviours associated with LGBT+ life being hidden – a 'heterosexual façade' (McPhail & Fisher, 2015) or 'passing as straight' (Howard, 2011a).

This is, however, not only an issue in migration contexts: oppression and marginalization of LGBT+ cultural groups are just as likely to occur *within* societies, not just across them; we can think of this in terms of 'cultures within cultures' (Jandt, 2016, p. 275). Howard, for example, illustrates her experience of attending a university environment shaped by very conservative Christian values, which led her to 'strategically negotiate' her sexual orientation (Howard, 2011b, p. 123). Strong institutional symbols of **heterosexism** (the discrimination against LGBT+ people based on the assumption that heterosexuality is the norm), be it at work, education or society as a whole, may deter LGBT+ people from disclosing their sexuality.

TASK

Critically reflect on your own gender identity in the light of the dominant gender ideologies of the culture you live in. To what extent does your own gender identity overlap with cultural expectations of gender? Are there any points of conflict?

9.3 Gay, Black, Migrant: Intersectionality Theory

Our discussion of gender has been deliberately brief, and so far we have also omitted an explicit discussion of race and ethnicity; factors that are usually extensively discussed in intercultural textbooks. This is not because we do not consider them important but because we consider them too important to be discussed in isolation.

For example, Howard's experience as a gay woman within a conservative Christian environment (Section 9.2.2) is exacerbated by her being of African-American descent. As such, the negotiation of her Black Lesbian identity takes place not only in the context of an environment that shows little welcome towards LGBT+ people, but also the fact that parts of the Black community are perceived to be homophobic (Howard, 2011a). Similarly, there have been high levels of racism observed within British gay male culture, a group historically dominated by privileged white men (Mowlabocus, 2010, p. 71). In both examples, being non-white intersects with being LGBT+, with lines of oppression running along both race/ethnicity *and* gender dimensions or sexual orientation.

We can best understand this phenomenon in terms of **intersectionality theory**: originally developed by Black feminist researchers, intersectionality argues that we cannot look at social categories in isolation, but need to consider how they intersect with each other in order to understand individual experiences (Hill Collins & Bilge, 2016; Levon, 2015). That is, people are not just male or female, or Black or White, or gay or straight, but female *and* black *and* gay, or White *and* male *and* straight etc. Kimberlé Crenshaw is often credited to have first formulated intersectionality as a social theory. As a legal scholar, Crenshaw used a range of examples from lawsuits to argue that Black women face more discrimination by the legal system not just because they are Black (as anti-discrimination laws forbid this), or because they are women (as anti-discrimination laws forbid that too), but because they fall into the intersection *of* Black *and* female (Crenshaw, 1989); yet, this space is not legally defined. Social inequality hence needs to be understood as multifaceted and influenced by interpersonal, cultural and structural power mechanisms (Durham, 2020, p. 46).

Notions of privilege and power depend, of course, on the context. As an example by Purkayastha shows, a Black Ugandan and an Indian Ugandan may both face discrimination in the US but for different reasons: the Black Ugandan based on race alone, much like many African Americans, but the Indian Ugandan on account of being 'Muslim-looking', bringing religion into the mix – a factor we have not so far discussed. In Uganda, the Black Ugandan is likely to be in a position of advantage, while the Indian Ugandan is in one of disadvantage (the Ugandan regime under Idi Amin expelled most Ugandans of Indian descent in 1972); in India, it is likely to be the reverse – but will also depend on the Indian Ugandan's religion and, in a society with a strong class system, class

(Purkayastha, 2012). As we have emphasised throughout this book, simple classification based on essentialist categories will not allow us to grasp the complexities of modern life.

We can also link our discussion of symbolic capital to an intersectionality framework: as we have seen in our Syrian example, in the context of migration, language is one of the key cultural capitals: in a study of migrant Moroccan women in Spain, Martínez illustrates how gender, low socioeconomic status and low levels of education directly impact on their development of Spanish as a second language, further compounding the socioeconomic inequalities and disempowerment they already face (Martínez, 2015). While middle-class migrants and those with higher qualifications had an initial advantage in terms of Spanish language development, linguistic gatekeeping within the host society leads to a 'de-classing' based on linguistic skills (2015, pp. 235–236). However, cultural capitals such as languages or cultural practices can also be used to migrants' advantage, that is, are deployed differently by different people, creating intra-migrant differentiations based on gender, class or ethnicity. Indeed, foreign language skills might be a crucial tool in finding a job: Erel provides the example of a Turkish migrant in Germany who secured graduate training and ultimately a job as a bilingual German-Turkish teacher by virtue of her Turkish language skills (Erel, 2010).

9.4 In Summary

In this chapter, we have focused on how we can explain power structures within a society, and, by extension, across cultures. We have seen that symbolic capital can play an important role in creating and maintaining inequalities. Our discussion of gender and intersectionality has provided us with a framework of explaining complex social realities by moving away from a traditional exploration of individual social categories. We will revisit these issues over subsequent chapters, and in particular in Part III (chapters 12 to 18), where we will look at intercultural communication in specific settings.

DISCUSSION QUESTIONS

In the cultures you know, what are common symbols of heterosexism/ heteronormativity? Do these symbols differ between cultures? What are the institutional mechanisms and discourses that reinforce them?

Considering your race/ethnicity, gender, sexual orientation, socioeconomic group and level of education, how high or low would you assess your own symbolic capital (and why)? Does that capital give you privileges, such as easier access to well-paid and potentially powerful jobs and/or political roles? Who has less symbolic power than you, and who has more (and why)?

CASE STUDY

The following is an abridged letter that was sent to the *Los Angeles Times* by Leo Guerra Tezcatlipoca, Director and founder of the Chicano Mexicano Empowerment Committee, Los Angeles. How does it relate to the concepts of race and symbolic power discussed in this chapter?

There is a daily insult that we Chicanos and Mexicanos *(Meh-hee-kah-nohs)* receive from the English- and Spanish-language media as well as government and business. They all refer to us as Hispanics and/or Latinos. We Mexicanos and Chicanos do this, too, parroting what we hear and read in the English- and Spanish-language media, mostly not knowing the damage we do to ourselves and our children. We supposedly all fit under Hispanic and/or Latino. We are supposedly all the same people. We are not!

Hispanic refers to the people, land, language and culture of Spain. Latino means Latin in Spanish. Latin is the language of the old Roman-dominated part of Europe. Latino is equivalent to *Hispano. Hispano* is equivalent to European. We Mexicanos and Chicanos are not Hispanic, Latino, Spanish or European.

Chicanos and Mexicanos who have pride in who we are do not want to be Hispanic or European. Chicanos are people of Mexican descent born in the United States. Some Central Americans identify with or (see themselves) as Chicano. Mexicanos are Mexicans born in Mexico. Mexicano comes from the word *Mexica (Meh-chi-ca),* which is what the original people of Mexico called themselves. Chicano comes from the word *Mechicano.* Chicano is more of an aggressive, proud and assertive political and cultural statement than Mexican American.

Chicanos and Mexicanos have a heritage that includes the long and proud history of the Olmec, Teotihuacano, Maya, Zapotec, Toltec, Aztec and the dozens of other native cultures and civilizations of Mexico, Central America and the Southwestern United States.

The terms *Hispanic* and *Latino* are insulting to Chicanos and Mexicanos because these words deny us our great Native Mexican heritage.

[...]

The majority of Chicanos and Mexicanos don't know our own history and we don't know that we're being insulted by Hispanic/Latino. Please give those other two persons their separate cultural identity – Peruvian, Argentine, Spaniard or whatever their cultural identity is. In general references, most of the time, use Chicano, Mexicano and Latino – all three words.

And please, never Hispanic.

(Guerra Tezcatlipoca, 1993)

References

Albirini, A. (2016). *Modern Arabic sociolinguistics: Diglossia, variation, codeswitching, attitudes and identity*. Abingdon: Routledge.

Ateek, M. & Rasinger, S. M. (2018). Syrian or non-Syrian? Reflections on the use of LADO in the UK. In I. M. Nick (ed.), *Forensic linguistics: Asylum-seekers, refugees and immigrants* (pp. 75–93). Wilmington: Vernon Press.

Berger, C. R. & Calabrese, R. J. (1974). Some explorations in initial interaction and beyond: Toward a developmental theory of interpersonal communication. *Human Communication Research*, 1(2), 99–112.

Bourdieu, P. (1991). *Language and symbolic power*. Cambridge: Polity.

Brown, F. J. (1939). Sociology and intercultural understanding. *The Journal of Educational Sociology*, 12(6), 328–331.

Butler, J. (1990). *Gender trouble: Feminism and the subversion of identity*. Abingdon: Routledge.

Crenshaw, K. (1989). Demarginalizing the intersection of race and sex: A black feminist critique of antidiscrimination doctrine, feminist theory and antiracist politics. *University of Chicago Legal Forum*, 139, 139–168.

Durham, A. (2020). Black feminist thought, intersectionality, and intercultural communication. In S. Eguchi, B. M. Calafell, & S. Abdi (eds.), *De-Whitening intersectionality: Race, intercultural communication, and politics* (pp. 45–58). Lanham: Lexington Books.

Dutta, U. & Martin, J. N. (2020). Sociological approaches to intercultural communication. In G. Rings & S. M. Rasinger (eds.), *The Cambridge handbook of intercultural communication* (pp. 170–186). Cambridge: Cambridge University Press.

Edgar, A., & Sedgwick, P. R. (2008). *Cultural theory: The key concepts* (2nd edition). Abingdon: Routledge.

Erel, U. (2010). Migrating cultural capital: Bourdieu in migration studies. *Sociology*, 44(4), 642–660. DOI:10.1177/0038038510369363

Flam, H. & Beauzamy, B. (2008). Symbolic violence. In G. Delanty & R. Wodak (eds.), *Identity, belonging and migration* (pp. 221–240). Liverpool: Liverpool University Press.

Gedro, J., Mizzi, R. C., Rocco, T. S. & van Loo, J. (2013). Going global: Professional mobility and concerns for LGBT workers. *Human Resource Development International*, 16(3), 282–297. DOI:10.1080/13678868.2013.771869

Gudykunst, W. B. (2004). *Bridging differences: Effective intergroup communication*. London: Sage.

Gudykunst, W. B. & Shapiro, R. B. (1996). Communication in everyday interpersonal and intergroup encounters. *International Journal of Intercultural Relations*, 20(1), 19–45.

Guerra Tezcatlipoca, L. (1993). We're Chicanos – not Latinos or Hispanics. *Los Angeles Times*. 22 November. https://lat.ms/38HPevp

Hill Collins, P. & Bilge, S. (2016). *Intersectionality*. Cambridge: Polity Press.

Howard, S. C. (2011a). Breaking the silence: An autoethnography of a single, Black, lesbian's interpersonal relationships at an HBCU. In E. Gilchrists (ed.), *Experiences of single African-American women professors: With this Ph.D., I thee wed* (pp. 159–172). Lanham, MD: University Press of America.

Howard, S. C. (2011b). Intercultural (mis)communication: Why would you 'out' me in class? *Sexuality & Culture*, 16(2), 118–133. DOI:10.1007/s12119-011-9112-3

Jackson, J. (2020). *Introducing language and intercultural communication* (2nd edition). Abingdon: Routledge.

Jandt, F. E. (2016). *An introduction to intercultural communication: Identities in a global community* (8th edition). Thousand Oaks, CA: SAGE.

Lee, S. K. (2014). The impact of social capital in ethnic religious communication networks on Korean immigrants intercultural development. *International Journal of Intercultural Relations*, 43, 289–303. DOI:10.1016/j.ijintrel.2014.10.001

Lengel, L., Atay, A. & Kluch, Y. (2020). Decolonizing gender and intercultural communication in transnational contexts. In G. Rings & S. M. Rasinger (eds.), *The Cambridge handbook of intercultural communication* (pp. 205–226). Cambridge: Cambridge University Press.

Lengel, L. & Martin, S. C. (2013). Situating gender in critical intercultural communication studies. In T. K. Nakayama & R. T. Halualani (eds.), *The handbook of critical intercultural communication* (pp. 334–347). Chichester: Wiley-Blackwell.

Levon, E. (2015). Integrating intersectionality in language, gender, and sexuality research. *Language and Linguistics Compass*, 9(7), 295–308.

Martínez, T. C. (2015). Intersectionality in language trajectories: African women in Spain. *Applied Linguistics Review*, 6(2), 217–239. DOI:10.1515/applirev-2015-0011

McPhail, R. & Fisher, R. (2015). Lesbian and gay expatriates' use of social media to aid acculturation. *International Journal of Intercultural Relations*, 49, 294–307. DOI:10.1016/j.ijintrel.2015.05.007

Mooney, A. & Evans, B. (2019). *Language, society and power: An introduction* (5th edition). Abingdon: Routledge.

Moore, R. (2008). Capital. In M. Grenfell (ed.), *Pierre Bourdieu: Key concepts* (pp. 101–117). Durham: Acumen.

Mowlabocus, S. (2010). *Gaydar culture: Gay men, technology and embodiment in the digital age*. Abingdon: Routledge.

Pöllmann, A. (2013). Intercultural capital: Toward the conceptualization, operationalization, and empirical investigation of a rising marker of sociocultural distinction. *Sage Open*, 3(2), 1–7.

Purkayastha, B. (2012). Intersectionality in a transnational world. *Gender & Society*, 26(1), 55–66. DOI:10.1177/0891243211426725

Simmel, G. (1950). The stranger. In K. H. Wolff (ed.), *The sociology of Georg Simmel* (pp. 402–406). Glencoe, IL: The Free Press.

Sloan, L. (2011). Women's oppression or choice? One American's view on wearing the hijab. *Affilia*, 26(2), 218–221. DOI:10.1177/0886109911405827

Yamak, S., Ergur, A., Özbilgin, M. F. & Alakavuklar, O. N. (2016). Gender as symbolic capital and violence: The case of corporate elites in Turkey. *Gender, Work & Organization*, 23(2), 125–146. DOI:10.1111/gwao.12115

Yep, G. A. (2013). Queering/quaring/kauering/crippin'/transing 'other bodies' in intercultural communication. *Journal of International and Intercultural Communication*, 6(2), 118–126.

Yep, G. A., Lescure, R. M. & Russo, S. E. (2019). Queer intercultural communication. *Oxford Research Encyclopedia of Communication*. DOI:10.1093/acrefore/9780190228613.013.170

10 Psychological Perspectives

In this chapter we would like to concentrate on contributions from psychology that help to reconstruct best practice in intercultural relations, rather than just assist with the deconstruction of monocultural obstacles (as in chapters 1 and 4). We argue that such constructive support is particularly explicit in positive psychology. Since Seligman's PERMA model has been widely accepted as pathbreaking for new directions in positive psychology, we discuss this model to examine potential reasons for enhanced cultural mediation. We finish with the exploration of a comparable shift of focus from the deconstruction of monocultural features to an elaboration of best practice in intercultural film, which comes with new directions in the construction of collective memory. To facilitate discussions, we provide examples of cultural encounters in films, with a focus on team sports. This links up to strong political support for the value of sport for intercultural development, for example through the United Nations Inter-Agency Task Force on Sport for Development and Peace, and recent studies on the impact of films on viewer behaviour.

AIMS

By the end of this chapter, you should be able to:

1. **outline contributions from positive psychology to understand and develop intercultural relations better;**
2. **demonstrate the shift from deconstruction to reconstruction in intercultural film and memory production;**
3. **explain the extent to which that shift is connected to questions of power.**

KEY TERMS
positive psychology – PERMA – transcultural memory

10.1 A Shift of Focus

When discussing critical intercultural communication in Chapter 4, we highlighted links to postcolonial studies because of their examination of cultural hierarchies and power structures. We also talked about the decolonising mission of critical intercultural communication to facilitate successful exchange and negotiation of common ground and differences between people from different cultural backgrounds. However, all this aims predominantly at the examination and destabilisation of monocultural patterns, that is, a weakening of obstacles to intercultural communication, while direct contributions to the development of intercultural relations remain limited.

We argue that **positive psychology** might be able to deliver such direct contributions, partly because it had to move away from the critical focus of mainstream psychology first. One of the key representatives and founding scholars, Martin Seligman, summarises this shift as follows: 'Historically and in my own intellectual history, psychology has been about what is wrong with life', which leads to a 'repairing pathology' focus, while positive psychology redirects scholarly attention to two basic questions: 'What makes life worth living, and how can we build it?' (Seligman, 2012, p. 232). *Intercultural education* provides some answers to these questions when aiming at the creation of an intercultural society shaped by 'understanding, tolerance and friendship among all nations, racial or religious groups', which includes an understanding 'of the necessity for international solidarity and cooperation' (UNESCO, 1974), as well as 'respect for the dignity and intrinsic equality of all human beings' (Council of Europe, 1981, p. 1). Key objectives are 'empathy, solidarity, recognition and respect for diversity', and maximum restraint of 'ethnocentrism, nationalism, racism and discrimination' (Bećirović, 2012, p. 153).

TASK

Think of a project, e.g. from your school, university or workplace, that aims to meet one of the above-mentioned aims or objectives of intercultural education.
- How far and how exactly could that project contribute to a better society?

- What role might sport be able to play in this context? Look at the illustration of rowers reaching calmer seas through teamwork (Figure 10.1). You might also want to compare the image's focus on people sitting in one boat with the illustration *Culture* in Figure 1.1.

Before we examine psychological contributions to intercultural aims and objectives, it is worth highlighting that positive psychology should not be misunderstood as a rejection of mainstream psychology, but as complementary research (Seligman, 2012, p. 233). Similarly, our discussion of positive psychology for the development of intercultural relations aims to amend the work done by critical intercultural scholars like Nakayama and Martin (discussed in Chapter 4).

Figure 10.1 *Psychological Perspectives* by Alíz Kovács-Zöldi

10.2 PERMA for Intercultural Analysis

In recent decades, positive psychology has evolved from discussions of happiness and life satisfaction, to a measurable examination of well-being, for which Seligman proposes five key aspects in his **PERMA** model: **p**ositive emotion, **e**ngagement, positive **r**elationships, **m**eaning and **a**ccomplishment (Seligman, 2011, p. 12).

Although these aspects do not cover all elements of well-being and marginalise for example the importance of physical health, basic income, humanity–nature relations and sustainability, for which other studies should be considered (e.g. Faulkner, 2019; Layard, 2020; Helne, 2021), they combine key aspects from earlier models (Ryff, 1989, Ryff & Keyes 1995; Keyes, 2002; 2005) and correspond to key objectives of intercultural education. Potential and limits of the model have been confirmed by research that builds on PERMA (Butler & Kern, 2016; Seligman, 2018). The latter includes Niemiec & Wedding's (2014) analysis of PERMA aspects in contemporary cinema, many of which focus on intercultural mediation, including sport films like *Remember the Titans* (Yakin, 2000) and *Invictus* (Eastwood, 2009). Both films present successful negotiations of ethnic boundaries, with *Invictus* drawing heavily on South African history in its portrayal of the joint intervention of black president Nelson Mandela (played by Morgan Freeman) and white rugby team leader Francois Pienaar (Matt Damon) to support the development of post-apartheid solidarity in South Africa through sport.

We will in the following discussion refer in particular to *Invictus* and two popular sport comedies, which have been examined for their intercultural dimensions: *Bend it like Beckham* (Chadha, 2002) and *Sink or swim* (Lellouche, 2018). *Bend it like Beckham* presents second generation British-Indian Jess (played by Parminder Nagra) as a protagonist who clashes with her family traditions while pursuing her personal ambitions as a footballer, but who can rely on support from her English team member Jules (Keira Knightly) and her Irish trainer Joe (Jonathan Rhys Meyers). It could be argued that the film indicates how ethnic and gender boundaries in football could be overcome, although Jess's and Jules's dreams of a professional football career are linked to images of the UK and the US as lead cultures (Rings, 2018, p. 70–71). *Sink or swim* explores psychological challenges of middle-aged men in crisis through depressed protagonist Bertrand (Mathieu Amalric) and his new friends Laurent (Guillaume Canet) and Marcus (Benoît Poelvoorde), who manage to negotiate gender, class and age boundaries in their synchronised swimming team led by sport coaches Delphine (Virginie Efira) and Amanda (Leïla Bekhti).

Here and in the following examples, 'sport' can be defined in broad terms, as suggested and promoted for enhanced intercultural understanding by the United Nations Inter-Agency Task Force on Sport for Development and Peace, to capture the widest possible range of physical actions 'from play and physical activity to competitive sport' (United Nations, 2003).

10.2.1 Positive Emotion

With *positive emotion* (**P**), Seligman's PERMA discussion addresses in particular hedonic dimensions, that is, aspects related to pleasure (Seligman, 2011, p. 16). The importance of positive emotions for social connection beyond cultural boundaries has been examined by other scholars well before and after the introduction of the PERMA model (e.g. Fredrickson, 2001 & 2013). However, Seligman's model helps to avoid reductions of well-being to such emotions and facilitates an examination of the interdependence between all five aspects addressed through PERMA.

MediCinema surveys (2019), with nearly 1,000 participants, highlight the impact of a wider spectrum of films on positive emotions, especially fictional comedies that present ways of overcoming cultural boundaries. This includes *Bend it like Beckham* and *Sink or swim*, which could be approached through Vallerand's model of harmonious and obsessive passions (Vallerand et al., 2003 & Vallerand, 2010). These passions have been examined with athletes, including synchronised swimmers (Vallerand et al. 2006), which brings us back to *Sink or swim*, but also with fans (Vallerand et al., 2008) and coaches (Lafrenière et al., 2008), which are important for both films.

Vallerand et al. (2006) and Vallerand (2015) present evidence that harmonious passion supports positive affective experiences, which are key for enhanced interaction and the mediation of cultural boundaries, while obsessive passion enhances negative affective experiences that are counterproductive. Massumi defines 'affect' as 'unformed and unstructured', and highlights that it shows in preconscious 'autonomic reactions' (Massumi, 2002, p. 260), for example in spontaneous mimicry or a different heartbeat. If we draw on this to explore *Bend it like Beckham* and *Sink or swim*, then we could argue that the blurring of ethnicity, class, age, and gender boundaries in these films is partially a consequence of preconscious learning. For example, Jules's friendly mimicry helps to motivate Jess to join the Hounslow Harrier football team, while the immediate connection to similarly troubled but welcoming middle-aged men stimulates Bertrand to join the synchronised swimming team. Overall, positive affect appears key to starting and developing intercultural mediation, be it between Jess, Jules and Joe, or between Bertrand, Laurent, Marcus, Delphine and Amanda, with the latter aggressively negotiating her disability (she is a wheelchair user), gender and French-Algerian background in a male French mainstream culture.

TASK

Discuss harmonious and obsessive passions in a sport in which you have taken part or which you have observed. Which positive and negative emotions were visible and what was their impact?

10.2.2 Engagement

With *engagement* (**E**), Seligman (2011) presents another aspect of well-being that focuses on the suspension of time and self-consciousness, which have been discussed as flow in different sport activities (Kimiecik et al., 2018) and beyond (Csikszentmihalyi, 1990). Sport research has shown that enjoyment of the activity, for example in training, tends to enhance flow, both in elite (Swann et al., 2016) and non-elite environments (Schüler & Brunner, 2009). However, flow is often retrospectively regarded as enjoyment, and there is evidence that this can strengthen the motivation for more training (Hogan et al., 2015). This implies enhanced cultural interaction and continuous mediation of cultural backgrounds in *Bend it like Beckham* and *Sink or swim*, because the footballers and swimmers train hard, forget about time while training and have a lot of fun, which enables discussion of cultural challenges.

10.2.3 Relationships

Relationships (**R**) examines the importance of social connections and group dynamics, including individual acceptance, respect and support (Seligman, 2011), which are key for team sports and intercultural education. Studies have shown a link between positive emotions and relationship building inasmuch as the former enhance smiling, sharing and openness vis-à-vis others as well as inclusion of those others, which can support the development of positive interactions and relationships across cultural boundaries (Johnson & Fredrickson, 2005; Waugh & Fredrickson, 2006). Sport research confirms this emotional link for athlete relationships (Vallerand, 2015) and for athlete–coach relationships (Jowett et al., 2013), which are key for *Invictus*, *Bend it like Beckham* and *Sink or swim*. Particularly interesting in this context is Janicke & Oliver's study (2017), because it demonstrates that positive relationships portrayed in meaningful films are able to inspire viewers to develop similar relationships themselves. This is in line with Baily & Ivory's research (2018), which highlights that hedonic and eudaemonic states, that is happiness through experiences of pleasure and meaning in viewers, can be stimulated through film exposure. This implies that intercultural films are able to enhance corresponding behaviour, if viewers embrace them for the pleasure and enjoyment or the meaning and purpose they (re-)create.

While there are hardly any quantitative studies of viewer responses to popular movies like *Bend it like Beckham* and *Sink or swim*, box office success and viewer ratings confirm that these films have been embraced by a wider audience: on a budget of less than $5 million, *Bend it like Beckham* grossed more than $76 million at the box office (Box Office Mojo, 2003) and keeps an impressive 73 per cent audience score based on nearly 470,000 users on Rotten Tomatoes (2020a). *Sink or swim* does not reach the British film's sales figure, but it grossed more than $39 million at the box office on a budget of less than $22 million (Box Office Mojo, 2019), and it has an audience score of 77 per cent, albeit based on fewer than 100 viewers (Rotten Tomatoes, 2020b).

10.2.4 Meaning

This brings us to *meaning* (**M**) as an important factor of well-being (Seligman, 2011). Niemiec and Wedding (2014) discuss sense of purpose, significance and order in life in Payne's *About Schmidt* (2002), and there is evidence of moral empowerment and helping behaviour as a result of elevation through films (Schnall & Roper, 2012). Furthermore, research within cultural sport psychology has explicitly highlighted the importance of cultural sensitivity (Schinke et al., 2012; Storm & Larson, 2020) and competence (Ryba et al., 2013; Storm, 2020) for the development of meaning. If individuals can be considered in a wider sense as 'cultural beings situated in a specific context' (Storm & Larson, 2020, p. 77), then an examination of the cultural impact of sport is essential for all sport films mentioned so far, and overcoming the artificial boundaries set by ethnic, class, gender and numerous other tribal constructs (Rings, in Trinder, 2021) is key for meaning in these films. All this is particularly obvious in *Invictus*, which features continuous mediation of tribal constructs, especially for the predominantly white rugby players, who are at first reluctant to represent the new post-apartheid Africa, but then discover a highly satisfying intercultural meaning, especially in their work with black children who are happy to accept them as role models.

10.2.5 Accomplishment

Finally, *accomplishment* (**A**) can be measured objectively, e.g. by awards received, but also subjectively, e.g. with focus on personal achievements (Seligman, 2011). In *Bend it like Beckham* and *Sink or swim* these boundaries are blurred, because success in a competition means major personal achievements for the protagonists, such as overcoming the boundaries set by ethnicity (Jess) and depression (Bertrand). Niemiec & Wedding's (2014) comments on *Invictus* include an exploration of achievement related to the film's presentation of the rugby team, and a short examination of work as calling, which connects to Mandela's attempt to unite South Africa. Overall, Niemiec & Wedding's book gives an overview about an impressive number of films and is, as such, a good starting point for the contextualisation of psychologically oriented intercultural cinema projects. However, its focus remains predominantly on Hollywood movies, and there are no in-depth explorations of individual films.

TASK

Select a UNESCO supported Sport for Development Coalition project, for example on *Sport en Commun* (sportencommun.org), which you would regard as particularly helpful for the development of intercultural communication. Then justify your selection by explaining the project's (already measured or potential future) impact through Seligman's PERMA model.

10.3 Shifts in Intercultural Cinema and Memory Construction

10.3.1 From Monoculturality to Positive Intercultural Relations as Focal Point

Prominent intercultural film makers like Werner Herzog and Wim Wenders have already embarked on a shift of focus from critical explorations of monocultural perspectives to (re-)constructions of intercultural worldviews, which can be examined through the positive psychology concepts elaborated above. In Herzog's work, this is reflected in the change from films like *Aguirre, the wrath of God* (1972) and *Cobra Verde* (1987) to *Queen of the desert* (2015) and *Salt and fire* (2016), which features a shift from (neo-)colonial and neoliberal critique as focal point to the elaboration of intercultural solidarity constructs (see Rings, 2021). This does not imply a break with previous criticism, but a step beyond the critical realm. Instead of homing in on yet another failed coloniser and 'homo œconomicus' (Foucault 2008, p. 226) like Aguirre, who is 'an interest-driven calculative being' generating 'his own origin, [...] his own self as well as his own living' (Giraudeau, 2012, p. 43), Herzog presents in *Queen of the desert* with Gertrude Bell an open-minded protagonist who wants to build a new society beyond colonial imperialism. Through her embrace of Middle Eastern landscapes and their peoples, viewers are guided towards the potential of a 'cooperative society', within which the supposedly uncivilised Bedouins are presented in the way Harvard Law School scholar Yochai Benkler outlines contemporary shared economy, that is 'fundamentally capable of empathy, of possessing sentiments that compel us to act morally, cooperatively' (2011, p. 5).

Wim Wenders's films show a comparable development from the critical examination of individual alienation in a neoliberal world reflected in *The goalkeeper's fear of the penalty* (1972) and *Paris, Texas* (1984) to the focus on pleasure through intercultural mediation in *Buena Vista Social Club* (1999) and *Pina* (2011).

TASK

Which other examples of shifts from critical examination of monocultural perspectives to intercultural mediation can you think of, e.g. in film or other media in your culture? Please explore one of these examples with the help of Seligman's PERMA model.

10.3.2 Revising Cultural Memory

Intercultural cinema contributes with such shifts to the development of public memories, which can be defined as 'creative and strategic responses to present needs and interests', that is, they are not 'static bodies of texts and/or objects that anyone or any group simply have but are active projects, performances and struggles with persuasive goals to shape the present and the future' (Drzewiecka, 2020, p. 157).

Just like nationalist commemorations, such as the major D-Day commemorations in the United States and the United Kingdom that are held without comparable events for the atomic bombings of Hiroshima and Nagasaki, these memories are highly selective and not always in line with historiographical research. For example, the portrayal of Aguirre in Herzog's *Aguirre, the wrath of God* departs from research on the historical conqueror, who 'decided to abandon the expedition to El Dorado [...] to conquer Peru' (Davis, 2012, p. 294), and who is shot by Spanish troops for his rebellion against the Spanish crown. However, fictional freedom allows Herzog to shed light on a highly egocentric (neo-)colonial and neoliberal take on humanity, which links up to 'the dominant assumption in Western society about human motivation: that human beings are basically selfish creatures, driven by their own interests' (Benkler, 2011, p. 2).

Herzog's Bell in *Queen of the desert* also shows substantial differences to research on Gertrude Bell. In particular, the historical Bell tends to be categorised as British spy (Muhanna, 2017), and her support for Kings Faisal and Abdullah is assessed within the context of efforts to enhance British imperial influence in the Middle East (Thomas, 2003). However, Bell's fictionalisation allows Herzog to construct an alternative character, who overcomes the tribal mentality of the British colonial elite through the development of intercultural solidarity. That concept draws on notions of the 'interlocking interdependence of cultures in the age of globalization' (Antor, 2010, p. 12), stresses the importance of a 'Third Space' to negotiate identities (Bhabha, 2004, p. 36) and focuses on interconnectedness, which provides alternatives to the ego- and ethnocentrism shaping *Aguirre, the wrath of God*.

Such a focus on 'transcultural and transnational connections' is essential for the development of what Rothberg now categorises as '**transcultural memory**' (Moses & Rothberg, 2014, p. 30), but which was elaborated originally as 'multidirectional memory' (Rothberg, 2009) and qualifies on the basis of our discussion in Chapter 2 as 'intercultural memory'. As highlighted in Chapter 1, the use of different terms is perfectly acceptable, but it is necessary to define the concepts behind them, and the acknowledgement of 'our implication in each other's suffering and loss' (Moses & Rothberg, 2014, p. 29) is essential for intercultural memory. This is particularly well reflected in the omnipresence of destruction in *Aguirre, the wrath of God*, and includes the murder of indigenous people by Spanish conquerors, the killing of conquerors by the indigenous and the self-destruction of the whole Spanish expedition through its irrational and compulsory greed for gold (Rings, 2021). It is, however, also visible in Bell's rejection of British imperialist tribalism in *Queen of the desert*, which is mirrored in the tribalism that has led to the decline of Ha'il and will lead to the decline of Europe in two world wars, with World War I being presented repeatedly as background to the plot (Rings, 2021). Above all, the definition of intercultural memory should be amended to include the acknowledgement of our implication in other people's happiness and well-being, which might trigger similar feelings in us, as Schwartz & Sendor's report (1999) on volunteers' satisfaction following their support of patients in need suggests. In this sense, *Queen of the desert* outlines – like *Buena Vista Social Club* – numerous 'possibilities for counter-narratives and new forms of solidarity' (Moses & Rothberg, 2014, p. 31) that go beyond the discussion of monocultural identity constructs in *Aguirre, the wrath of God* and *Cobra Verde*.

TASK

Research US American President George W. Bush's Cuba policy and summarise which public memory of Cuba he reconstructs to justify that policy. Now watch Wim Wenders's *Buena Vista Social Club*. Which cultural memory is being reconstructed here and in what respects is it different from Bush's construct? Which role (if any) do positive psychology and intercultural concepts play in the two public memories?

10.4 In Summary

As complementary research to mainstream psychology and critical intercultural communication, positive psychology can redirect our focus to key aims of intercultural education, including cross-cultural empathy, cooperation and solidarity, for which recognition, tolerance and respect for cultural diversity are central. A good starting point for examinations and active support of such aspects is Seligman's PERMA model, since positive emotions, engagement, relationships, meaning and accomplishment are measurable factors for successful intercultural solidarity.

All this complements our discussion of monocultural politics as a challenge to intercultural developments in Chapter 1, in which we considered contributions from evolutionary psychologists on human tribalism as particularly helpful in understanding monocultural patterns better. More psychological insights on desires and fantasies linked especially to monocultural identity construction can be found in Chapter 12.

DISCUSSION QUESTIONS

The United Nations General Assembly established the World Day for Cultural Diversity for Dialogue and Development in 2002, and since then there are annual activities on 21 May to promote intercultural understanding.

Discuss one example of these activities on the UNESCO website (e.g. https://en.unesco.org/commemorations/culturaldiversityday/2020). How exactly does your chosen example promote intercultural aims, and to what extent does that involve positive psychology? How could you improve that example by drawing on PERMA concepts? How could you help to promote intercultural values, and to what extent could you make use of the PERMA model for that?

CASE STUDY

Please watch the Heineken beer advert *Worlds apart* (Dye, 2017) on Vimeo. Draw on key concepts from this chapter to explain, e.g. in a two-page long written report, how far and how exactly the Heineken experiment helps to bridge cultural boundaries. Finish the report with a paragraph (or two) on how the results of this experiment could be used to reduce interethnic friction. The films from this chapter have provided you with numerous examples of such friction.

References

Antor, H. (2010). From postcolonialism and interculturalism to the ethics of transculturalism in the age of globalization. In H. Antor, M. Merkl, K. Stierstorfer & L. Volkmann (eds.), *From interculturalism to transculturalism: Mediating encounters in cosmopolitan contexts* (pp. 1–14). Heidelberg: Universitätsverlag Winter.

Bailey, E. J. & Ivory, J. D. (2018). The moods meaningful media create: Effects of hedonic and eudaimonic television clips on viewers' affective states and subsequent program selection. *Psychology of Popular Media Culture*, 7(2), 130–145. DOI:10.1037/ppm0000122

Bećirović, S. (2012). The role of intercultural education in fostering cross-cultural understanding. *Epiphany Journal of Transdisciplinary Studies*, 5(1), 138–156.

Benkler, Y. (2011). *The penguin and the leviathan: How cooperation triumphs over self-interest*. New York: Crown Business.

Benkler, Y. (2013). Foreword. In M. L. Smith & K. M. A. Reilly (eds.), *Open development: Networked innovations in international development* (pp. vii–ix). Cambridge, MA: MIT Press.

Bhabha, H. (2004 [1994]). *The location of culture*. Abingdon: Routledge.

Box Office Mojo (2003). Bend it like Beckham. www.boxofficemojo.com/release/rl3074721281 (last accessed 18 April 2022).

Box Office Mojo (2019). Sink or swim. www.boxofficemojo.com/title/tt7476116 (last accessed 18 April 2022).

Butler, J. & Kern, M. L. (2016). The PERMA-profiler: A brief multidimensional measure of flourishing. *International Journal of Wellbeing*, 6(3), 1–48. DOI:10.5502/ijw.v6i3.1

Chadha, G. (2002). *Bend it like Beckham*. United Kingdom: Kintop Pictures.

Council of Europe (1981). Declaration regarding intolerance – A threat to democracy. 14 May. Council of Europe. https://bit.ly/3MdKwUz (last accessed 18 April 2022).

Csikszentmihalyi, M. (1990). *Flow: The psychology of optimal experience*. New York: Harper & Row.

Davis, J. E. (2012). Lope de Aguirre, the tyrant, and the prince: Convergence and divergence in postcolonial collective memory. *Journal of International and Intercultural Communication*, 5(4), 291–308.

Drzewiecka, J. (2020). Psychoanalytic approaches to memory and intercultural communication. In G. Rings & S. M. Rasinger (eds.), *The Cambridge handbook of intercultural communication* (pp. 155–169). Cambridge: Cambridge University Press.

Dye, T. (2017). *Heineken – Worlds apart*. London: Ben Porter Production Company. https://vimeo.com/222330551 and www.youtube.com/watch?v=dKggA9k8DKw (last accessed 18 April 2022).

Eastwood, C. (2009). *Invictus*. USA: Warner Bros.

Faulkner, G. (2019). Physical activity: Positive psychology in motion. *Journal of Science and Medicine in Sport*, 22(2), 1–9. https://doi.org/10.1016/j.jsams.2019.08.027

Foucault, M. (2008) *The birth of biopolitics: Lectures at the Collège de France, 1978–79*. Edited by M. Senellart. Translated by G. Burchell. New York: Palgrave Macmillan.

Fredrickson, B. L. (2001). The role of positive emotions in positive psychology: The broaden-and-build theory of positive emotions. *American Psychologist*, 56(3), 218–226. DOI: 10.1037//0003-066X.56.3.218

Fredrickson, B. L. (2013). *Love 2.0. Creating happiness and health in moments of connection*. New York: Hudson Street Press.

Giraudeau, M. (2012). Remembering the future: Entrepreneurship guidebooks in the US, from meditation to method (1945–1975). *Foucault Studies*, 13, 40–66.

Helne, T. (2021). Well-being for a better world: The contribution of a radically relational and nature-inclusive conception of well-being to the sustainability transformation. *Sustainability: Science, Practice and Policy*, 17(1,) 221–231, DOI: 10.1080/15487733.2021.1930716

Herzog, W. (1972). *Aguirre, the wrath of God*. Federal Republic of Germany: Werner Herzog Filmproduktion.

Herzog, W. (1987). *Cobra Verde*. Federal Republic of Germany: Werner Herzog Filmproduktion.

Herzog, W. (2015). *Queen of the desert*. USA: Benaroya Pictures.

Herzog, W. (2016). *Salt and fire*. Germany: Skellig Rock.

Hogan, C. L., Catalino, L. I., Mata, J. & Fredrickson, B. L. (2015). Beyond emotional benefits: Physical activity and sedentary behaviour affect psychosocial resources through emotions. *Psychology & Health*, 30, 354–369.

Janicke, S. H. & Oliver, M. B. (2017). The relationship between elevation, connectedness and compassionate love in meaningful films. *Psychology of Popular Media Culture*, 6(3), 272–289.

Johnson, K. J. & Fredrickson, B. L. (2005). 'We all look the same to me'. Positive emotions eliminate the own-race bias in face recognition. *Psychological Science*, 16(11), 875–881.

Jowett, S., Lafrenière, M-A. K. & Vallerand, R. J. (2013). Passion for activities and relationship quality: A dyadic approach. *Journal of Social and Personal Relationship*, 30, 734–749.

Keyes, C. L. M. (2002). The mental health continuum: From languishing to flourishing in life. *Journal of Health and Social Behavior*, 43, 207–222.

Keyes, C. L. M. (2005). Mental illness and/or mental health? Investigating axioms of the complete state model of health. *Journal of Consulting and Clinical Psychology*, 73, 539–548.

Kimiecik, J., Vealey, R. S., Wright, E. & Morrison, D. (2018). As positive as it gets: Flow and enjoyment in sport and physical activity. In A. Brady & B. Grenville-Cleave (eds.), *Positive psychology in sport and physical activity: An introduction* (pp. 115–128). Abingdon: Routledge.

Lafrenière, M.-A. K., Jowett, S., Vallerand, R. J., Donahue, E. G. & Lorimer, R. (2008). Passion in sport: On the quality of the coach–player relationship. *Journal of Sport & Exercise Psychology*, 30, 541–560.

Layard, R. (2020). *Can we be happier?* London: Penguin.

Lellouche, G. (2018). *Le Grand Bain [Sink or swim]*. France: Trésor Films.

Massumi, B. (2002). *Parables for the virtual*. Durham, NC: Duke University Press.

MediCinema (2019). MediCinema. Feel better with film. www.medicinema.org.uk/what-we-do (last accessed 18 April 2022).

Moses, D. & M. Rothberg (2014). A dialogue on the ethics and politics of transcultural memory. In L. Bond (ed.), *The transcultural turn: Interrogating memory between and beyond borders* (pp. 29–38). Berlin: De Gruyter.

Muhanna, E. (2017, June 14). What Gertrude Bell's letters remind us about the founding of Iraq. *The New Yorker.* https://bit.ly/36tacxo (last accessed 18 April 2022).

Niemiec, R. M. & Wedding, D. (2014). *Positive psychology at the movies 2: Using films to build character strengths and well-being* (2nd edition). Boston: Hogrefe Publishing.

Payne, A. (2002). *About Schmidt.* USA: New Line Cinema.

Rings, G. (2018). *The other in contemporary migrant cinema: Imagining a new Europe?* New York: Routledge.

Rings, G. (2021). From neoliberal crime in 'Aguirre, the Wrath of God' to transcultural solidarity in 'Queen of the Desert'. In Y. Temelli, ed., *Narratives of money & crime: Neoliberalism in literature, film and popular culture* (pp. 111–133). Berlin: Peter Lang.

Rothberg, M. (2009). *Multidirectional memory: Remembering the Holocaust in the age of decolonization.* Redwood City, CA: Stanford University Press.

Rotten Tomatoes (2020a). Bend it like Beckham. www.rottentomatoes.com/m/bend_it_like_beckham (last accessed 18 April 2022).

Rotten Tomatoes (2020b). Sink or swim. www.rottentomatoes.com/m/sink_or_swim_2018 (last accessed 18 April 2022).

Ryba, T. V., Stambulova, N. B., Si, G. & Schinke, R. J. (2013). ISSP position stand: Culturally competent research and practice in sport and exercise psychology. *International Journal of Sport and Exercise Psychology*, 11, 123–142.

Ryff, C. (1989). Happiness is everything, or is it? Explorations on the meaning of psychological well-being. *Journal of Personality and Social Psychology*, 57, 1069–1081. DOI:10.1037/0022-3514.57.6.1069

Ryff, C. & Keyes, C. (1995). The structure of psychological well-being revisited. *Journal of Personality and Social Psychology*, 69, 719–727.

Schinke, R. J., McGannon, K., Parham, W. & Lane, A. M. (2012). Toward cultural praxis and cultural sensitivity: Strategies for self-reflexive sport psychology practice. *Quest*, 64, 34–46.

Schnall, S. & Roper, J. (2012). Elevation puts moral values into action. *Social Psychological and Personality Science*, 3, 373–378. DOI:10.1177/1948550611423595

Schüler, J. & Brunner, S. (2009). The rewarding effect of flow experience on performance in a marathon race. *Psychology of Sport and Exercise*, 10, 168–174.

Schwartz, C. E. & Sendor, R. M. (1999). Helping others helps oneself: Response shift effects in peer support. *Social Science & Medicine*, 48(11), 1563–1575.

Seligman, M. (2011). *Flourish: A visionary new understanding of happiness and well-being.* New York: Free Press.

Seligman, M. (2012). Flourish: Positive psychology and positive interventions. In M. Matheson (ed.), *The Tanner Lectures on Human Values* (Vol. 31, pp. 229–243), Salt Lake City: The University of Utah Press.

Seligman, M. (2018). PERMA and the building blocks of well-being. *The Journal of Positive Psychology*, 13(4), 333–335. DOI:10.1080/17439760.2018.1437466

Storm, L. K. & Larson, C. H. (2020). Context-driven sport psychology: A cultural lens. In D. Hackfort & R. J. Schinke (eds.), *The Routledge international encyclopedia of sport and exercise psychology Vol. 1: Theoretical and methodological concepts.* (pp. 73–83). New York: Routledge.

Swann, C., Keegan, R. J., Crust, L. & Piggott, D. (2016). Psychological states underlying excellent performance in professional golfers: 'Letting it happen' vs. 'making it happen.' *Psychology of Sport and Exercise*, 23, 101–113.

Thomas, M. (2003). Bedouin tribes and the imperial intelligence services in Syria, Iraq and Transjordan in the 1920s. *Journal of Contemporary History*, 38(4), 539–561.

Trinder, S. (2021). Interview with Guido Rings: 'We need intercultural solidarity if we want to survive and prosper in a world hit by ultranationalism'. *Disjuntiva*, 2(1), 74–80.

UNESCO (1974). Recommendation concerning education for international understanding, co-operation and peace and education relating to human rights and fundamental freedoms. https://bit.ly/37mCaeJ (last accessed 18 April 2022).

United Nations Inter-Agency Task Force on Sport for Development and Peace (2003). *Sport for development and peace: Towards achieving the millennium development goals.* New York: United Nations.

Vallerand, R. J. (2010). On passion for life activities: The dualistic model of passion. In M. P. Zanna (ed.), *Advances in experimental social psychology* (Vol. 42, pp. 97–193). New York: Academic Press.

Vallerand, R. J. (2015). *The psychology of passion: A dualistic model.* Oxford: Oxford University Press.

Vallerand, R. J., Blanchard, C., Mageau, G. A., Koestner, R., Ratelle, C., Léonard, M., et al., (2003). Les passions de l'âme: On obsessive and harmonious passion. *Journal of Personality and Social Psychology*, 85, 756–767.

Vallerand, R. J., Rousseau, F. L., Grouzet, F. M. E., Dumais, A. & Grenier, S. (2006). Passion in sport: A look at determinants and affective experiences. *Journal of Sport & Exercise Psychology*, 28, 454–478.

Vallerand, R. J., Ntoumanis, N., Philippe, F. L., Lavigne, G. L., Carbonneau, N., Bonneville, A. & Maliha, G. (2008). On passion and sports fans: A look at football. *Journal of Sports Sciences*, 26, 1279–1293.

Waugh, C. E. & Frederickson, B. L. (2006). Nice to know you: Positive emotions, self–other overlap, and complex understanding in the formation of a new relationship. *Journal of Positive Psychology*, 1(2), 93–106. DOI:10.1080/17439760500510569

Wenders, W. (1972). *The goalkeeper's fear of the penalty.* Federal Republic of Germany: Filmverlag der Autoren.

Wenders, W. (1984). *Paris, Texas.* Federal Republic of Germany: Roadmovies Filmproduktion.

Wenders, W. (1999). *Buena Vista Social Club.* Germany: Road Movies Filmproduktion.

Wenders, W. (2011). *Pina.* Germany: Neue Road Movies.

Williams, D. (2010). *Men who swim.* UK: Met Film Production.

Yakin, B. (2000). *Remember the Titans.* USA: Jerry Bruckheimer Films.

11 Raising Intercultural Awareness through Storytelling

In Chapter 6, we examined how far stories disseminated through literature and film can contribute to the development of intercultural awareness and competence. We also mentioned that storytelling is not limited to established authors and directors, and we encouraged you to tell an intercultural story based on your own experiences. In this chapter, we want to examine storytelling further as a key feature of human interaction and identity construction, and we explore alternative ways of storytelling, for example through proverbs, adverts and flash fiction.

AIMS

By the end of this chapter, you should be able to:

1. explain the extent to which and how exactly storytelling can contribute to critical intercultural communication;
2. demonstrate how storytelling can be used to support monocultural worldviews;
3. describe the relation between storytelling and power.

> **KEY TERMS**
> story circle – ubuntu – flash fiction – consumer ethnocentrism

11.1 Humans as Storytelling Animals

In his million-copy bestseller *Sapiens: A brief history of humankind*, historian Yuval Noah Harari elaborates on fictional storytelling abilities as key features that allowed homo sapiens to conquer the world (Harari, 2015, pp. 36–44). While this could be regarded as a simplification of the historical development of humans from *homo naledi*, *habilis* and *erectus* to *neanderthalensis* and *sapiens* with ever-growing brain volumes (Wood, 2016), the concomitant growth in the ability to tell stories about imagined qualities and supernatural connections of particular tribes, that is, 'tribal spirits' (Harari, 2015, p. 41), gives modern humans an enormous advantage over archaic humans and non-human animals.

This is in line with Ricoeur's categorisation of storytelling as the 'strongest medium in human history' (1983, p. 45), although it is worth considering that its impact might depend as much on the actual stories being told as on the social and interactional contexts in which they are told. Often inspired by Labov and Waletzky's framework of narrative analysis (1967), scholars have concentrated on the function of canonical vis-à-vis under-represented or excluded stories and their role in the stabilisation or destabilisation of particular identity constructs (Ochs & Capps, 2001; Rings, 2010). While this research has been essential for an examination of cultural, sociopolitical and economic power, which is key for critical intercultural communication studies (see Chapter 4), it has led to a marginalisation of contextual aspects that are at the centre of more recent research (De Fina & Georgakopoulou, 2008, 2015; Deardorff, 2020).

This shift in narrative studies towards a 'social interactional approach' (De Fina & Georgakopoulou, 2008, p. 379) is also visible in film studies (Turner, 2006), and should inform current and future analyses of storytelling, whether these stories are about inclusionary inter- and transcultural beliefs or exclusionary monocultural tribalism. We will start our exploration with a focus on intercultural storytelling before returning to the latter.

11.2 Intercultural Storytelling

As lead agency for the International Decade for the Rapprochement of Cultures (2013–2022), UNESCO aims to fight 'the current surge of flaring conflicts, acts of violence and intolerance' through a commitment to principles of 'human dignity, conviviality and solidarity' (UNESCO, 2021), which relates to sustainable educational and peace-building goals in its 2030 agenda (see goals 4 and 16, UNDP, 2021). In this context, the organisation has identified the importance of intercultural competence development (UNESCO, 2013), established an e-platform on intercultural dialogue to help 'positively manage diversity and pluralism' (UNESCO, 2018), and supported projects on intercultural storytelling that aim to serve the same purpose. The latter includes Deardorff's *Manual for developing intercultural competencies* (2020), which is based on UNESCO-funded storytelling projects in Thailand, Tunisia, Zimbabwe and Austria, and is introduced by UNESCO's Director-General Audrey Azoulay and an UNESCO editorial team.

All this builds on a recognition of the importance of cultural storytelling since ancient times as a tool to enhance conviviality and solidarity, and there is an established history of storytelling for intercultural development reflected in publications by DuBois & Li (1963), Holliday et al. (2010) and Wang et al. (2017). Deardorff (2020) draws on such work when emphasising the benefits of personal storytelling in smaller culturally mixed groups with a focus on intercultural competence development. In particular, this **story circle** methodology might facilitate 'demonstrating respect for others, practicing listening for understanding, cultivating curiosity about similarities and differences with others, gaining increased cultural self-awareness, developing empathy, and developing relationships with culturally different others' (Deardorff, 2020, p. 16).

Most of the benefits of telling stories in circles are neither new nor limited to intercultural competence development in a narrow sense, as confirmed by the history of Alcoholics Anonymous and numerous other self-help circles. A circle with a triangle inside it has also been the crucial part of the AA symbol since 1955, and it is precisely the circle–triangle combination that establishes a link to much older traditions, including seers and priests' interventions against evil (W., 1985, p. 139). However, there is clear evidence that storytelling has been marginalised in contemporary intercultural research as an important tool for understanding 'cultural attitudes, customs or habits' (Wolting, 2020, p. 283), both in traditional circles and in a great variety of other contexts, which we would like to explore in this chapter.

TASK

Describe an intercultural story that you have heard.
- What exactly did you learn from that story?
- To what extent did the storytelling context (e.g. traditional circle, face-to-face communication with the storyteller/your father/best friend) have an impact on what you learned?

- Look at the storytelling circle in Figure 11.1 and outline potential advantages and disadvantages of that method. How could online communication tools be adapted to integrate that method?

11.2.1 The Power of Proverbs

Proverbs are part of the oldest and at the same time shortest stories told to others, and educational scholar Jeylan W. Hussein highlights the ongoing importance of African proverbs as 'the most widely used pieces of oral artistry' and 'repositories of social and cultural wisdom' (Hussein, 2005, p. 61). Sociolinguist Azubuike Onwe confirms this for Nigeria and provides through his analysis of Ikwo proverbs a wide spectrum of examples that aim to enhance 'communalism as lifestyle option' (Onwe, 2018, p. 68), including 'When people are many, they can pull the boat' ('A du igwe a kputa ugbo') and 'If one hand brings and another hand brings, the mouth is full' ('Eka wota eka wota onu eji') (2018, pp. 69, 73). Such solidarity-enhancing proverbs reflect the sociocultural perspective of most of Onwe's Nigerian interviewees, but they are also mirrored in texts and connected philosophical concepts in South Africa (Kanwangamalu, 1999), Senegal (Gleason, 2003) and the Middle East (Zeffane, 2014).

While we have to consider access limitations to and hierarchies within the communities that draw on such micro-stories, which include the original development, memorisation, public narration and elaboration of the stories as the particular domain of older males (see Section 11.3), there is ample evidence for the crossing of cultural boundaries. For example, the common ground between different

Figure 11.1 *Intercultural Storytelling* by Alíz Kovács-Zöldi

generations is brought to the fore by a proverb like 'The okra does not grow taller than the person who planted it' ('Okfuru t'akajedu onye kuru iya'), while the rigidity of age-related hierarchies is questioned through proverbs that put each other into perspective, for example 'What the elder sees sitting down, a youth cannot see even from a tree top' ('Iphe ogerenya nodu anodu phu be nwata nyihuru eli oshi t'aphudu') compared with 'The adventurous youth is often wiser than the sedentary elder' ('Nwaije ka onye ishi ewo omaru iphe') (Onwe, 2018, p. 94, 105).

If the communalist approach manages to blur tribal boundaries, then it could be described as an expression of **ubuntu**, that is, a concept that is often associated with post-apartheid South Africa in so far as it aims at a transformative society characterised by social cohesion, social justice and equality (Rapatsa, 2016, p. 15). While the return of large-scale corruption and infighting under Jacob Zuma's presidency cast doubts about South Africa as an exemplar of solidarity, his successor Cyril Ramaphosa has explicitly reconnected with the sociocultural heritage left by Nelson Mandela, and that is – according to former US president Barack Obama – an ubuntu heritage: 'Ubuntu [...] captures Mandela's greatest gift: his recognition that we are all bound together in ways that are invisible to the eye; that there is a oneness to humanity; that we achieve ourselves by sharing ourselves with others, and caring for those around us' (Obama, 2013).

Short stories, novels and other literary genres have provided a wealth of more elaborate stories, which were originally also frequently disseminated in groups, for example tales of medieval knights at camp fires of Spanish conquerors in the New World (Ife, 1985, p. 16; Pastor-Bodmer, 1992, p. 153). Kramsch highlights the potential of literary stories to enhance *symbolic competence*, which includes the 'awareness of the symbolic values of words, ability to find the most appropriate subject position, ability to grasp the larger social and historical significance of events and to understand the cultural memories evoked by symbolic systems, ability to perform and create alternative realities by reframing the issues' (Kramsch, 2009, p. 113).

Such basic concepts could be transferred to film as the key form of storytelling since the twentieth century, with literary contexts worth considering (e.g. in filmic adaptations of short stories, novels and comic books). Especially in interaction, literature and film can effectively support the dissemination of particular stories, for example about Tarzan, Harry Potter and Aladdin, which might (or might not) lead to more 'tolerance of ambiguity' (Kramsch, 2006, p. 251) and 'empathy with the Other' (Wolting, 2020, p. 279). A discussion of such narratives in 'story circles' (Deardorff, 2020), including literary reading groups and film viewing circles at universities and in cultural centres, might further enhance that intercultural potential, especially when different versions of a popular story are compared (e.g. 'Aladdin' in Berger et al., 1940, Clements & Musker, 1992, Napoli & Moore, 2017; Ritchie, 2019). Surprisingly, such circles tend to focus on longer stories, especially novels and full-length fictional movies, which marginalises numerous genres. Despite their growth in numbers in recent decades, frequent repeats and millions of viewers, television adverts remain particularly under-represented in scholarship and are therefore briefly discussed in Section 11.2.2.

11.2.2 Storytelling in Adverts

Intercultural narratives are increasingly disseminated through international advertising, which is an indication that prosocial behaviour and cross-cultural solidarity constructs sell well. One example is Milka's 'Tenderness is inside' campaign, which focuses on examples of solidarity in the fictional town Lilaberg that helped the Swiss–US American chocolate producer to increase its European sales and enter the Chinese market. The advertising agency Wieden+Kennedy Amsterdam describes Lilaberg as 'a world where everyone is as kind as kind can be, air is a little cleaner, the sky a little bluer and where the extraordinary is never unexpected when the magic of Milka is there to bring people together' (LBB Lab, 2016).

Video clips like *Lost & found* and *The time machine* (Milka, 2016a, 2016b), which highlight the blurring of cultural boundaries, are part of the campaign. In *Lost & found*, the child protagonist helps her father keep his job at the rarely visited railway station lost property office by motivating villagers of all ages, classes and genders to leave some of their valuables with her, so that she can place them in a train as if they were lost. The villagers then retrieve their valuables from her father's office, thereby creating the illusion that it is very important to the town. In *The time machine*, a clip developed by *Amélie* director Jean-Pierre Jeunet, the child protagonist receives overwhelming support from his family and local businesspeople in his efforts to make Christmas come sooner by an imagined invention of a time-travelling machine. In this context, numerous age and gender boundaries are blurred in the context of child and adult play (Brown & Vaughan, 2009), and the fact that Milka continues to invest substantial amounts in adverts that link its chocolate to stories of human solidarity are an indication that the stories sell. While there are reports on the contribution of such clips to Milka chocolate sales, there is to date little research on their value as a tool for intercultural communication, for which both qualitative and quantitative studies are needed.

11.2.3 Flash Fiction

Finally, there are endless opportunities to develop new intercultural stories from individual experiences, which students and teachers of intercultural studies might especially want to use to augment textbook-based learning. A particularly successful tool for narrative self-expression has more recently been called **flash fiction**, which is comparable to proverbs inasmuch as it can be defined as a micro-story or 'story miniature' (Masih, 2009, p. xi). These stories are not clearly defined in length but tend to range from six-word stories to a maximum of 1,500 words (Gil, 2017; Tarrayo, 2019, p. 10), and there are numerous possibilities for dissemination through open access e-journals or e-(maga)zines like *3 AM Magazine*, *Flash Fiction Online* and *Word Riot*, which in 2016 had nearly 150,000 visitors per month (2019, p. 11).

Examples of mostly anonymous and undated six-word stories from a *Hitrecord* challenge that led to more than 20,000 text contributions include 'That feeling of home was him' (entitled 'Him'), 'It ended before it even started' ('The Stranger') and 'Love yourself enough to love another' ('Love') (see Taralabovich, 2021). The first micro-story could be used to discuss the dynamic meaning of home and belonging, which should be contrasted with more static and territorial notions of home that can be found in monocultural slogans like 'Britain first' and 'British jobs for British people' (see Chapter 1). The second story could lead to an exploration of stereotypical categorisations of strangers, with which cultural encounters could end, unless these categorisations are questioned. It might, however, also trigger a discussion of the 'stranger' as key concept from Simmel (1908) to Amin (2012) and beyond. The third story could be used to question egocentrism and ethnocentrism and define 'love' from sociocultural perspectives, which might include examinations of its frequent use in biblical and other religious contexts. Above all, these and many other examples (for flash fiction on Twitter, see Gil, 2017), could prepare students to write their own six-word stories (or longer narratives) as contributions to intercultural communication, and such shorter stories could – like proverbs – be more easily used for story circles, for example in the classroom.

11.3 Monocultural Storytelling

The development of personal intercultural stories supports the integration of student and teacher experiences into the teaching and learning process, and their dissemination in the above-mentioned e-journals and e-zines could help to strengthen intercultural knowledge in the digital environment, which might facilitate the destabilisation of often dominant monocultural stories. We discussed in Chapter 4 the ongoing popularity of racist fake news as well as nationalist stories that homogenise, essentialise and separate migrants and other strangers from members of the host society through stereotypical portrayals, for example as criminals or parasites. Unfortunately, monocultural stories can also shape proverb knowledge, advertising and flash fiction.

In particular, monocultural proverbs can help to reconstruct, stabilise and enhance traditional tribal boundaries. This is particularly visible in the portrayal of the 'supremacy of the group' and the importance given to kinship, which is reflected in Ikwo proverbs like 'One tree does not make a forest' ('Oshi lanu teme-jedu oswa') and 'The lion does not kill its own kind' ('Agu tegbudu ogbo') (Onwe, 2018, pp. 98, 95). In Ikwo culture these tribal traditions are linked to a focus on elderly men's perspectives and a strong gender hierarchy. Examples of related proverbs are 'If the elder's speech is not allowed to come first, it will certainly come last' ('Okfu ogerenya evudu uzo yokperu azu') and 'When a girl outgrows "who is her father?" she enters "who is her husband?"' ('Nwamgboko tseswee "bu onye muru?" yobahu le "bu onye alu?"') (2018, pp. 83, 74). Studies of proverbs in other African cultures, from the Maasai in Tanzania and Kenya to the Oromo in Ethiopia and the Igbo (of which the Ikwo people are sometimes considered to be part) in Nigeria confirm strong gender hierarchies (Hussein, 2005; Mmadike, 2014), which are based on patriarchal tribal structures that have repeatedly been highlighted as a major problem for socio-economic development (Moriba & Edwards, 2009).

In advertising, we have to consider **consumer ethnocentrism**, that is, 'consumers' tendency to buy a locally made good over a foreign product' (Ma et al., 2019, p. 1), which has been examined in detail by Moon & Jain (2002), Jiménez & San Martín (2010) and Ma et al. (2019). Consumer ethnocentrism tends to be heavily supported by the meat industry, which often joins farmers in organisations that then often aggressively market national products. One major lobbyist in the UK is Love British Food, which is proud to serve as an umbrella for organisations like the British Premium Sausage Company, and appeals to viewers' national sentiments with pages entitled 'Why buy British lamb?', 'Why buy British beef?' and 'Why buy British pork?' (Love British Food, 2021).

Figure 11.2 Lidl in Cambridge, UK, 20 February 2020
Source: @guidorings

In this narrative, the suffering of animals is erased through abstract comments about high welfare standards and a focus on 'production' (see Stibbe, 2001, 2012), while environmental damage is suppressed through statements about imported products having higher carbon footprints. Researchers have also found a link between the construction of hyper-masculinity and high meat consumption, that is, a 'real men eat meat' narrative disseminated through magazines like *Men's Health* (Stibbe, 2004; Rogers, 2008; Rothgerber, 2012), which supports aggressive nationalist images through a culture-gender link ('real British men eat British meat'). A key symbol of the Love British Food lobbyist is the British flag presented in the form of a heart, which many supermarkets have adopted to attract ethnocentric consumers. For example, Figure 11.2 is a photograph of the Cambridge branch of the German supermarket Lidl, which had decorated its entrance with three enormous Union Jack-emblazoned hearts.

Finally, flash fiction, which we highlighted as a strong medium for intercultural expression in Section 11.2, can also be used to express cultural hierarchies, for example when 'anxiety' becomes female in 'Dear Miss Anxiety, we meet again' (Cjdubria in Taralabovich, 2021).

TASK

Search for examples of ethnocentric stories in your own culture(s) under a working title like 'My tribe first' or 'Make my tribe great again'. How popular are these stories? Which alternative stories do you know and how popular are they? How can the monocultural stories be fought more effectively?

11.4 In Summary

Our analysis highlights that storytelling tools can be used in very different ways, and there is certainly no linear development towards interculturality considering the sharp rise of neo-nationalism and other forms of tribalism in recent decades that are reflected in consumer ethnocentrism. However, there is suggestive evidence that intercultural storytelling is gaining ground, for example through international advertising and flash fiction, and the dense description of cultural features in the latter shows parallels with proverb traditions that might be ideal for development, reconstruction and discussion in educational circles, such as classrooms or seminar rooms. Furthermore, we can all make use of the power of storytelling by disseminating our own intercultural stories and by encouraging others to do so.

DISCUSSION QUESTIONS

Write three six-word-stories that summarise key aspects of your intercultural encounters. Discuss them with members of your class to see if they are understood and help trigger a debate. Then upload the final version of these stories in a flash fiction writing challenge, e.g. on Hitrecord or Twitter, or submit them to an e-zine like *3 AM Magazine* or *Flash Fiction Online*, where you will get many more readers and comments.

CASE STUDY

Please discuss the following story, which was told to a group of international students in a seminar room at a German university, by drawing on intercultural, monocultural and psychological concepts (see Chapters 1 and 10).

Soon after I moved into my flat in Cambridge, the neighbours invited me for tea. 'Ah, yes, the famous English tea', I thought. As German and European,

I was looking forward to that. It was, after all, a chance to get to know my neighbours, Joe and Emily – a couple around my age, and an opportunity to know about that famous English 'tea at 5'.

When I arrived, Joe put his hand forward as for a handshake, so I tried to grab his hand, but he went backwards, mumbling something about where I could sit. Weird. And something else was surprising: Only tea and a few biscuits on the table? I mean, every decent 'Kaffee und Kuchen' in Germany includes a good cake .... Was it more like the simple 'merienda' in Spain or Italy ...? – but that wouldn't explain the fuss about the 'tea at 5', would it? Then I looked closer at my hosts – their old jeans, old sweaters, and I imagined that a lack of financial means might be the best explanation, ... or did they just not care? Anyway, I was not here for the cake – I was here to get to know my neighbours.

Then they asked me if I wanted milk and sugar with my tea. 'Sure', I said, although I did not really like milk in my tea, but 'when you are in Rome, do as the Romans ...', and now I was in England, the land of Mr Bean, so .... Suddenly, the lady started pouring milk into my cup of tea, then put sugar into it, always staring at me and waiting for me to say stop. She even stirred it all in my cup of tea! That was really weird. I mean, I had seen people do that for their child – with hot chocolate, but never for an adult. Did they take me for a child? Was it an English thing? Or were they just weird?

Then the conversation: Weather here, weather 'in my country', weather in the Lake District where they were on holidays ... Weird, and boring .... I changed the subject and we talked a bit about Cambridge, which museums to visit, which pubs to go (my hosts were good at that), but I did not feel comfortable. I smiled, drank my tea and went back to my flat with the excuse that I still had work to do. From then on, I kept my distance.

References

Amin, A. (2012). *Land of strangers*. Cambridge: Polity Press.

Berger, L., Powell, M. & Whelan, T. (1940). *The thief of Bagdad*. United States: Alexander Korda Films.

Brown, S. & Vaughan, C. (2009). *Play: How it shapes the brain, opens the imagination, and invigorates the soul*. New York: Avery.

Clements, R. & Musker, J. (1992). *Aladdin*. United States: Walt Disney Feature Animation.

De Fina, A. & Georgakopoulou, A. (2008). Analysing narratives as practices. *Qualitative Research*, 8(3), 379–387.

De Fina, A. & Georgakopoulou, A. (2015). *The handbook of narrative analysis*. Hoboken, NJ: Wiley.

Deardorff, D. (2020). *Manual for developing intercultural competencies: Story circles*. New York: Routledge.

DuBois, R. & Li, M. (1963). *The art of group conversation: A new breakthrough in social communication*. New York: National Board of Young Men's Christian Associations.

Gil, N. (2017). People are writing 6-word stories on Twitter. *Refinery29*. 12 May. https://r29.co/3McHL5Y (last accessed 19 April 2022).

Gleason, M. R., 2003. Cultural models of individualism and collectivism in a context of development: Self-efficacy versus interdependence in rural Senegal. PhD. University of Georgia.

Harari, Y. N. (2015). *Sapiens: A brief history of humankind*. London: Penguin.

Holliday, A., Hyde, M. & Kullman, J. (2010). *Intercultural communication: An advanced resource book for students*. New York: Routledge.

Hussein, J. W., 2005. The social and ethno-cultural construction of masculinity and femininity in African proverbs. *African Study Monograph*, 26(2), 59–87.

Ife, B. W. (1985). *Reading and fiction in golden-age Spain: A Platonist critique and some picaresque replies*. Cambridge: Cambridge University Press.

Jiménez, N. H. & San Martín, S. (2010). The role of country-of-origin, ethnocentrism and animosity in promoting consumer trust: The moderating role of familiarity. *International Business Review*, 19, 34–45. DOI:10.1016/j.ibusrev.2009.10.001

Kamwangamalu, N. M. (1999). Ubuntu in South Africa: A sociolinguistic perspective to a Pan-African concept. *Critical Arts*, 13(2), 24–27.

Kramsch, C. & Huffmaster, M. (2008). The political promise of translation. *Fremdsprachen lehren und lernen*, 37, 283–297.

Kramsch, C. (2006). From communicative competence to symbolic competence. *The Modern Language Journal*, 90(2), 249–252.

Kramsch, C. (2009). Discourse, the symbolic dimension of Intercultural Competence. In A. Hu & M. Byram (eds.), *Interkulturelle Kompetenz und fremdsprachliches Lernen: Modelle, Empirie, Evaluation* [Intercultural Competence and Foreign Language Learning: Models, Empiricism, Assessment] (pp. 107–121). Tübingen: Narr.

Labov, W. and Waletzky, J. (1967). Narrative analysis: Oral versions of personal experience. In J. Helm (ed.), *Essays on the verbal and visual arts*. Seattle: University of Washington Press.

LBB Lab (2016). W+K Amsterdam brings idyllic Alpine tales to life for new Milka campaign. 4 April. https://bit.ly/38Q55YM (last accessed 19 April 2022).

Love British Food (2021). Love British Food. www.lovebritishfood.co.uk (last accessed 19 April 2022).

Ma, Q., Abdeljelil, M. H. & Hu, L. (2019). The influence of consumer ethnocentrism and cultural familiarity on brand preference: Evidence of event-related potential (ERP). *Frontiers in Human Neuroscience*, 13(220), 1–9.

Masih, T. L. (2009). *Field guide to writing flash fiction: Tips from editors, teachers, and writers in the field*. Brookline, MA: Rose Metal Press.

Media Smart (2015). An introduction to advertising. Lesson 1: Advertising and you. *TES*. https://bit.ly/3820pij (last accessed 19 April 2022).

Meeus, W., Walrave, M. & Van Ouytsel, J. (2014). Advertising literacy in schools: Evaluating free online educational resources for advertising literacy. *Journal of Media Education*, 5(2), 5–12.

Milka (2016a). Lost & found. www.youtube.com/watch?v=4ErY9weJbRQ (last accessed 19 April 2022).

Milka (2016b). The time machine. www.youtube.com/watch?v=UZASx5A21rA (last accessed 19 April 2022).

Mmadike, B. I., 2014. The Igbo perception of womanhood: Evidence from sexist proverbs. *Research on Humanities and Social Sciences*, 4(18), 98–104.

Moon, B. J. & Jain, S. C. (2002). Consumer processing of foreign advertisements: Roles of country-of-origin perceptions, consumer ethnocentrism, and country attitude. *International Business Review*, 11, 117–138. DOI:10.1016/s0969-5931(01)00052-x

Moriba, S. & Edwards, M. C. (2009). Tribalism and its consequences: A cancer infecting the corpus of educational leadership in many West African countries. In A. W. Wiseman & I. Silova (eds.). *Educational leadership: Global contexts and international comparisons – International perspectives on education and society*, Vol. 11, Chapter 3 (pp. 81–122). Bingley: Emerald Group Publishing Limited. DOI:10.1108/S1479-3679(2009)0000011006

Napoli, D. J. & Moore, C. (2017). *Tales from the Arabian nights: Stories of adventure, magic, love, and betrayal.* Washington, DC: National Geographic.

Obama, B. (2013). Remarks by President Obama at memorial service for former South African president Nelson Mandela. The White House Office of the Press Secretariat. 10 December. https://bit.ly/3jP7lBN (last accessed 19 April 2022).

Ochs, E. & Capps, L. (2001). *Living narrative.* Cambridge, MA: Harvard University Press.

Onwe, A. (2018). *Proverbs and worldviews: An analysis of Ikwo proverbs and their worldviews.* Cambridge: ARRO. https://arro.anglia.ac.uk/id/eprint/704208 (last accessed 19 April 2022).

Pastor Bodmer, B. (1992). *The armature of conquest: Spanish accounts of the discovery of America, 1492–1589.* Redwood City, CA: Stanford University Press.

Rapatsa, M. (2016). Ubuntu and capabilities approach: Basic doctrines for calibrating humanitarian action. *European Review of Applied Sociology*, 9(12), 12–19.

Ricoeur, P. (1983). *Narrative fiction: Contemporary poetics.* London: Methuen.

Rings, G. (2010). *La Conquista desbaratada: Identidad y alteridad en la novela, el cine y el teatro hispánicos contemporáneos.* Madrid: Iberoamericana.

Ritchie, G. (2019). *Aladdin.* United States: Walt Disney Pictures.

Rogers, R. (2008). Beasts, burgers, and hummers: Meat and the crisis of masculinity in contemporary television advertisements. *Environmental Communication: A Journal of Nature and Culture*, 2, 281–301.

Rothgerber, H. (2012). Real men don't eat (vegetable) quiche: Masculinity and the justification of meat consumption. *Psychology of Men & Masculinity.* 14(4), 363–375. DOI:10.1037/a0030379

Simmel, G. (1908). *Soziologie: Untersuchungen über die Formen der Vergesellschaftung.* Leipzig: Duncker & Humblot.

Stibbe, A. (2004). Health and the social construction of masculinity in *Men's Health Magazine. Men and Masculinities*, 7, 31–51. DOI:10.1177/1097184X03257441

Stibbe, A. (2001). Language, power, and the social construction of animals. *Society and Animals*, 9(2), 145–162.

Stibbe, A. (2003). As charming as a pig: The discursive construction of the relationship between pigs and humans. *Society and Animals*, 11(4), 375–392.

Stibbe, A. (2012). *Animals erased: Discourse, ecology, and reconnection with the natural world.* Middletown, CT: Wesleyan University Press.

Stibbe, A. (2015). *Ecolinguistics: Language, ecology and the stories we live by.* Abingdon: Routledge.

Taralabovich (2021). Write a story in six words (No more, no less.) https://hitrecord.org/challenges/2412674 (last accessed 19 April 2022).

Tarrayo, V. N. (2019). What's in a flash? Teaching reading and writing (and beyond) through flash fiction. *ELTAR-J*, 1(1), 9–15.

Turner, G. (2006). *Film as social practice* (4th edition). Abingdon: Routledge.

UNDP (2021). The SDGS in action. www.undp.org/sustainable-development-goals (last accessed 19 April 2022).

UNESCO (2013). *Intercultural competencies: Conceptual and operational framework*. Paris: UNESCO.

UNESCO (2018). Intercultural dialogue. https://en.unesco.org/interculturaldialogue/about (last accessed 19 April 2022).

UNESCO (2021). International decade for the rapprochement of cultures (2013–2022). https://en.unesco.org/decade-rapprochement-cultures/about (last accessed 19 April 2022).

W., B. (1985). *Alcoholics Anonymous comes of age: A brief history of A.A.* New York: Alcoholics Anonymous World Services.

Wang, Y., Deardorff, D. K. & Kulich, S. (2017). Chinese perspectives on intercultural competence in international higher education. In D. K. Deardorff & L. Arasaratnam-Smith (eds.), *Intercultural competence in higher education: international approaches, assessment and application* (pp. 95–109). Abingdon: Routledge.

Wolting, S. (2020). Enhancing intercultural skills through storytelling. In G. Rings & S. M. Rasinger (eds.), *The Cambridge handbook of intercultural communication* (pp. 276–285). Cambridge: Cambridge University Press.

Wood, T. C. (2016). Estimating the statistical significance of hominin encephalization. *Journal of Creation, Theology and Science Series B: Life Sciences*, 6, 40–45.

Zeffane, R., 2014. Does collectivism necessarily negate the spirit of entrepreneurship? *International Journal of Entrepreneurial Behaviour and Research*, 20(3), 278–296.

 PART III

APPLICATION

12 Communicating in the Digital Sphere

We have already touched a little bit on digital communication and the role digital technology plays in intercultural communication in the preceding chapters. It seems unquestionable that 'new media has been the main force accelerating the trend of globalisation in human society during the last few decades' (Chen, 2012, p. 1) but also that it 'affects how people understand each other in the process of human communication, especially for those from different cultural or ethnic groups' (2012, p. 3). In this chapter, we want to explore this in more detail.

AIMS

By the end of this chapter, you should be able to:

1. **explain some of the key aspects of intercultural communication in the digital sphere;**
2. **explain some of the challenges and opportunities of digital intercultural communication;**
3. **describe the role of power in digital intercultural communication;**
4. **identify some of the ethical issues in digital intercultural communication.**

KEY TERMS
lingua franca – bonding social capital – Web 2.0 – ethics – digital divide

12.1 Going Digital

TASK

Take a look at all your social media contacts: social networking sites, messaging services, online gaming communities etc.
– How many people share your first language?

– How many people come from your own cultural background?
– How many of your contacts have you actually met in real life, not just online?

Figure 12.1 *Digital Communication* by Alíz Kovács-Zöldi

Let's start this chapter with some figures: social media and social networking sites (we will use these terms interchangeably) have seen a steep rise in usage (Figure 12.1). Kemp (2020) reports there are around 5.54 billion internet users in 2020 – that is 59 per cent of the world's population. An estimated 3.8 billion (49 per cent) are considered active social media users, and 89 per cent of internet users between 16 and 64 reported to have used social networking, chat or messenger apps. Across the globe, people in 2020 spent an average of two hours twenty-four minutes using social media, ranging from four hours per day in the Philippines, to forty-five minutes in Japan. Facebook tops the league of most-used platforms, followed by YouTube, with Pinterest and Kuaishou bringing up the rear (Kemp, 2020). That is a lot of social media use! Statista, a global business data provider, estimated that in 2020, around 306.4 billion emails would be sent worldwide, up from around 269 billion in 2017 (Statista, 2020).

The increase in internet and social media use, of course, leads to an increase in communication across cultures too. To illustrate this, we will take a quick look at the Facebook profile of one of the authors (Sebastian): my Facebook friends currently *live* in twelve different countries (which is not necessarily an indication of *where they are from*), covering a lot of Europe but also as far away as Nepal, Ecuador and Australia. Twenty different first languages are represented, amongst them Arabic from a range of different regions, both Mandarin and Cantonese, Catalan, Korean, Farsi and Yoruba. Only 7 per cent have the same first language as me

(German); with 19 per cent of them I use English as a **lingua franca**, that is, neither my friend nor I have English as our first language. So there is a lot of diversity and a lot of opportunity for potential issues around intercultural communication. That said, I have met every single one of my Facebook friends in person. The latter is not always the case: as an avid scuba diver, I have digital connections on other online platforms with fellow divers across the world without ever having met them, mainly to share tips on underwater photography. Social networking sites are versatile and 'can facilitate Western-style networking with strangers, but they can equally well support the family and other trust relationships' (Hooker, 2012, p. 406). These communication patterns are, of course, also the case in my professional life: I regularly communicate with colleagues in other countries, though mostly by email rather than social media, but have never met many of them in 'real life'.

The increase in digital communication does not, however, necessarily equate to an increase in intercultural encounters. For example, at the heart of social media use amongst many migrants is what is known as **bonding social capital**: strong and substantive social links, associated with 'higher levels of trust, support, and intimacy' (Ellison et al., 2014, p. 856). In a migration context, people often use digital technologies to maintain links to friends and families back home, which can counteract home-sickness and feelings of isolation, and for many migrants, maintaining existing relationships is often more important than forming new ones (Callahan et al., 2018). Amongst the Basque diaspora, Oiarzabal observed that many diaspora Basques 'tend to reproduce their offline networks and friendships' (Oiarzabal, 2012, p. 1479), which in turn boosts pre-existing offline relationships, but also leads to the strong maintenance of cultural identity. Such online connections with close relationships, however, are not necessarily an indicator of how often contact is made: 'Migrants, like most others, maintain strong attachments to close kin relations, even if they did not contact them very often or very effectively' (Komito, 2011, p. 1081). Strong social connections with family play a particularly important role in the context of young migrants: around 2015, a large number of unaccompanied child and adolescent refugees arrived in Europe, and social media played a large part in 'doing family' online (Kutscher & Kreß, 2018, p. 5). So while digital technologies, and the Internet in particular, can lead to increasing communication between people from different cultures, they also facilitate communication *within* a culture across geographic distance.

We will approach the topic of intercultural communication in the digital sphere from two angles: we start with a look at how individuals or groups of people communicate across different cultures using digital technology. We will then look at digital communication more widely, focusing on discourses of power and dominance.

12.2   The Pen Pal Goes Digital

Using written language to communicate with people from other cultures is nothing new. Global business has always meant communicating with other languages and cultures in writing as much as face to face. Generations of students have engaged in pen pal programmes, exchanging letters with peers from across the globe, developing both their linguistic skills (especially when writing in another language) but also their intercultural competence (Barksdale et al., 2007). The use of email is therefore to an extent just a modern development of a well-established practice. Digital technology, however, makes the exchange a lot more efficient and quicker, but, as Levy reminds us, comes with its own dangers: information overload, that is, having to deal with too much information, can result in a range of problems including reduced productivity and increased stress levels (Levy, 2008).

At the start of this book, we suggested an approach to intercultural communication that focuses on situations of mediation aimed at creating mutual understanding between individuals or groups of different cultural backgrounds; we also looked at how power relationships impact on this process. Incelli (2013) investigated the email interaction between a British and an Italian company to illustrate how native speakers of English and Italian non-native English speakers (with intermediate level of English proficiency) negotiated in the context of business communication. Incelli found that problems with communication between the two companies arose from linguistic issues, that is, the Italians' comparatively low English proficiency hindered clear communication at times. As such, the Italian company was significantly disadvantaged as the linguistically weaker participant. There were also cultural differences, for example the level of formality at different points of the exchange: 'cultural norms played a part in the differences in communication strategies and the degree of formality or informality used in the emails differed considerably between the two companies' (Incelli, 2013, p. 529). Yet, Incelli also observed aspects of accommodation, whereby participants adjusted, particularly linguistically, in order to facilitate negotiations.

Differences in email interaction are also visible when looking at people who communicate using a *lingua franca*: Huang (2016) studied 768 emails between Taiwanese, Japanese and Italian students of English as a Foreign Language, with a particular focus on email opening and closings. The study found a considerable number of similarities across students from the three different countries: for example, salutations such as 'Dear *x*' were the most frequent opening across both groups, followed by simple greetings ('Hi', 'Hello'). However, on closer inspection, Taiwanese and Japanese students used formal salutation-type openings more frequently, while Italian students preferred more informal greetings. Huang concluded that 'Italian students employed more informal opening strategies to consolidate friendship' (Huang, 2016, p. 202). There were also differences in the use of closings: Taiwanese students used fewer 'farewell salutations' than Japanese and Italian students. In terms of how such a lack might be perceived in communication, Huang argues that '[t]hese farewell markers, such as regards, best wishes, and sincerely, are regarded as politeness signals to end a conversation. It seems that more instruction on ending a message politely will be necessary to ensure the flow of conversation' (p. 202).

Digital technology has also allowed us to communicate de facto face to face while we are hundreds or thousands of miles apart: there is a plethora of platforms and apps that facilitate video calls and require little more than a smartphone. Hsu and Beasley (2019) investigated how Taiwanese students use computer-mediated communication (CMC) tools, such as Skype, to interact with people from other cultures, and found that CMC helped students to develop 'their intercultural knowledge, skills, attitudes, and critical cultural awareness, the vital elements of [intercultural competence], and [become] successful intercultural speakers' (Hsu & Beasley, 2019, p. 159). In Chapter 17, we will look at how we can develop intercultural competence in more detail.

As with face-to-face interaction, there is significant scope for things to go wrong in an online setting. In his chapter on the use of telecollaboration in the educational context, O'Dowd highlights that online intercultural exchange can 'often result in negative attitudes towards the partner group and their culture, misunderstandings and unachieved objectives' (O'Dowd, 2014, p. 248), with different communication styles between groups being one part of the problem. But contextual issues, including access to technology, also play a role: both macro- and micro-level aspects of the environment influence intercultural exchanges (2014, p. 248).

12.3 The Rise of Social Media

We have so far looked at digital communication that is focused on a small number of individuals being in direct exchange: spam emails or emails coming via large email distribution lists aside, we usually write emails or text messages to a small(er) number of individuals, and the communication is generally more directed towards these individuals. The emergence of **Web 2.0** opened new opportunities:

> Web 2.0 harnesses the Web in a more interactive and collaborative manner, emphasizing peers' social interaction and collective intelligence, and presents new opportunities for leveraging the Web and engaging its users more effectively.
> (Murugesan, 2007, p. 34)

With the Web 2.0, we have also seen the rise of social media platforms. Instant messaging services such as WhatsApp, WeChat or SnapChat allow us to connect and communicate instantaneously with people from around the world; Instagram, Facebook and YouTube, to name but a few, let us share photographs and videos of our surroundings and experiences, and so on. Moreover, we increasingly see what is known as *transmedia storytelling*: the same story appears across multiple digital platforms, 'in an attempt to create synergy between the content and a focus on an emotional, participatory experience for the audience' (Pratten, 2015, p. 3).

However, not all services and platforms are available in all countries (often because of governments blocking certain platforms), and some countries and cultures prefer different services. For example, in many Asian countries, such as Thailand, LINE is the preferred instant messaging service, with more people using LINE than WhatsApp (Kunaboot et al., 2015; Ruangkanjanases & Wutthisith, 2017). So intercultural communication in this context is dependent not only on the message, but also the tool. A quick word of 'warning' at this point: as we have seen throughout the book, cultures are anything but homogeneous, where everyone acts and thinks the same; and analogously, of course, this means that not everyone within each culture uses social media in the same way. Jitpaisarnwattana (2018), for example, found gender differences in the way people in Thailand use the LINE messaging app not only in terms of how men and women use language, but also in how they use LINE's virtual stickers (which are like large emojis); the author also showed that social factors other than gender, such as level of familiarity, play a role in the way people communicate using the app. In a study of young Dutch users, Waterloo et al. (2018) identified distinct differences in the norms of expressing emotions on different social media platforms:

> The expression of negative emotions was rated as most appropriate for WhatsApp, followed by Facebook, Twitter, and Instagram. For positive emotion expression, perceived appropriateness was highest for WhatsApp, followed by Instagram, Facebook, and Twitter.
>
> (Waterloo et al., 2018, p. 1813)

Jackson reminds us that a considerable part of meaning in interaction is conveyed through non-verbal communication such as gestures, body language, facial expressions etc., with some of them being universal across cultures (Jackson, 2020). Smiling, for example, is generally associated with positive emotions. Non-verbal communication is also an area where things go spectacularly wrong in intercultural encounters, with misinterpretation of nonverbal communication being a major barrier to intercultural communication (Jandt, 2016, p. 101). Touching your thumb and your index finger, for example, can signify 'okay' in large parts of the world, but is considered vulgar with strong sexual connotations in others. The 'thumbs up' sign often signals agreement, while in others, it is offensive. While communication in the digital sphere these days also includes voice or video, a considerable proportion is still through writing. As a communication system, writing lacks non-verbal channels beyond basic punctuation (!!!!, ?!?!?!), spelling ('you gotta be JOKING!?!?'), and basic combinations to express feelings, like :-) (happy) :-((sad) or ;-) (wink).

Japanese designer Shigetaka Kurita is credited with being the inventor of the 'modern' emoji: the little digital pictograms that allow us to convey significantly more than the traditional typographic emoticons could ever do. Danesi's (2016) book provides us with a great discussion of emojis as a new visual language. It should come as no surprise that, as with any language, there are differences as well as similarities in the way different cultures use and/or perceive emojis. Li et al. looked at more than 100 million posts from Weibo in China and Twitter in the USA, and found, for example, that 'Twitter and Weibo users have different views towards Surprise and Trust, at least in terms of Emojis associated with them' and concluded that 'Twitter users and Weibo users indeed take different sets of Emojis as suitable to each emotion' (Li et al., 2019, p. 466). This, then, is no different from different cultures interpreting different gestures differently. Similarly, Cheng's study in Spain found that young people of Spanish origin and those of Chinese origin considerably overlap in their perceptions of emojis, such as associating the happy face emoji with positive emotions and friendliness; however, Spanish users opted for the angry emoji more often than the Chinese (Cheng, 2017, p. 222). Cheng argues that 'unlike the universal attribution of the emotion of happiness to the positive situations experienced by different individuals, there are clear cultural differences associated with the communication of sadness' (2017, p. 222), and suggests that this is a result of Chinese 'high context' culture, which prefers an indirect communication style – the 'angry emoji' in this case is perceived as being too direct.

The exponential increase in digital communication has also impacted on cultures and cultural identities; we have seen in the first few chapters that this is a complex area already. Singh discusses how the arrival of the Internet and the growth of social media allows people to create new cultural identities as 'networked individuals' with their own new communities, based on shared interests, but independent from the requirements of a physical space (Singh, 2010, p. 88). Surveying research on how people construct their own identity online, Beinhoff and Rasinger conclude that 'for some, online identities can be very different from their "real life" identity, while for others their online identities are an extension of their identities in work and/or home domains' (Beinhoff & Rasinger, 2016, p. 580). Jackson summarises this concisely: 'When you become a member of an online community, you usually have some control over how much personal information, if any, you wish to reveal about yourself', and this includes decisions as to whether you want other people to see what you actually look like (Jackson, 2020, p. 153). However, Shuter (2012) argues that the exact processes are not quite clear. According to him, it is not clear how cultural identities – and in particular hybrid identities – are constructed in virtual communities, and suggests the dynamics of maintaining cultural identity may be different in virtual communities from those in offline ones (Shuter, 2012). Much of this will also depend on the kind of online community: a WhatsApp group consisting of a group of friends who know each other well in 'real life' is very different from a Facebook group with thousands of members from across the globe. In the former, creating an 'online identity' will be significantly different from doing so in the latter.

TASK

As we have seen, cultural differences can influence how emojis are interpreted. Can you think of an incident where you either did not understand the use of an emoji in a message you received, or where you misunderstood its intended meaning? To what extent was this an issue of culture?

12.4 Megxit, Brexit and Black Lives Matter: Power, Dominance and the Internet

While we all enjoy sharing pictures from our holidays and dinners in fancy restaurants, or videos of kittens and puppies, it is inevitable that not everything in the digital sphere is tasty, cute and fluffy. Throughout this book, we draw upon the question of power in intercultural communication, and the digital environment is no exception to this. Ladegaard and Phipps argue that language and intercultural research is in a strong position to advocate social activism and social justice, especially counteracting 'skewed narratives' from 'elite groups', and placing the emphasis on the narratives of 'disenfranchised groups like forced migrant workers, those seeking refuge or humanitarian assistance, sex workers and other victims of human trafficking' (Ladegaard & Phipps, 2020, p. 71).

Nakayama (2020) identifies three aspects related to power and the resistance to domination; in an earlier paper, he also used them to illustrate the spread of whiteness on the Internet (Nakayama, 2017). First, content on the Internet, especially in the era of Web 2.0, is often *user-generated*, and this means that it allows any user to create and distribute content without the editorial control of traditional media. Nakayama uses the example of the debate around former US president Barack Obama's country of birth: in the run-up to Obama's election in 2008, the so-called 'birther movement', spearheaded by Donald Trump, who in 2016 would become his successor, made extensive use of digital platforms to spread rumours that Obama was not in fact a US-born citizen (a constitutional requirement for US presidency) and hence ineligible for office: '"birtherism" – the belief that Obama is constitutionally disqualified from holding Presidential office' (Hughey, 2012, p. 163) featured prominently in public discourse (see also Chapter 4). Crucially, the movement was strongly based on race, targeting the first non-white president of the United States: 'the Birther rhetoric of constitutional protection relies on racial logics used in previous discourses about foreignness to delineate acceptable citizenship for the presidency and mark Obama as untrustworthy' (Pham, 2015, p. 86).

Second, the Internet provides *pseudo-anonymity* (Nakayama, 2020, p. 88). We have looked at the aspect of anonymity in the previous section implicitly in our discussion of online identities, but Nakayama reminds us that user-generated content together with anonymity 'can be a very powerful force in creating tension across cultural differences' and can 'create or enhance dominant groups on the basis of powerful fake news' (Nakayama, 2020, pp. 88, 89). We can use the example of former actress and now wife of Prince Harry, Meghan Markle, as an example: an American of mixed racial heritage, she is subject to at times extreme criticism and hatred across the social media spectrum (and parts of the British traditional media, too, for that matter). A quick search for the Twitter hashtags #Megxit and #snarkle unearths a myriad of negative tweets, often around race, but also around authenticity and trustworthiness:

Wally @▆▆▆▆▆▆   21 Sep   ⌄
Oh here she goes again, in full psycho mode....changing the world, one lie at
a time. #MeghanVsMail **#megxit**

Roccosmum @▆▆▆▆▆▆   20 Sep
Oh Barf. Meghan Markle's name in the same sentence as Ruth Bader
Ginsburg is sacrilege. RBG had integrity in every act, in every fight she told
on. The other is... well the other is Meghan Markle **#megxit**

Third, *status levelling*: 'social media has made communication with people up and
down various hierarchies much easier' (Nakayama, 2020, p. 89). The fact that
anyone with a Twitter account and an internet connection can directly respond
to a tweet by the US president constitutes a significant departure from traditional
communication channels with high levels of gatekeeping; yet, as we have already
seen above, this is not without consequence: one of the first tweets by Obama was
followed by a barrage of racist and hateful messages (Nakayama, 2017).

At this point in the chapter, we want to look briefly at opportunities the Internet offers for social action and to initiate social change. Horvath and Bako, for
example, illustrate how artists use Facebook and blogs for online artistic projects in the multi-ethnic region of Transylvania in Romania to foster intercultural
dialogue between different ethnic groups (Horváth & Bakó, 2016). Hon (2015)
shows us how the fatal shooting of black American teenager Trayvon Martin by
a white neighbourhood watchman in 2012 led to the development of an entire
digital media ecosystem in support of the 'Justice for Trayvon' campaign, which
later developed into the Black Lives Matter movement with the #BlackLivesMat-
ter or #BLM hashtag on social media. Carney's study of the early #BlackLives-
Matter movement 'reveals the ways in which youth of color actively engaged in
debates over race in the nation, strategically and adeptly negotiating signs and
language to control the public discourse' (Carney, 2016, p. 17). Hence, digital
media provide important platforms that support sociopolitical movements (De
Choudhury et al., 2016) that allow a wide range of people to participate, and to
coordinate joint action.

TASK

Pick a current event or a current sociopolitical debate. At the time of writing this chapter, the Black Lives Matter movement (#BLM) and Britain's exit from the European Union (#Brexit) were good examples. Search for postings about the event on a range of social media platforms. What are the dominant narratives and positions? How do they relate to notions of race, culture, and racial and cultural identities?

12.5 Intercultural Ethics in the Digital World

TASK

In your culture, what would be considered unethical behaviour? And what makes it unethical?

In this chapter, we have raised some aspects of digital intercultural communication – such as online versus 'real life' identities, or around power and dominance – which in turn raise a different issue altogether: that of **ethics** or more specifically *digital media ethics* (Ess, 2017). Ethics is a highly complex concept and includes elements from philosophy and law. Hammersley and Traianou provide an attempt to define ethics as:

> A set of principles that embody or exemplify what is good or right, or allow us to identify what is bad or wrong. [...] '[E]thical' can mean: What is good or right, as contrasted with the *unethical*, what is bad or wrong.
>
> (Hammersley & Traianou, 2012, pp. 16–17, original emphasis)

12.5.1 Ethics in Intercultural Communication

Ethics, and intercultural ethics in particular, focuses on the norms that govern the behaviour of, and relationships between, different groups of people, both formally and informally organised (Evanoff, 2020, p. 187). Yet, there is considerable debate as to whether ethics forms part of a culture, or is separate from it (Ting-Toomey, 2011): for example, while there are certain underlying norms that seem to be universal across cultures, the interpretation and application of these norms need to reflect different cultural settings (Ess, 2017, p. 2). It appears that at least some cultural value orientations, such as Trompenaars and Hampden-Turner's ideas of *universalism* versus *particularism* (Trompenaars & Hampden-Turner, 1997; also see Chapter 2), play a role in ethical decision making processes (Ting-Toomey, 2011).

Nam et al. (2015) surveyed intercultural communication professionals on what they perceived to be the main ethical challenges in the field. The perpetuation of stereotypes was considered one of the most important ethical issues, but also the most frequently observed violation. So clearly, the avoidance of cultural stereotypes is an important facet of intercultural communication and training. At the same time, respondents agreed that ethics are culturally relative, which makes the creation of a set of universal ethical standards difficult, if not impossible. But this does not mean that all behaviour is considered ethical simply because it is a cultural practice: using the example of female infanticide (the practice of killing newborn girls), the authors argue that such practices need to be *understood* within their cultural context – but this does not mean they should be *accepted*. As a less drastic example, we may want to consider culturally different approaches to eating animals which in some cultures are perceived to be pets: on my first trip to

Ecuador, I was somewhat shocked to see guinea pigs on the menu of several restaurants, as they are seen as a delicacy in parts of South America; yet this does not
make Ecuadorians less ethical than Western Europeans. At the same time, we need
to be wary of stereotypes: not all South Americans are 'pet eaters', just like not
every Spanish person loves bullfighting (in fact, most Ecuadorians and Spaniards
I know despise both practices).

12.5.2 Intercultural Ethics in the Digital World

Different conceptions of what is considered ethical are, of course, an issue for
any type of intercultural communication. But it is arguably more of a challenge
than ever when it comes to intercultural communication in the digital sphere. For
example, as we have seen above, the relative anonymity of the Internet has given
rise to racial aggression and abuse; practices that have – fortunately – become
less common in face-to-face interaction. It also allows the creation of powerful
narratives that serve to disenfranchise both individuals and entire groups. What
we need then is to consider some of the issues under the umbrella of *Intercultural
Digital Ethics* (Ess, 2020).

In the introduction of a special issue on intercultural digital ethics, Aggarwal
highlights the dangers of the dominance of Western ethical perspectives in the
context of digital technologies, and argues for a broader approach that brings
together 'a range of cultural, social and structural perspectives' (Aggarwal, 2020,
p. 547). Capurro (2009) identifies privacy, security, information overload, the
digital divide and censorship as some of the main ethical topics in the context of
digital intercultural communication. The **digital divide** manifests itself in two
forms: the first relates to basic access to the Internet. Access to the Internet equals
access to information, which, to an extent, equals power – imagine if you had to
do research for an essay without access to even a basic online library catalogue. At
the start of this chapter, we reported that 59 per cent of the world's population has
internet access, but this also entails that 41 per cent do not. This leaves a large part
of the world's population without access to vital information and global communication networks, leading to a range of different forms of digital inclusions and
exclusions (Seah, 2020, p. 127). This problem is not only confined to the developing world either: the Office for National Statistics estimated that in 2019, 93 per
cent of households in the UK had access to the Internet – which means seven out
of 100 did not (Office for National Statistics, 2019). This might not seem a lot. But
when the COVID-19 pandemic of 2020–21 saw schools moving their lessons away
from face-to-face to online teaching for considerable periods of time, this became
a striking challenge. In a report on British children's access to digital technology
during lockdowns, Simone Vibert, Senior Policy Analyst at the British Children's
Commissioner's office, highlights that an 'estimated 9 per cent of families in the
UK do not have a laptop, desktop or tablet at home' and concludes that 'proper
access to the internet is not a luxury, but a necessity' (Vibert, 2020). Yet, for many
children, the reality is rather different: Despite government schemes to supply

digital devices and internet access to the children most in need, of the more than half a million children eligible, only 37 per cent were provided with a device (Vibert, 2020).

But, as Capurro highlights, the digital divide also brings with it 'dangers of cultural exploitation, homogenisation, colonialism, and discrimination' (Capurro, 2009). Language is a basic but potent example of this: as of January 2020, English was the most commonly used language on the Internet, with 25.9 per cent of all internet users using English, followed by Chinese (19.4 per cent).[1] In fact, only ten languages make up more than 76.9 per cent of all internet users: English, Chinese, Spanish, Arabic, Indonesian, Portuguese, French, Japanese, Russian and German; the remainder is divided by all other languages of the world (Clement, 2020). If the Internet is dominated by only a few languages, it inevitably leads to a power imbalance. How can we ensure that the voices of those speaking other languages, and by extension their cultures, are adequately represented in the digital domain? Individual societies need to reflect critically – and act – upon these risks.

This cultural dominance, however, goes beyond the use of language on the Internet. In the field of Artificial Intelligence (AI), there is a strong prevalence of whiteness (Cave & Dihal, 2020). For example, a quick Google image search (though other search engines are available!) for 'humanoid robot' shows that the vast majority of robots resembling humans are designed with white-coloured bodies and other ethnically/racially White features. This pattern continues with AI applications such as virtual assistants, who are predominantly designed to sound and behave as if 'White' (Cave & Dihal, 2020). Apple's 'Siri' virtual assistant, for example, offers a range of options of English varieties (American, Australian, British, Indian, Irish and South African), but even the American and South African options are based on what would generally be associated with a White speaker – there is no African-American or 'Black' option.

A further example is privacy: Capurro (2009) illustrates how '[w]hile in Western cultures privacy is closely related to the self having an intrinsic value, Buddhism relies on the tenet of non-self'. Yet, this is shifting: even in Western cultures, the concept of 'self' is moving from something very individualistic to something that is much more relational – our self depends very much on our relationship with other people (Ess, 2017). This in turn will have different implications for how online privacy is perceived, but also how it is regulated: while within the European Union, for example, data and privacy – including online data such as IP addresses – are protected and enshrined in law, this is less so in the United States, as there are cultural differences in the way that data is perceived. In Chapter 3, we briefly looked at the sub-Saharan concept of *ubuntu* – a sense of community consensus, where group solidarity and sharing is a key component; whatever affects the individual affects the entire group (Reviglio & Alunge, 2020, pp. 603–604). This, in turn, would imply that a Western, individual concept of privacy is difficult to apply in an ubuntu context. However, as Reviglio and Alunge argue, the strong focus of ubuntu on community could also serve to develop a stronger sense of privacy as a collective endeavour that includes the development of group privacy and 'a more communitarian conception and protection of privacy' (Reviglio & Alunge, 2020, p. 609).

12.6 In Summary

In this chapter, we have taken a whistle-stop tour of some of the key issues around intercultural communication in the digital environment. We have seen that digital communication can pose challenges for its users, at times mirroring traditional face-to-face interaction, but that it also offers new opportunities. We have also explored some of the ethical issues that emerge in the context of digital intercultural communication, and how these link to our cultural understanding and power relationships. We will revisit some of these aspects in subsequent chapters when we look at migration (Chapter 13), and the development of intercultural competence (Chapter 17).

DISCUSSION QUESTIONS

1. From your own experience of using the Internet and social media, can you provide examples of when you have been affected by any of the issues raised in this chapter?
2. If you have ever witnessed what you would class as unethical behaviour in the digital world, did you intervene? Why, or why not?

CASE STUDY

Critically evaluate the following incident, taking into account the various aspects we have discussed in this chapter.

Following England's loss in the finals of the European football championships in 2021 after a penalty shootout, several Black English players saw themselves faced with massive racist abuse on social media. These tweets, and one Twitter user in particular, created considerable outrage, with users not only targeting the original racist Tweeter, but also his employer.

Tweet A: example of racist abuse

Replying to ▮

Fucking ell man send them back where they came from

23:25 · 11/07/2021 · Twitter for Android

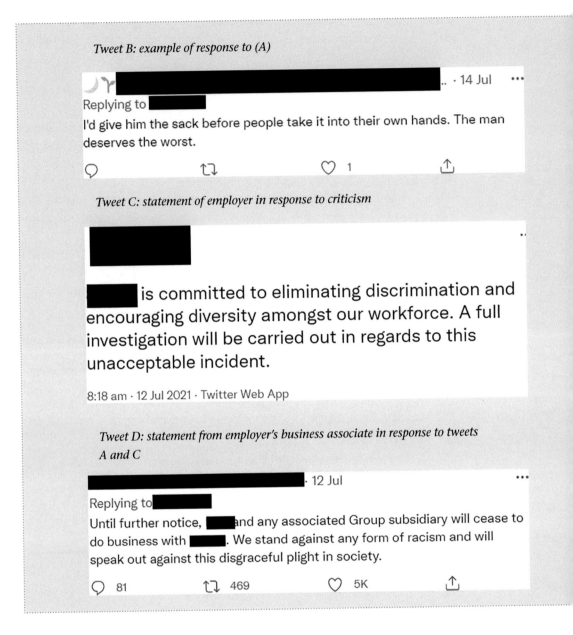

Tweet B: example of response to (A)

Replying to █████████

I'd give him the sack before people take it into their own hands. The man deserves the worst.

Tweet C: statement of employer in response to criticism

████████ is committed to eliminating discrimination and encouraging diversity amongst our workforce. A full investigation will be carried out in regards to this unacceptable incident.

8:18 am · 12 Jul 2021 · Twitter Web App

Tweet D: statement from employer's business associate in response to tweets A and C

· 12 Jul

Replying to █████

Until further notice, ██████and any associated Group subsidiary will cease to do business with ██████. We stand against any form of racism and will speak out against this disgraceful plight in society.

81   469   5K

Note

1   The term 'Chinese' is in itself reductionist and hence problematic. The Chinese language consists of a range of at times very different dialects. Of those, Mandarin Chinese is often considered the 'Standard Chinese' of China's mainland (and is likely what is being referred to by Capurro here), while Cantonese is widely spoken in Hong Kong and Macau.

References

Aggarwal, N. (2020). Introduction to the special issue on intercultural digital ethics. *Philosophy & Technology*, 33(4), 547–550. DOI:10.1007/s13347-020-00428-1

Barksdale, M. A., Watson, C. & Park, E. S. (2007). Pen pal letter exchanges: Taking first steps toward developing cultural understandings. *The Reading Teacher*, 61(1), 58–68. DOI:10.1598/rt.61.1.6

Beinhoff, B. & Rasinger, S. M. (2016). The future of identity research. In S. Preece (ed.), *The Routledge handbook of language and identity* (pp. 572–585). Abingdon: Routledge.

Callahan, C., Robinson, T. & Trachmann, K.-A. (2018). Migrant perceptions of social media. *Journal of Intercultural Communication*, 46, 1–12.

Capurro, R. (2009). Digital ethics. *Global Forum on Civilization and Peace*. Retrieved from www.capurro.de/korea.html

Carney, N. (2016). All lives matter, but so does race. *Humanity & Society*, 40(2), 180–199. DOI:10.1177/0160597616643868

Cave, S. & Dihal, K. (2020). The whiteness of AI. *Philosophy & Technology*, 33(4), 685–703. DOI:10.1007/s13347-020-00415-6

Chen, G.-M. (2012). The impact of new media on intercultural communication in global context. *China Media Research*, 8(2), 1–10.

Cheng, L. (2017). Do I mean what I say and say what I mean? A cross-cultural approach to the use of emoticons & emojis in CMC messages. *Fonseca, Journal of Communication*, 15, 2017–2226. DOI:10.14201/fjc201715207226

Clement, J. (2020). Most common languages used on the internet as of January 2020, by share of internet users. Online. www.statista.com/statistics/262946/share-of-the-most-common-languages-on-the-internet (last accessed 22 April 2022).

Danesi, M. (2016). *The semiotics of emoji: The rise of visual language in the age of the internet*. London: Bloomsbury.

De Choudhury, M., Jhaver, S., Sugar, B. & Weber, I. (2016). Social media participation in an activist movement for racial equality. *Proceedings of the International AAAI Conference on Weblogs and Social Media* (pp. 92–101): NIH Public Access. www.ncbi.nlm.nih.gov/pmc/articles/PMC5565729

Ellison, N. B., Vitak, J., Gray, R. & Lampe, C. (2014). Cultivating social resources on social network sites: Facebook relationship maintenance behaviors and their role in social capital processes. *Journal of Computer-Mediated Communication*, 19(4), 855–870. DOI:10.1111/jcc4.12078

Ess, C. (2017). Digital media ethics. *Oxford research encyclopedia of communication*. Oxford: Oxford University Press.

Ess, C. (2020). Interpretative pros hen pluralism: From computer-mediated colonization to a pluralistic intercultural digital ethics. *Philosophy & Technology*, 33(4), 551–569. DOI:10.1007/s13347-020-00412-9

Evanoff, R. (2020). Introducing intercultural ethics. In G. Rings & S. M. Rasinger (eds.), *The Cambridge handbook of intercultural communication* (pp. 187–201). Cambridge: Cambridge University Press.

Hammersley, M. & Traianou, A. (2012). *Ethics in qualitative research: Controversies and contexts*. London: SAGE.

Hon, L. (2015). Digital social advocacy in the Justice for Trayvon campaign. *Journal of Public Relations Research*, 27(4), 299–321.

Hooker, J. N. (2012). Cultural differences in business communication. In C. B. Paulston, S. F. Kiesling & E. S. Rangel (eds.), *The handbook of intercultural discourse and communication* (pp. 389–407). Malden, MA: Wiley-Blackwell.

Horváth, G. & Bakó, R. K. (2016). Online artistic activism: Case-study of Hungarian–Romanian intercultural communication. *Coactivity: Philosophy, Communication*, 24(1), 48–58. DOI:10.3846/cpc.2016.237

Hsu, S.-Y. & Beasley, R. E. (2019). The effects of international email and Skype interactions on computer-mediated communication perceptions and attitudes and intercultural competence in Taiwanese students. *Australasian Journal of Educational Technology*, 35(1), 149–162.

Huang, H.-C. (2016). Openings and closings in intercultural email communication: A case study of Taiwanese, Japanese, and Italian students. In Y.-S. Chen, D.-H. V. Rau & G. R. Rau (eds.), *Email discourse among Chinese using English as a lingua franca* (pp. 185–204). Heidelberg: Springer.

Hughey, M. W. (2012). Show me your papers! Obama's birth and the whiteness of belonging. *Qualitative Sociology*, 35, 163–181.

Incelli, E. (2013). Managing discourse in intercultural business email interactions: A case study of a British and Italian business transaction. *Journal of Multilingual and Multicultural Development*, 34(6), 515–532. DOI:10.1080/01434632.2013.807270

Jackson, J. (2020). *Introducing language and intercultural communication* (2nd edition). Abingdon: Routledge.

Jandt, F. E. (2016). *An introduction to intercultural communication: Identities in a global community* (8th edition). Thousand Oaks, CA: SAGE.

Jitpaisarnwattana, N. (2018). Gender-differential tendencies in LINE use: A case of Thailand. *Journal of English Studies*, 13(1), 53–70.

Kemp, S. (2020). Digital trends 2020: Every single stat you need to know about the internet. TNW. Online. https://bit.ly/3KAPA4W

Komito, L. (2011). Social media and migration: Virtual community 2.0. *Journal of the American Society for Information Science and Technology*, 62(6), 1075–1086. DOI:10.1002/asi.21517

Kunaboot, W., Chaipoopirutana, S. & Combs, H. (2015). A study of the factors influencing LINE stickers purchase intention in Thailand. *Proceedings of ASBBS*, 22, 261–268.

Kutscher, N. & Kreß, L.-M. (2018). The ambivalent potentials of social media use by unaccompanied minor refugees. *Social Media + Society*, 4(1). DOI:10.1177/2056305118764438

Ladegaard, H. J. & Phipps, A. (2020). Intercultural research and social activism. *Language and Intercultural Communication*, 20(2), 67–80. DOI:10.1080/14708477.2020.1729786

Levy, D. M. (2008). Information overload. In K. E. Himma & H. T. Tavani (eds.), *The handbook of information and computer ethics* (pp. 497–516). Hoboken, NJ: Wiley.

Li, M., Guntuku, S., Jakhetiya, V. & Ungar, L. (2019). Exploring (dis-)similarities in emoji-emotion association on Twitter and Weibo. *Companion Proceedings of the 2019 World Wide Web Conference (WWW '19 Companion)*, 461–467. DOI:10.1145/3308560.3316546

Murugesan, S. (2007). Understanding Web 2.0. *IT Professional*, 9(4), 34–411.

Nakayama, T. K. (2017). What's next for whiteness and the Internet. *Critical Studies in Media Communication*, 34(1), 68–72.

Nakayama, T. K. (2020). Critical intercultural communication and the digital environment. In G. Rings & S. M. Rasinger (eds.), *The Cambridge handbook of intercultural communication* (pp. 85–95). Cambridge: Cambridge University Press.

Nam, K.-A., Weaver, G. & del Mas, R. (2015). Major ethical issues in the field of intercultural relations: An exploratory study. *International Journal of Intercultural Relations*, 48, 58–74. DOI:10.1016/j.ijintrel.2015.03.015

O'Dowd, R. (2014). Intercultural communicative competence through telecollaboration. In J. Jackson (ed.), *The Routledge handbook of language and intercultural communication* (pp. 340–356). Abingdon: Routledge.

Office for National Statistics. (2019). *Internet access: Households and individuals, Great Britain, 2019.* Online. https://bit.ly/36273nQ

Oiarzabal, P. J. (2012). Diaspora Basques and online social networks: an analysis of users of Basque institutional diaspora groups on Facebook. *Journal of Ethnic and Migration Studies*, 38(9), 1469–1485. DOI:10.1080/1369183x.2012.698216

Pham, V. N. (2015). Our foreign President Barack Obama: The racial logics of birther discourses. *Journal of International and Intercultural Communication*, 8(2), 86–107. DOI:10.1080/17513057.2015.1025327

Pratten, R. (2015). *Getting started with transmedia storytelling: A practical guide for beginners* (2nd edition). Seattle: CreateSpace.

Reviglio, U. & Alunge, R. (2020). 'I am datafied because we are datafied': An Ubuntu perspective on (relational) privacy. *Philosophy & Technology*, 33(4), 595–612. DOI:10.1007/s13347-020-00407-6

Ruangkanjanases, A. & Wutthisith, M. (2017). Factors influencing intention to purchase stickers in a messaging application: A comparative study between male and female customers in Thailand. *Advanced Science Letters*, 23(1), 634–639. DOI:10.1166/asl.2017.7280

Seah, K. M. (2020). COVID-19: exposing digital poverty in a pandemic. *International Journal of Surgery*, 79, 127–128. DOI:10.1016/j.ijsu.2020.05.057

Shuter, R. (2012). Intercultural new media studies: The next frontier in intercultural communication. *Journal of Intercultural Communication Research*, 41(3), 219–237.

Singh, C. L. (2010). New media and cultural identity. *China Media Research*, 6(1), 8690.

Statista. (2020). Number of sent and received e-mails per day worldwide from 2017 to 2025. Online. https://bit.ly/3E5sAbZ

Ting-Toomey, S. (2011). Intercultural communication ethics: Multiple layered issues. In G. Cheney, S. May & D. Munshi (eds.), *The ICA handbook of communication ethics* (pp. 335–352). Mahwah, NJ: Lawrence Erlbaum Publishers.

Trompenaars, F. & Hampden-Turner, C. (1997). *Riding the waves of culture* (2nd edition). London: Nicholas Brealey.

Vibert, S. (2020). *Children without internet access during lockdown.* Online. https://bit.ly/37HaXDi

Waterloo, S. F., Baumgartner, S. E., Peter, J. & Valkenburg, P. M. (2018). Norms of online expressions of emotion: Comparing Facebook, Twitter, Instagram, and WhatsApp. *New Media Society*, 20(5), 1813–1831. DOI:10.1177/1461444817707349

13 Migration and Intercultural Communication

In Chapter 12 we moved our discussion to the exploration of intercultural communication in different contexts by looking at the digital domain. In the current chapter, we will consider intercultural communication in the context of migration: we start with a discussion of migration in more general terms, taking into account increases in global mobility where people live in more than one place and culture during their lifetime. We will also take a look at the various different shapes and forms that migration can take in our current day and age, including digital nomadism, academic migration and study abroad, and forced displacement.

AIMS
By the end of this chapter, you should be able to:

1. identify some of the main forms of migration;
2. explain some of the key intercultural issues migrants face;
3. reflect on how some of the key aspects discussed in the book so far relate to the migration context.

> ### KEY TERMS
> push and pull factors – transnationalism – culture shock – acculturation – panethnicity – global/intercultural citizenship – network capital – return migration – myth of return

13.1 Setting the Scene: Is the World Getting Smaller?

WARM-UP TASK

In your class, how many of you are currently living in a country that is not the country of their birth? How many of you have parents who were not born in the country you are currently living in? How many countries and continents are represented in your class?

Figure 13.1 *Migration* by Alíz Kovács-Zöldi

It is estimated that approximately 272 million people around the globe are migrants, that is, live in a country that is not that of their origin – a total of about 3.5 per cent of the world's total population (International Organization for Migration, 2019, p. 3). People migrate for a variety of reasons, and traditionally, these have been divided into **push *and* pull factors**: economic, environmental and demographic factors that push people out of one location, and pull them to another (Castles et al., 2013, p. 28). More recent theories of migration have focused on globalisation and increasing cross-border flows (2013, p. 34), an approach that is of interest to us here, too. For a more comprehensive overview of migration theories, Castles et al.'s (2013) *The age of migration* provides a good introduction.

A comparatively recent development is the very substantial increase in highly skilled migration (Bailey & Mulder, 2017), that is, the global mass movement of people who are highly educated with strong skills and knowledge sets (as opposed to more 'traditional' migration that saw migrants purely as a source of cheap labour). In particular where there are skills shortages, highly skilled migrants can be beneficial for the economy of the host society, and, unlike unskilled migrants, are usually more welcome and wanted (Hercog, 2019). Transnational networks can also be beneficial for the home countries as skills (and money) are often transferred back home, and might incentivise education; but on the other hand, mass emigration can lead to 'brain drain' (Hercog, 2019, pp. 166–167). Highly skilled migrants also often inhabit 'privileged legal and socio-economic positions' (2019, p. 169) with good access to social networks; we will pick up this particular issue a bit later on in this chapter. This development in migration patterns has also seen a marked shift in migration policy in many countries (Hercog & Sandoz, 2018), such as for example the Australian merit-based immigration system that awards points based on education and skills set: the higher the level of education and experience in 'skilled' jobs, the more points potential migrants receive (see Sumption, 2019, for an overview), with visas awarded on a points basis.

13.2   From Adaptation to Assimilation

In Chapter 1, we introduced the concept of transculturality; the idea that all cultures interconnect and overlap in some respects. Within the context of migration study, the related notion of **transnationalism** emerged in the 1960s and 1970s. While an in-depth discussion of the concept goes beyond the scope of this book (Steven Vertovec's 2009 *Transnationalism* provides a good and more detailed overview), the basic idea behind transnationalism is that contemporary migrants' networks and activities span both home and host societies. Unlike migration in the past (think of the first European settlers in the Americas or Australia), modern migration does not entail a complete breaking of all ties to the home country: it is now 'a boundary-breaking process in which two or more nation states are penetrated by, and become a part of, a singular new social space' (Faist & Bilecen, 2019, p. 502).

This does not mean, however, that migration is without challenges, and cultural differences can play a major role. Around 30–40 per cent of migrants and expatriates suffer from **culture shock** to some degree: 'the feelings of disorientation and anxiety that many people experience for a time while living in a foreign country' (Jandt, 2016, p. 279). Anthropologist Kalervo Oberg (1960) was one of the first to describe the phenomenon of culture shock, and divided it into four distinct phases which are still often referred to in this context: a *honeymoon period*, during which the fascination of the new environment outweighs any negatives, is followed by *anxiety*, *uncertainty* and *frustration*. The third phase is one of *adjustment*, followed by a final phase, *acceptance* or *adaptation*. We will mainly focus on the final two.

A key concept in the context of migration is that of **acculturation**: just like acclimatisation is about adjusting to a new climate, acculturation involves migrants' adjustments to the new environment, including the development of new customs, activities, values and language (Bornstein, 2017, p. 4). Acculturation occurs at both individual and group level. For example, those of Indian descent in the UK are often considered acculturated (for example, linguistically by speaking English), but that does not apply to every individual of the Indian community (Bornstein et al., 2019). At the same time, in situations of cultural contact, some degree of acculturation also takes place in the host society, which might adopt certain cultural practices of the migrant community (Berry, 2001).

How well someone acculturates is based on a variety of factors, such as social networks, both within the host society and the diaspora. For example, it has been shown that whether someone works for an international or a local employer can make a difference in terms of how well people acculturate (Selmer et al., 2015). Of course, the host society's attitude towards migrants also plays a role: in a study of Luxembourgers, Goedert et al. showed that those with fearful negative attachment styles (that is, people who are generally negatively disposed towards social interaction and relationships) are generally unwelcoming towards foreigners and reject the cultural influences migrants bring with them; instead, migrants are expected to adjust to the host culture, or at least not interfere with it, 'hence shielding the receiving culture from change due to cultural contact' (Goedert et al., 2019, p. 25). In this context, acculturation is a one-sided process. Those with generally positive attachment style displayed a more positive and indeed multicultural outlook on migration and acculturation. Social networking and acculturation also has a geographic dimension: Large cities such as Amsterdam or New York have well-established multi-ethnic neighbourhoods that promote contact between different ethnic and linguistic groups (Bornstein et al., 2019, p. 26).

Gender is one factor that impacts on acculturation, as is age: Güngör and Bornstein have shown how girls of Turkish heritage living in Belgium showed better adaptations than boys; in particular, 'older girls reported higher proficiency in the mainstream language and being more "Belgian" in both their private and public stances than older boys' (Güngör & Bornstein, 2008, p. 544). Similarly, younger people are more likely to adapt, older people less so; and there are often differences between first generation, who migrated to the host country, and second generation, who were born and raised in the host country (Bornstein et al., 2019, p. 21).

Unsurprisingly, cultural differences and acculturation have a direct impact on people's identities: young third generation (that is, those born to second generation migrants) Bangladeshis in East London, for example, often struggle to reconcile the multiple cultural spheres of their daily lives, leading to a 'story of non-belonging to neither a national British space nor a cultural Bangladeshi community' (Hoque, 2018, p. 192). In other words, those born to people of migrant descent often feel part neither of the host, nor the heritage culture.

A related phenomenon is that of **panethnicity**, sometimes known as 'racial lumping', 'the generalization of solidarity among ethnic subgroups that are perceived to be homogeneous by outsiders' (Espiritu, 2019, p. 261). For example, in the USA, Blacks, Asian Americans, Hispanics and Native Americans are often considered 'the same' (that is, non-White), which has led to these groups acting collectively and forming a collective voice, especially when it comes to securing rights. However, while collective voice and action can certainly be a positive outcome, at close inspection, this is not unproblematic: by 'lumping' groups of people together into artificial categories, this type of essentialist generalisation does not always reflect the lived experience of the people affected. As Espiritu explains, Latinos in the USA are racially diverse, and racial lines run along socio-economic groups: those looking 'more European' are often in higher socio-economic classes, which in turn can lead to racism even within Hispanic groups (Espiritu, 2019).

TASK

The acronym 'BAME' – Black, Asian and Minority Ethnic – has often been used as an umbrella term in Britain to refer to people who are non-White, especially in the context of tackling discrimination and disadvantage. Critically reflect on the term: can you identify problems with its use?

Above we have introduced the notion of transnationalism: the fact that in today's globalised world, people's lives often span several countries, with boundaries between 'home' and 'away' being increasingly blurred. In Chapter 1 we looked at different conceptualisations of culture and saw how national (and nationalist) ideas about culture have developed into inter- and transcultural concepts – of course, this does not mean that nationalist concepts of culture have disappeared! We can move these ideas forward and introduce the concept of **global** or **intercultural citizenship**, which can be understood as 'an extension of citizenship beyond national borders' (Baker & Fang, 2020, p. 3). The charity Oxfam defines a global citizen as someone who:

- is aware of the wider world and has a sense of their own role as a world citizen;
- respects value and diversity;
- has an understanding of how the world works;
- is passionately committed to social justice;
- participates in the community at a range of levels, from the local to the global;
- works with others to make the world a more equitable and more sustainable place;
- takes responsibility for their actions.

(Oxfam, 2015, p. 4)

While global citizenship has increasingly become part of national school curricula, for example in the UK (Davies, 2006), as with many of the concepts we have encountered in this book, the definition of global citizenship is contested, since 'there is neither an essential set of necessary and sufficient criteria for the correct use of such concepts nor a calculus for their application in particular cases' (Tully, 2014, p. 4). Global citizenship has sometimes been seen as a spectrum, ranging from the vague, such as an affiliation with certain global groups like Greenpeace, to a legal framework, and ultimately to a world government (Davies et al., 2005). Much of the Oxfam definition is based on the non-legal end of the spectrum.

TASK

Look at the Oxfam definition of global citizenship. Which of the seven characteristics do you meet? Provide specific examples. To what extent do you see yourself as a 'global citizen'?

13.3 Life on the Move: Digital Nomads

We briefly touched on the role digital communication plays in the context of migration and diaspora in Chapter 12. Technological advances have also created a new type of migrant: the *digital nomad*. Digital nomads work remotely, traditionally often in IT or fields such as digital marketing (and are highly educated – see Section 13.1), while travelling the world in search of a better work–life balance, professional and spatial freedom, and independence, often following a period of dissatisfaction in the home environment (Reichenberger, 2017; Thompson, 2018). The Covid-19 pandemic of 2020–21 with its global lockdowns that saw physical offices closed down has resulted in a large number of people across a range of sectors move to working online, and there is evidence that this trend will persist even beyond the acute pandemic (de Almeida et al., 2021); digital nomadism is now an option for more people than ever before, especially for traditional office workers. Digital nomads differ from expats by showing a high degree of transience and frequent changes of residential location.

Digital nomadism shows traditional multicultural tendencies in so far as coexistence with the host population seems to be more common than intercultural or transcultural lifestyles, in which nomads and people of the host culture exchange perspectives and negotiate meaning. Thompson's (2018) research showed that especially digital nomads who live and work in popular tourist destinations such as Thailand often follow a pattern that is not dissimilar to that of tourists and expats, with few links and little socialisation and cultural integration with the local population. Although some digital nomads actively pursue a lifestyle that is different from that of tourists, and seek to align themselves with locals, real cultural immersion can be rare (Mouratidis, 2018). With many digital nomads coming from affluent industrialised societies (Olga, 2020), the socio-economic differences between often more privileged nomads and locals can exaggerate this divide (Thompson, 2018): higher buying power means that they are often 'exactly as alienated from their environment as tourists' (Mouratidis, 2018, p. 45). This can frequently lead to the formation of 'communities within communities' (Olga, 2020, p. 345) where digital nomads form close social networks away from the host population.

While some digital nomads attempt to be involved with the local communities, in the long-term, constant relocation can lead to loneliness and isolation (Fernandes Barroso & Moreira da Silva, 2020). Smercina concludes that digital nomads in her study 'are constantly searching for a sense of belonging, for a community to generate social solidarity' (Smercina, 2019, p. iii), with digital communities alone being unfulfilling. Similarly, Haking's study in Bali showed that cultural adjustment, the strain on relationships and dating, loneliness and homesickness form common experiences amongst digital nomads (Haking, 2017).

Yet, digital nomads often possess valuable assets: in Chapter 9, we looked at the Bourdieuian notion of *capital*, and in Chapter 12 we expanded that concept by looking at bonding social capital. Following Urry (2007), Mancinelli (2020) shows how in the context of digital nomads, **network capital** becomes an important resource:

> a set of competences that are both a prerequisite and a consequence of a mobile life, such as having the appropriate documents and contacts, the networking tools and the appropriate meeting places, the physical and financial access to communication devices, means of transportation, and time as a resource to manage the whole set. (Mancinelli, 2020, p. 433)

Together with high levels of education and skills (education and qualifications being other forms of cultural capital), this network capital forms not only a valuable tool for digital nomads, but also for the hosting communities. Considerable efforts have been made in parts of the world to increase digital infrastructure to create working spaces and 'digital hubs' for those able to work remotely – accelerated dramatically during the Covid-19 pandemic – and in particular in rural and remote areas (Rundel et al., 2020; Tomaz et al., 2021): 'Digital technologies create urban–rural linkages and challenge the traditional perspective on urban–rural dichotomies' (Bürgin & Mayer, 2020, p. 91). On the island of Arranmore on the west coast of Ireland, for example, a new digital hub has been specifically created to target a technological workforce in order to counteract a falling population as a result of the decline of the traditional fishing and farming industries (Glass et al., 2020).

13.4 Academic Migration and Study Abroad

So far in this chapter, we have looked at highly skilled migration in general, and then through the lens of digital nomads. In this section, we want to return to this topic by looking at it from a very focused angle: that of academic migration. Academia (universities and research institutes) is a sector that sees large numbers of people move across the globe. For example, in the UK alone, in 2019/20, there were 538,600 overseas students studying at universities, a proportion of 22 per cent of the total student population (Hubble & Bolton, 2021, p. 5). Of those, more than 100,000 students came from China (ibid.). Around 4 per cent of UK students studied abroad in 2018 (2021, p. 7). Much more strikingly, the Royal Society reports that '28% of academic staff in UK universities are non-UK nationals' (Frenk et al., 2016, p. 4). This is not a uniquely British phenomenon: Germany registered close to 111,000 international students at its universities in 2019/20, slightly higher than in the year before; as in the UK, students from China formed the largest group (10 per cent of the total), followed by those from India (8.8 per cent) (Bundesamt für Migration und Flüchtlinge, 2020, p. 7). At the same time, China itself has been developing as an international higher education provider: between 2001 and 2015, the number of international students studying at its universities rose by more than 542 per cent to 397,600 (Wang, 2017, p. 45), with the highest numbers coming from South Korea (50,600), Thailand (28,600) and Pakistan (28,000) (Statista, 2021).

In particular, study abroad – spending a semester or a year at a university in a different country – is closely linked to the development of both linguistic and (intercultural) skills (we will discuss the development of intercultural competence in more detail in Chapter 17). That said, a study abroad experience is very much an individual one, and outcomes can differ: the way students experience study abroad 'is moderated by their prior experiences, both international and domestic' (Anderson & Lawton, 2011, p. 97). Of course, just as with other migration processes, issues such as culture shock and acculturation also apply in a study abroad context; for example, homesickness is a common phenomenon amongst international students (Saravanan et al., 2019). In a study of international students in the Netherlands, Taušová and colleagues showed how aspects such as strong orientation to their own culture can lead to students struggling with cultural adjustment, while a positive orientation towards the host culture has a positive impact on adjustment (Taušová et al., 2019); student migration and studying abroad, therefore, follows patterns we have already seen in our discussion in this chapter so far. Adequate preparation before departure, such as preparatory workshops that include cultural aspects, is therefore essential, as is a requirement for students to reflect on their experiences critically during the period abroad, and appropriate support on returning home, since 'returnees may experience re-entry woes as they readjust to their life in their home country' (Jackson, 2020, p. 342). The use of digital technologies, already discussed in this chapter, also plays an increasing role in supporting those studying abroad pre-, during and post-sojourn (Jackson, 2020).

However, as Jackson highlights, much of traditional preparation reinforces otherisation and essentialism, with little attention being paid to the nuances and complexities of culture (Jackson, 2020). Such essentialist conceptions of culture and cultural differences have also been observed by students themselves: in interviews, Spanish students in South Korea, and South Korean students in Spain, paint fairly fixed and stereotypical pictures of their host culture, such as Koreans paying close attention to hierarchy and respect; however, as the stay in the host country progressed, some of these cultural boundaries become less rigid (Montalban et al., 2020). There is also yet another issue we need to consider: universities are host to a multicultural and multilingual population of staff and students, but as we have made clear throughout this book, societies across the globe are hardly culturally homogeneous entities but increasingly diverse. This is particularly true for large metropolitan areas: international students' desire to interact with native speakers and 'true locals' in these multilingual and multicultural contexts can hence be challenging (Jang, 2020).

Studying and working abroad relates, of course, not only to students but also to teachers. In particular for trainee teachers, study abroad has been shown to benefit their intercultural development (Marx & Moss, 2011). American preservice teachers participating in a study abroad programme in Italy, for example, showed increased intercultural competence, which was also reflected in increased empathy towards their students (Hauerwas et al., 2017). Temporarily working in another country can also be beneficial for researchers more generally, although the actual value of international experience for an academic career may vary considerably, and, at times, be a hindrance rather than an advantage. While evidence suggests that a stint working abroad – especially towards a doctorate – might be beneficial for career progression, this is not always the case, and reintegration into the academic system in the home country can be challenging (Delicado, 2011). Particularly for those who are forced to work abroad due to lack of opportunities in their home country, the benefits are more likely to be limited (Teichler, 2015). Unsurprisingly, the issues for researchers working abroad are similar to those who study abroad, and those of migrants generally. Kurek-Ochmańska and Luczaj's study of 'Western' academics moving to work at universities in Poland identified language barriers, different institutional cultures and culture shock more generally as common issues (Kurek-Ochmańska & Luczaj, 2021).

13.5 Forced Migration and Displacement

In our discussion so far, we have, maybe implicitly, assumed that migration is a predominantly voluntary process: people migrate for education, jobs, love, or a desire for adventure, and while there are often a range of push and pull factors behind migration decisions, there cannot be any stronger push factor than when our lives, or those of our loved ones, are at stake. The United Nations estimates that in 2020, around 82.4 million people around the world were forced to leave their homes (UNHCR, 2021), that is 'people who have fled war, violence, conflict or persecution and have crossed an international border to find safety in another country' (UNHCR, 2019) were just under one-third of all migrants. The migration experience that refugees face is considerably more dramatic than that of other migrants, and often includes perilous journeys with many threats to their lives.

Refugees are by no means the 'digital nomads' we looked at above, but smartphones and social media also play an integral part in the lives and journeys of those forced to leave their home countries: Gillespie and colleagues have shown how for Syrian and Iraqi refugees in France, digital technology and social media 'are lifelines, as important as water and food' (Gillespie et al., 2018, p. 1). Syrian asylum seekers, for example, prefer 'social media information that originates from existing social ties and information that is based on personal experiences' (Dekker et al., 2018, p. 1) to make decisions both pre-migration and during the journey – both bonding and bridging social capitals are at work here (see Chapter 9), with social media being important for what type of information is considered trustworthy.

In addition to those who leave – or even flee – their home countries, the International Organization for Migration estimates that there are around 740 million *internal* migrants; people who move *within* a country (International Organization for Migration, 2019). Of those, around 48 million are *internally displaced* people: people who are forced to leave their home because of regional armed conflicts and violence, economic hardship, natural disasters etc. but remain in the same country (UNHCR, 2021). The armed conflict in the Tigray region of Ethiopia, for example, has led to more than 2.7 million people being internally displaced in 2020 alone (2021). But it is Colombia that leads the table with 8.3 million internally displaced people at the end of 2020, followed by Syria, ravaged by a decade of conflict, with 6.7 million. Climate change, too, is a growing factor in forcing people out of regions that have become increasingly uninhabitable due to consistent droughts, rising sea-levels etc. (Berchin et al., 2017). It is estimated that by 2050, around 200 million people will be 'climate refugees' (Merone & Tait, 2018, p. 1).

Internal displacement can be just as traumatic and result in severe psychological and social consequences; it often affects those already vulnerable and marginalised, such as those living in remote rural areas (Heugh, 2019). Displacement can have a considerable negative impact on linguistic and cultural practices: in countries with high levels of ethnic and linguistic heterogeneity, as is for example the case in large parts of sub-Saharan Africa or Asia, moving to the other end of the country can put considerable pressure on maintaining language and culture, in particular if the displaced group is already vulnerable. Dunn (2014) provides an example from a camp of displaced people in the Republic of Georgia, where ethnic Georgians were forcibly displaced from the breakaway province of South Ossetia during a war of independence in 2008. Their situation is characterised by a deep sense of all-encompassing loss that goes beyond the lack of material objects:

> *nothingness* had become a central category through which the IDPs [Internally Displaced People] had come to understand their new lives in the settlement, their new social status as displaced people, and their new political relationships to the state and the international community.
>
> (Dunn, 2014, pp. 287–288)

Forced migration and displacement, then, work as amplifiers of the challenges surrounding culture and intercultural communication we have discussed in this chapter and the book so far.

13.6   Going Home? The Myth of Return

In the last section of this chapter, we will look at a phenomenon that has frequently been observed in migration contexts across the world: **return migration** and the **Myth of Return**, the idea of staying in the host country for only a period of time before returning to the homeland – an idea that is both a material objective and an aspiration, and one that can significantly contribute to in-group cohesion of migrant groups (Zetter, 1999, p. 4).

Return migration – the process of moving back to the original home country – is driven by factors that often mirror that of out-migration, including push-and-pull factors, such as lack of socio-economic success in the host country, and new opportunities or a change of circumstance in the home country. '[F]amily situations, including issues of adaptation, decisions on where the children should be educated, and requests for the migrant to be present in the family' are amongst many of the personal factors that play a role in the decision whether to migrate back or not (Battistella, 2018, p. 4). In a study on Moroccan migrants across Europe, de Haas et al. (2015) identified strong social ties to Morocco as factors that positively influence return migration, while good sociocultural integration in the host country tends to influence return intentions negatively. Similarly, participants in Paparusso and Ambrosetti's study of Moroccans in Italy showed often exaggerated positive and nostalgic views of the homeland, yet few showed clear and concrete intentions to return to Morocco (Paparusso & Ambrosetti, 2017).

At the same time, people of migrant descent born in the host country as second generation might choose to migrate to the country of their cultural ancestry:

> The term 'return' is therefore used to denote otherness from a place of birth, reflecting ignorance, racism, or xenophobia on the part of a dominant population or in some cases, a sense of identity with a place other than one's birth.
>
> (Kobayashi, 2019, p. 526)

To this end, it is less of an actual and more of a metaphorical 'return' to cultural, linguistic and religious heritage. For example, some of those of second and third-generation Pakistani heritage in northern England see a 'return' to Pakistan as a response to increasing levels of Islamophobia, and feelings of affiliation to Pakistan remain strong across generations (Bolognani, 2007).

But, as Kobayashi points out, modern transnationalism means that many people consider more than one place 'home' (Kobayashi, 2019, p. 524). Return for many migrants means striking a careful balancing act between a desire for permanent resettlement in the home country, and the benefits offered by staying in the host country, leading to increasingly transnational lives with comings and goings between home and host countries (Sinatti, 2011) – and, in fact, the boundaries between 'home' and 'host' country disappear. In a study of Turkish migrants in North London, Cakmak illustrates how regular visits to Turkey replaced traditional concepts of return but enabled the maintenance of strong links, with a permanent return to Turkey occurring only after death for burial in the homeland (Cakmak, 2021).

Traditionally, the myth of return has been seen as a key driver for maintaining links with the homeland, and, by proxy, cultural and linguistic practices. Yet, for those migrants who are minority groups within their home countries, return can often be a less desirable objective, and for those forced to leave their country because of war or violence, it is often near-impossible (Byle, 2018); and especially after prolonged armed conflicts, the homeland may have changed beyond recognition (Žíla, 2015). The permanent return to the home country, for many, becomes no more than a myth.

13.7   In Summary

In this chapter, we have taken a closer look at migration and its impact on intercultural communication. As we have shown, migration as a phenomenon intersects with many of the key concepts and approaches we have looked at in this book so far, and will continue with in subsequent chapters. We have seen that modern migration patterns are characterised not by simple A to B movements, but by complex and often transnational flows of people. Traditional concepts such as 'home' become increasingly blurred. Migration is no longer motivated only by economic or safety factors, but modern technologies enable people to pursue lifestyles that allow the combination of work and travel.

TASK

'Migrants' and 'expatriates' (or 'expats') essentially refer to the same group of people: those who live in a country that is not their native one. Conduct a quick internet search of how different media outlets such as online newspapers, social media or discussion forums use the terms. Where are the similarities? Where are the differences?

Then, contrast the use of 'migrant'/ 'expat(riate)' with 'asylum seeker' and 'refugee'.

DISCUSSION QUESTIONS

The *CIA World Factbook* provides some information about the population of Nigeria:

ETHNICITY: Hausa 30%, Yoruba 15.5%, Igbo (Ibo) 15.2%, Fulani 6%, Tiv 2.4%, Kanuri/Beriberi 2.4%, Ibibio 1.8%, Ijaw/Izon 1.8%, other 24.7%
LANGUAGE: English (official), Hausa, Yoruba, Igbo (Ibo), Fulani, over 500 additional indigenous languages
RELIGION: Muslim 53.5%, Roman Catholic 10.6%, other Christian 35.3%, other 0.6% (Central Intelligence Agency, 2022)

Drawing on what we have discussed in this chapter, what kind of issues related to intercultural communication can you identify within this context?

CASE STUDY

Critically contrast the migration experiences of Sameena and Monika outlined below, drawing on the issues we have discussed in this chapter.

Sameena is a 32-year-old woman. She moved from her native Bangladesh to the UK at the age of 18. She lives with her husband, who is also from Bangladesh and works as a delivery driver for a courier company, and their three young children in East London – an area where there is a large Bangladeshi community. Despite having lived in the UK for more than a decade, her English language proficiency is quite low, and she puts this down to a lack of opportunities to practise the language.

She laments that 'Everyone here is Bangladeshi, everyone speaks Bengali. There are no English people.'

Monika is from Poland. She is 28 and moved to the UK six years ago to pursue a postgraduate degree. With her Spanish boyfriend, she lives in Cambridgeshire, a county in England with a considerable number of migrants from Eastern Europe, and she works as an administrator and supply teacher in a local secondary school. In an interview, she complains 'There are so many Polish people here. Everyone is Polish. Everyone only mixes with other Polish people. Everyone speaks Polish. What's wrong with people?'

(adapted from Rasinger, 2007, 2012)

References

Anderson, P. H. & Lawton, L. (2011). Intercultural development: Study abroad vs. on-campus study. *Frontiers: The Interdisciplinary Journal of Study Abroad*, 21(1), 86–108.

Bailey, A. & Mulder, C. H. (2017). Highly skilled migration between the global north and south: Gender, life courses and institutions. *Journal of Ethnic and Migration Studies*, 43(16), 2689–2703. DOI:10.1080/1369183x.2017.1314594

Baker, W. & Fang, F. (2020). 'So maybe I'm a global citizen': Developing intercultural citizenship in English medium education. *Language, Culture and Curriculum*, 34(1), 1–17. DOI:10.1080/07908318.2020.1748045

Battistella, G. (2018). Return migration: A conceptual and policy framework. In J. K. Appleby & D. Kerwin (eds.), *Perspectives on the content and implementation of the global compact for safe, orderly, and regular migration* (pp. 3–14). New York: Scalabrini Migration Study Centers.

Berchin, I. I., Valduga, I. B., Garcia, J. & de Andrade Guerra, J. B. S. O. (2017). Climate change and forced migrations: An effort towards recognizing climate refugees. *Geoforum*, 84, 147–150. DOI:10.1016/j.geoforum.2017.06.022

Berry, J. W. (2001). A psychology of immigration. *Journal of Social Issues*, 57(3), 615–631.

Bolognani, M. (2007). The myth of return: Dismissal, survival or revival? A Bradford example of transnationalism as a political instrument. *Journal of Ethnic and Migration Studies*, 33(1), 59–76. DOI:10.1080/13691830601043497

Bornstein, M. H. (2017). The specificity principle in acculturation science. *Perspectives on Psychological Science*, 12(1), 3–45. DOI:10.1177/1745691616655997

Bornstein, M. H., Bernhard, J. K., Bradley, R. H., Chen, X., Farver, J. M., Gold, S. J., Hernandez, D. J., Spiel, C., van de Vijver, F. & Yoshikawa, H. (2019). Psychological acculturation: Perspectives, principles, processes, and prospects. In S. J. Gold & S. J. Nawyn (eds.), *Routledge international handbook of migration studies* (2nd edition), (pp. 19–31). Abingdon: Routledge.

Bundesamt für Migration und Flüchtlinge. (2020). *Migrationsbericht 2019: Zentrale Ergebnisse*. Nuremberg: Bundesamt für Migration und Flüchtlinge.

Bürgin, R. & Mayer, H. (2020). Digital periphery? A community case study of digitalization efforts in Swiss mountain regions. In S. Patnaik, S. Sen & M. S. Mahmoud (eds.), *Smart village technology: Concepts and developments* (pp. 67–98). Cham: Springer.

Byle, J. J. (2018). Chaldean Christian refugees & the myth of return: A narrative study. *Digest of Middle East Studies*, 27(2), 185–204. DOI:10.1111/dome.12136

Cakmak, M. (2021). 'Take me back to my homeland dead or alive!': The myth of return among London's Turkish-speaking community. *Frontiers in Sociology*, 6. DOI:10.3389/fsoc.2021.630558

Castles, S., Haas, H. d. & Miller, M. J. (2013). *The age of migration: International population movements in the modern world* (5th edition). London: Palgrave Macmillan.

Central Intelligence Agency. (2022). *The world factbook: Nigeria*. Online. www.cia.gov/the-world-factbook/countries/nigeria/#people-and-society (last accessed 22 April 2022).

Davies, I., Evans, M. & Reid, A. (2005). Globalising citizenship education? A critique of 'Global Education' and 'Citizenship Education'. *British Journal of Educational Studies*, 53(1), 66–89.

Davies, L. (2006). Global citizenship: Abstraction or framework for action? *Educational Review*, 58(1), 5–25. DOI:10.1080/00131910500352523

de Almeida, M. A., Correia, A., Schneider, D. & de Souza, J. M. (2021). COVID-19 as opportunity to test digital nomad lifestyle. *Proceedings of the 2021 IEEE 24th International Conference on Computer Supported Cooperative Work in Design*, 1209–1214. DOI:10.1109/cscwd49262.2021.9437685

de Haas, H., Fokkema, T. & Fihri, M. F. (2015). Return migration as failure or success? The determinants of return migration intentions among Moroccan migrants in Europe. *Journal of International Migration and Integration*, 16(2), 415–429. DOI:10.1007/s12134-014-0344-6

Dekker, R., Engbersen, G., Klaver, J. & Vonk, H. (2018). Smart refugees: How Syrian asylum migrants use social media information in migration decision-making. *Social Media + Society*, 4(1). DOI:10.1177/2056305118764439

Delicado, A. (2011). The consequences of mobility: Careers and work practices of Portuguese researchers with a foreign PhD degree. In F. Dervin (ed.), *Analysing the consequences of academic mobility and migration* (pp. 163–180). Newcastle: Cambridge Scholars Publishing.

Dunn, E. C. (2014). Humanitarianism, displacement, and the politics of nothing in postwar Georgia. *Slavic Review*, 73(2), 287–306.

Espiritu, Y. L. (2019). Panethnicity. In S. J. Gold & S. J. Nawyn (eds.), *Routledge international handbook of migration studies* (2nd edition), (pp. 261–271). Abingdon: Routledge.

Faist, T. & Bilecen, B. (2019). Transnationalism. In S. J. Gold & S. J. Nawyn (eds.), *Routledge international handbook of migration studies* (2nd ed., pp. 498–511). Abingdon: Routledge.

Fernandes Barroso, C. & Moreira da Silva, M. (2020). From backpacker to digital nomad – footpaths of a digital transformation. *RTIC-Revista de Tecnologias, Informação e Comunicação*, 1(2), 5–14.

Frenk, C., Hunt, T., Partridge, L., Thornton, J. & Wyatt, T. (2016). *UK research and the European Union: The role of the EU in international research collaboration and researcher mobility*. London: The Royal Society. https://bit.ly/3Kx1n4l

Gillespie, M., Osseiran, S. & Cheesman, M. (2018). Syrian refugees and the digital passage to Europe: smartphone infrastructures and affordances. *Social Media + Society*, 4(1). DOI:10.1177/2056305118764440

Glass, J., McMorran, R., Jones, S., Maynard, C., Craigie, M. & Weeden, A. (2020). *Case studies of island repopulation initiatives*. Scotland's Rural College (SRUC). Online. https://bit.ly/3E72IMR

Goedert, C., Albert, I., Barros, S. & Ferring, D. (2019). Welcome or not? – Natives' security feelings, attachment and attitudes toward acculturation of immigrants. *International Journal of Intercultural Relations*, 69, 24–31. DOI:10.1016/j.ijintrel.2018.12.001

Güngör, D. & Bornstein, M. H. (2008). Gender, development, values, adaptation, and discrimination in acculturating adolescents: The case of Turk heritage youth born and living in Belgium. *Sex Roles*, 60(7–8), 537–548. DOI:10.1007/s11199-008-9531-2

Haking, J. (2017). Digital nomad lifestyle: A field study in Bali. (Dissertation MSc Industrial Management), KTH Royal Institute of Technology, Stockholm.

Hauerwas, L. B., Skawinski, S. F. & Ryan, L. B. (2017). The longitudinal impact of teaching abroad: An analysis of intercultural development. *Teaching and Teacher Education*, 67, 202–213. DOI:10.1016/j.tate.2017.06.009

Hercog, M. (2019). High-skilled migration. In S. J. Gold & S. J. Nawyn (eds.), *Routledge international handbook of migration studies* (2nd edition), (pp. 164–177). Abingdon: Routledge.

Hercog, M. & Sandoz, L. (2018). Highly skilled or highly wanted migrants? Conceptualizations, policy designs and implementations of high-skilled migration policies. *Migration Letters*, 15(4), 453–460.

Heugh, K. (2019). Displacement and language. In S. J. Gold & S. J. Nawyn (eds.), *Routledge international handbook of migration studies* (2nd edition), (pp. 186–206). Abingdon: Routledge.

Hoque, A. (2018). Third-generation British-Bangladeshis from east London: Complex identities and a culturally responsive pedagogy. *British Journal of Sociology of Education*, 39(2), 182–196.

Hubble, S. & Bolton, P. (2021). *International and EU students in higher education in the UK FAQs*. Briefing paper. London: House of Commons Library. Online. https://bit .ly/3O88T7P

International Organization for Migration. (2019). *World migration report 2020*. Geneva: International Organization for Migration.

Jackson, J. (2020). Intercultural education in study abroad contexts. In G. Rings & S. M. Rasinger (eds.), *The Cambridge handbook of intercultural communication* (pp. 335–349). Cambridge: Cambridge University Press.

Jandt, F. E. (2016). *An introduction to intercultural communication: Identities in a global community* (8th edition). Thousand Oaks, CA: SAGE.

Jang, I. C. (2020). The stratification of English speakers in a study-abroad program: An ethnography of South Koreans studying English in multilingual Toronto. *The Canadian Modern Language Review*, 76(2), 155–173. DOI:10.3138/cmlr-2018-0208

Kobayashi, A. (2019). Return migration. In S. J. Gold & S. J. Nawyn (eds.), *Routledge international handbook of migration studies* (2nd edition), (pp. 523–535). Abingdon: Routledge.

Kurek-Ochmańska, O. & Luczaj, K. (2021). 'Are you crazy? Why are you going to Poland?' Migration of western scholars to academic peripheries. *Geoforum*, 119, 102–110. DOI:10.1016/j.geoforum.2020.12.001

Mancinelli, F. (2020). Digital nomads: Freedom, responsibility and the neoliberal order. *Information Technology & Tourism*, 22(3), 417–437. DOI:10.1007/s40558-020-00174-2

Marx, H. & Moss, D. M. (2011). Please mind the culture gap: Intercultural development during a teacher education study abroad program. *Journal of Teacher Education*, 62(1), 35–47. DOI:10.1177/0022487110381998

Merone, L. & Tait, P. (2018). 'Climate refugees': Is it time to legally acknowledge those displaced by climate disruption? *Australian and New Zealand Journal of Public Health*, 42(6), 508–509. DOI:10.1111/1753-6405.12849

Montalban, F. M., Llorenta, F. M. & Zurita, E. (2020). Intercultural dimensions in academic mobility. In G. Rings & S. M. Rasinger (eds.), *The Cambridge handbook of intercultural communication* (pp. 475–490). Cambridge: Cambridge University Press.

Mouratidis, G. (2018). Digital nomadism: Travel, remote work and alternative lifestyles. (Dissertation Master of Applied Cultural Analysis), Lund University, Lund.

Oberg, K. (1960). Cultural shock: Adjustment to new cultural environments. *Practical Anthropology*, 4, 177–182.

Olga, H. (2020). In search of a digital nomad: Defining the phenomenon. *Information Technology & Tourism*, 22(3), 335–353. DOI:10.1007/s40558-020-00177-z

Oxfam. (2015). *Global citizenship in the classroom: A guide for teachers*. Oxford: Oxfam.

Paparusso, A. & Ambrosetti, E. (2017). To stay or to return? Return migration intentions of Moroccans in Italy. *International Migration*, 55(6), 137–155. DOI:10.1111/imig.12375

Rasinger, S. M. (2007). *Bengali–English in East London: A study in urban multilingualism*. Oxford: Peter Lang.

Rasinger, S. M. (2012). 'And everything is Polish': narrative experiences of 'new' migrants. *European Journal of Applied Linguistics and TEFL*, 1(2), 33–49.

Reichenberger, I. (2017). Digital nomads – A quest for holistic freedom in work and leisure. *Annals of Leisure Research*, 21(3), 364–380.

Rundel, C. T., Salemink, K. & Strijker, D. (2020). Exploring rural digital hubs and their possible contribution to communities in Europe. *The Journal of Rural and Community Development*, 15(3), 21–44.

Saravanan, C., Mohamad, M. & Alias, A. (2019). Coping strategies used by international students who recovered from homesickness and depression in Malaysia. *International Journal of Intercultural Relations*, 68, 77–87. DOI:10.1016/j.ijintrel.2018.11.003

Selmer, J., Lauring, J., Normann, J. & Kubovcikova, A. (2015). Context matters: Acculturation and work-related outcomes of self-initiated expatriates employed by foreign vs. local organizations. *International Journal of Intercultural Relations*, 49, 251–264. DOI:10.1016/j.ijintrel.2015.05.004

Sinatti, G. (2011). 'Mobile transmigrants' or 'unsettled returnees'? Myth of return and permanent resettlement among Senegalese migrants. *Population, Space and Place*, 17(2), 153–166. DOI:10.1002/psp.608

Smercina, V. R. (2019). Living on the move: The digital nomad mobile phenomenon identity and practice. (Dissertation MA Anthropology), University of Nevada, Las Vegas.

Statista. (2021). Number of foreign students studying in China in 2018, by selected country of origin. Online. https://bit.ly/3JBSaGJ

Sumption, M. (2019). *The Australian points-based system: What is it and what would its impact be in the UK?* Migration Observatory report. Oxford: COMPAS, University of Oxford.

Taušová, J., Bender, M., Dimitrova, R. & van de Vijver, F. (2019). The role of perceived cultural distance, personal growth initiative, language proficiencies, and tridimensional acculturation orientations for psychological adjustment among international students. *International Journal of Intercultural Relations*, 69, 11–23. DOI:10.1016/j.ijintrel.2018.11.004

Teichler, U. (2015). Academic mobility and migration: What we know and what we do not know. *European Review*, 23(S1), 6–37. DOI:10.1017/s1062798714000787

Thompson, B. Y. (2018). The digital nomad lifestyle: (Remote) work/leisure balance, privilege, and constructed community. *International Journal of the Sociology of Leisure*, 2(1–2), 27–42. DOI:10.1007/s41978-018-00030-y

Tomaz, E., Moriset, B. & Teller, J. (2021). Rural coworking spaces in the Covid-19 era. A window of opportunity? *halshs, 03235464*. Online. https://halshs.archives-ouvertes.fr/halshs-03235464

Tully, J. (2014). On global citizenship. In J. Tully (ed.), *On global citizenship: James Tully in dialogue* (pp. 3–100). London: Bloomsbury.

UNHCR. (2019). *What is a refugee?* Online. www.unhcr.org/afr/what-is-a-refugee.html (last accessed 22 April 2022).

UNHCR. (2021). *Global trends: Forced displacement in 2020*. Copenhagen: UNHRC Global Data Service.

Urry, J. (2007). *Mobilities*. Cambridge: Polity Press.

Vertovec, S. (2009). *Transnationalism*. Abingdon: Routledge.

Wang, Y. (2017). Language policy in Chinese higher education: A focus on international students in China. *European Journal of Language Policy*, 9(1), 45–66. DOI:10.3828/ejlp.2017.4

Zetter, R. (1999). Reconceptualizing the myth of return: Continuity and transition amongst the Greek-Cypriot refugees of 1974. *Journal of Refugee Studies*, 12(1), 1–22.

Žíla, O. (2015). The myth of return: Bosnian refugees and the perception of 'home'. *Geographica Pannonica*, 19(3), 130–145.

14 Intercultural Business Communication

This chapter explores the importance of intercultural communication in business, which might be regarded as an example for the growing acceptance of intercultural communication in other specific application contexts like health and the military (Chapters 15 and 16). We will first discuss the key aims and scope of intercultural business communication, before we approach its main areas of application. The chapter will conclude with comments on challenges for intercultural training and coaching, which continue to hinder business developments.

AIMS
By the end of this chapter, you should be able to:

1. describe the key aims and scope of intercultural business communication;
2. summarise the main areas of application;
3. outline challenges for the implementation of intercultural training and coaching.

> ### KEY TERMS
> intercultural business communication – intercultural management –
> flexpatriates – inpatriates – expatriates – guanxi – zhong dao

14.1 Key Aims and Scope

According to Jürgen Bolten, who was appointed to the first professorship in **intercultural business communication** at Jena University in 1992, this relatively new academic subject aims to examine and support business-related communication between participants of different cultural origins, with a focus on leadership, organisation, marketing and internal corporate communication (2006, p. 167). However, developments towards *industry 4.0*, also known as the *fourth industrial revolution*, that is, increasing the automation of manufacturing, product management and communication through customer-driven smart technology networks (Luo & Störmer 2018, p. 192), widen the scope for intercultural interventions.

After all, it is essential to develop 'a lot of collaborative and cross-cultural competencies [...] to work in network environments sustainably' that address the challenges of a highly dynamic customer-driven market with the necessary flexibility (Blanchet et al. 2014, p. 13). Examples are driverless train developments for smart cities, which help to run more trains at peak time traffic, autonomous farming support, which facilitates 24/7 farming, and modular assembly development for smart car factories, which allows for a more flexible integration of new car features. In parallel, the development from presentational Web 1.0 platforms to more interactive and customer perspectives including Web 2.0 sites opens up new opportunities for intercultural business communication input (Montiel Alafont, 2011, pp. 215–216). For example, Chang et al. (2021) elaborate on cultural differences in user-driven business networks with personal social circles as starting points in Chinese networks ('inside-out cycle') that tend to come last in 'Western' business culture ('outside-in cycle').

Academic interest in the impact of culture on business communication is considerably older than intercultural business communication as a university subject, with its blurred boundaries with economics, ethnology, philology, social psychology and other social studies. While Bolten (2006, p. 168) refers to early studies from linguistics and economics in the 1920s and 1930s (Messing, 1928; Levy, 1931; Schirmer, 1932), it could be argued that the development of intercultural communication has been significantly driven throughout its history by business interests. Examples are the comparative work by Hall, Hofstede, Trompenaars and Hampden-Turner, as well as the World Values Survey, which we examined in chapters 2 and 6. There is also a wide range of interactive studies, including business applications that draw on Brown & Levinson (1987), such as Victoria (2009), Holmes and Stubbe's analysis of workplace communication (2003) and Bolten's contributions to *intercultural coaching, competence development* and *diversity management* (2003, 2011, 2020), which illustrate the reach of intercultural business communication.

For example, in his reading of Hall's high and low context communication approach, Hooker argues that 'business practices are shaped by deeply-held cultural attitudes toward work, power, trust, wealth – and communication' (Hooker, 2012, p. 389), and then moves on to examine the extent to which the inability to cope with differences in such attitudes can lead to substantial loss of business, hence proving the need for intercultural coaching and competence development. The importance of the latter is also stressed by Blazevski, who regards intercultural competence in management as crucial for 'the success of many western companies operating in different parts of the world, and to the success of mergers and acquisitions' (Blazevski, 2018, p. 1681), although it might be worth adding that the same applies to other globally operating companies in a world that cannot be convincingly separated into West and East.

Figure 14.1 *Intercultural Business Communication* by Alíz Kovács-Zöldi

---

INDIVIDUAL TASKS

Please write down one of your own (or your friends'/family's) intercultural business experiences.
– If there was a conflict, explain how it was overcome (or how it could be overcome if that did not happen at the time).
– If the experience went smoothly, elaborate on common ground and cultural similarities, which might have facilitated that experience.

– Now, discuss the impact of that experience, for example on your knowledge, affect or skills when dealing with members of that particular culture and/or other cultures.
– Figure 14.1 highlights the potential importance of time when doing international business. Could you elaborate on that with reference to differences in time zones, annual festivities and concepts of time?

In their *Country Report Germany*, Müller and colleagues specify that 'Germany faces a skills shortage which causes nowadays an estimated macroeconomic loss of 20 billion EUR per year', especially in engineering, software development and the medical professions (Müller et al., 2017, pp. 72, 65). This has to be seen in the context of an increasing *global skills shortage* examined by the Society for Human Resource Management, which cannot be sufficiently addressed by better education and training provision at national level, but needs a wider response that includes 'supplementing the existing workforce with foreign-born talent' (2019, p. 2). All this is a strong argument for enhanced intercultural diversity management in most globalised societies at national and organisational level. In particular, it means facilitating international migration and integration of an appropriately skilled and large enough workforce, rather than erecting more artificial boundaries at national border control and company recruitment level as populist ultranationalists demand with reference to tribal traditions (see Chapter 1 on monocultural tribalism).

14.2 Areas of Application

Thomas et al. elaborate in their *Handbook of intercultural communication and cooperation* (2010) on key areas of application like **intercultural management**, *human resource development* in international organisations and *marketing* that benefit particularly from intercultural competence development and assessment.

For *management* to work most efficiently in the context of an increasing number of business partners, customers and employees with different cultural backgrounds, the handbook proposes to address intercultural negotiation, conflict management and mediation as well as project management, leadership and teamwork, with separate chapters devoted to mergers and acquisitions as well as the challenges expatriates and their families face in international assignments (Thomas et al., 2010, pp. 243–366). In the *Cambridge handbook of intercultural training*, Moeller and Harvey argue that in addition to traditional expatriates, who come back after a few years abroad, there is now a growing demand to work with **flexpatriates** and **inpatriates**, who help develop a global mindset 'that is necessary to compete beyond domestic borders' (Moeller & Harvey, 2020, p. 475). The concepts refer to flexible assignments, which might involve international commuting, rotational mobility and/or extended business travel ('flex'), as well as more mobility from subsidiaries to headquarters ('in', rather than 'ex' in **expatriates**). The Relocate Editorial highlighted such trends in manufacturing, construction, engineering, energy and technology as early as 2012, and a more recent Mercer survey (2020) confirms long-term moves in different directions and for different purposes.

A related key area for intercultural business communication is *human resource development* in international organisations. If human resources are supposed to help recruit employees who 'ensure the company's efficiency and effectiveness', then this includes for international organisations above all 'interculturally competent individuals for international assignments', because the failure rate in these assignments is particularly high (Thomas et al. 2010, p. 217). According to estimates, '40 to 70% of international projects fail, and 10 to 40% of all specialists and senior executive staff terminate their international assignment prematurely' (Thomas et al., 2010, p. 216). It is therefore highly recommendable to complement established evaluation methods in recruitment with tools for the assessment of intercultural competence (see Chapter 17). However, Thomas et al. go well beyond necessary adaptations in recruitment when they recommend the development of a human resource cycle framed by strategic qualification diagnosis, a clear leadership model, and an international strategy that starts at personnel marketing level and accompanies key employees from recruitment to training for assignments and potential reintegration with a view to creating a pool of competent staff for future assignments (Thomas et al., 2010, pp. 217–227). To develop and assess the intercultural communicative competences of those staff, shifts in most recent research should be taken into account, which consider more fully processual, contextual, relational, interpersonal and emic (relating to concepts from within a partner culture, e.g. guanxi) as well as emotional value and well-being perspectives (Szkudlarek et al., 2020). Finally, companies that work increasingly with employees from different cultural backgrounds might also benefit from interculturally competent staff in their human resource department, for which the training of existing staff and/or appropriate new recruitment should be considered.

Marketing is another key area for intercultural business communication. While basic socio-psychological principles and techniques of consumer guidance are universal (see Montiel Alafont, 2020, p. 152 on face-saving as a pragmatic social function rather than an Asian particularity), culture tends to act as a major moderator variable both in *standardised and differentiated marketing*, that is, it shapes the way such principles and techniques are applied. IKEA is an example of *standardised marketing*, inasmuch as it works from Sweden to China with images of Scandinavian landscapes and lifestyles as well as a comparable product range that focuses on functional simplicity (Daxue, 2021). However, it has to consider *cultural values*, *preferences* and *taboos*, which means that intercultural input is essential from the translation of the brand name to the design of playgrounds for children in its subsidiaries (Felser, 2010, pp. 228–229). Similar challenges hit brands like Coca Cola and McDonald's, as they have to strike a balance between their marketing of a particular vision of the American way of life and adaptation to cultural differences. Interconnected with cultural frames of reference are political, legal, economic and socio-psychological dimensions, and Felser sees dissimilarities in particular in the degree of individualism, the importance of time, attitudes with regard to taking action, and concepts of Self and Other (2010, pp. 235–238; see also Chapter 5).

GROUP TASKS

Search for popular McDonald's videoclips on YouTube and select three from the United States and three from China.

- What similarities can you see, and what differences, e.g. in the people shown, their interaction, camera perspectives and/or music in the background?

- How would you explain these similarities and differences in marketing? You might want to draw on contrastive, interactive and/or psychological approaches for this (Chapters 5, 7 and 10).

In the case of IKEA, Daxue (2021) reports the need to consider also the *location of shops, furniture delivery options* and *food offers* in China: for example, selecting locations with good metro or train connections and establishing smaller 'click and collect' shops in city centres is a response to the vastly greater use of public transport in Chinese cities than in European or US American cities. Special delivery deals with Amazon and others have also been struck to ease the difficulties of bringing larger furniture home by public transport, while at the same time addressing strong online shopping trends. Finally, a mixed food offer consisting of IKEA standards like Swedish meatballs and local Chinese specialities like the Sichuan hotpot help to keep customers in the shop for longer and generate extra revenue through cafeterias (Daxue, 2021).

TASKS

Search for national differentiation at McDonald's, for example through menu adaptation from the United States to China, India and your place of origin.

– Which national cultural differences have already been considered when marketing McDonald's in these cultures, and which differences and/or similarities might be worth adding?

Be it management, human resource development or marketing, intercultural business communication should not only be approached from European or US American perspectives, especially if one of the business partners comes from other parts of the world. In the case of IKEA's work in China, it might be particularly helpful to include the social capital based **guanxi** concept, which is an important topic in Chinese management studies due to its link to human resource management (Lin, 2011), risk, conflict and knowledge management (Pearce, 2011, Wong & Tjosvold, 2010, Buckley et al., 2010) and industrial marketing management (Gao et al., 2010). A study by Wang & Chen (2009, p. 87) defines Guanxi as relationship marketing that is associated with long-term engagement, cooperation, trust and mutual benefit.

Luo draws on this research to develop his Guanxi-based model of intercultural competence, which indicates the potential impact of a harmony-based cultural framework on economic, individual and social dimensions, such as mutual benefit and fairness, empathy and adaptation, as well as reciprocity, trust, bonding and favour exchange (Luo, 2013, pp. 75–76). Going the non-linear circular middle-way (**zhong dao**) is essential to achieve the necessary harmony for 'a mutually-defining and complementary relationship' (Chen, 2013, p. 3; see also Chapter 3). This circle concept goes well beyond traditional monocultural binaries, within which rule- or task-based 'Westerners' encounter relationship-based Chinese (see Hooker, 2012, p. 394). In particular, it helps to understand interrelated aspects of social capital in China and identify the common ground on which long-lasting business relations could be built, such as *reciprocity, trust, bonding* and *favour exchange*, which are also important concepts in the so-called West.

The competence to understand and act on such common ground is essential to reject (neo-)colonial hierarchies, within which 'Westerners' are presented as superior rational (task-oriented) beings in contrast to an irrational 'Orient' (Said, 2003, p. 48 on Orientalism; see Chapter 4), or 'Easterners' are projected as superior human beings in contrast to aggressive, imperialist and non-human 'Westerners'

(Buruma & Margalit, 2005, p. 11 on Occidentalism). Such artificial monocultural hierarchies have to be rejected in order to open up a Third Space for the negotiation of genuine business partnerships that consider socio-economic key concepts of all parties involved. In Chapter 3, we outlined as competing and partially complementary concepts South African **ubuntu**, Māori **whānau**, Kichwa **alli kawsay**, Japanese **kizuna**, Malayan **silaturahmi** and Hindu **vishwa roopa darshanam**.

Such an open approach, accepting partners as equals, allows for a more competent and successful business exchange in the context of contemporary demands for decolonisation and multi-perspectivity. Academic research in intercultural business communication, which is still very US-centric, is likely to follow global business practice.

14.3 Challenges for Intercultural Training and Coaching

At the beginning of this millennium, Bolten had already noticed an increase in specific on the job *coaching* and a decrease in preparatory off the job *training*, which he links to increasingly short-term decisions on international ventures and assignments, a lack of specific job-oriented intercultural training, scepticism regarding intercultural competence assessment, and the competition of intercultural offers with supposedly more important foreign language programmes (Bolten, 2003, p. 1). It is worth examining the extent to which the relatively slow advance or even decline of intercultural training in other areas, like the health and military services, can also be explained in such terms. However, the reduction of the Defence Centre for Languages and Culture in the Defence Academy in Shrivenham (UK) to a language centre (see Section 16.3) suggests that similar reasons, starting with rivalry between intercultural and foreign language provisions, might have played a significant role.

Intercultural training providers like CORE Languages have reacted to these challenges by highlighting the value of a coaching approach to help clients 'set and meet goals in their work environment', think through 'situations in a critical – as opposed to reactive – manner' and develop intercultural competence (CORE, 2022). How far and how exactly intercultural competence skills can be acquired solely from a specific and relatively unique job-related problem is not convincingly explained. However, the value of coaching is likely to increase with a transparent structure and a methodology that involves client and participants in a culturally challenging situation, such as for example inefficient multinational teamwork.

For this purpose, Bolten suggests a five-phase structure consisting of coordination between coach–team and client, recording of the situation, pre-analysis, joint analysis and joint setting of targets (Bolten, 2003, p. 3). In the coordination phase, the coaches – who should be selected with regard to their knowledge and experience of the cultures involved – might also want to accompany the team members in their everyday work, for example, for two days (coaches as learners). Team interactions should then be video recorded before coaches run a pre-analysis of the situation. This is followed up by a joint analysis with team members, and a joint setting of targets (2003, pp. 3–6).

All this does not necessarily compensate for the loss of training, and the BFC Group remains clear in its presentation of coaching as a strategy that it should follow training, that is, 'coaching is more suited to employees who already have the knowledge and skills, but are encountering issues or barriers which are preventing them from utilising them to full effect and achieving their maximum potential in the workplace for the company' (BFC, 2021).

GROUP TASK

Design a SMART (Specific, Measurable, Appropriate, Realistic, Time-restricted) training programme for IKEA management trainees in Stockholm. They will come from Sweden, Germany and the UK with ample IKEA sales experience, but have now been assigned to support the establishment of a new IKEA shop in China. Lead questions:

– What intercultural knowledge, skills and attitudes do you want to teach, for what personal, social, strategic and specialised competence development (see Chapter 3)?
– What should the trainers' qualifications be?

However, if training is not an option at the beginning, coaching might also be a valuable starting point that could trigger managerial interest in more intercultural provision. After all, a survey of more than 360 recruitment decision-makers at larger companies in nine nations, including the United States, China and India, confirms that employers regard intercultural skills as essential to boost earnings, with one interviewee outlining that 'employees with these skills bring in new clients, work within diverse teams and support a good brand and reputation' (British Council, 2013).

14.4 In Summary

Although the development of most theories and key concepts in the history of intercultural communication have been influenced by cultural challenges in business, intercultural business communication, which focuses on the reduction of these difficulties, is a relatively new academic discipline. So far, most studies in that discipline examine ways of improving intercultural management, human resource development and international marketing, but they are limited due to their US-centrism and Eurocentrism. In order to open up to a decolonised version of global business genuinely, key concepts from other parts of the world, such as Chinese *guanxi* and *zhong dao*, South African *ubuntu*, and Hindu *vishwa roopa darshanam*, have to be fully incorporated in global as well as country specific training programmes. The notable decline in preparatory off-the-job training is in this context very regrettable, as specific on-the-job coaching cannot fully compensate for the concepts and skills development originally provided by training programmes.

DISCUSSION QUESTIONS

– From your own experience, whether as employer, employee or customer, which business – and/or exemplary companies, departments and employees – would particularly benefit from more intercultural training or coaching, and why?
– Considering that 'time is money', in which situation might training, coaching or a combination of both be most appropriate for which business?

Now that you are well aware of the importance and reach of intercultural business communication, please read the following case study on a clash between US-American and Japanese managers, and answer these questions:

a. How would you explain the following situation?
b. What would you do differently to avoid similar challenges?

CASE STUDY

Donald T., a manager of a US firm, and selected Japanese executives had agreed on key policies and strategies for a joint venture, when the review meeting came.

It was chaired by Mr Tanaka, the president of the Japanese firm, who had helped advance the negotiations, but his grandfather, the preceding president, attended it as well. After more constructive discussions, the 80-year-old grandfather stood up and outlined in detail, the extent to which some of the plans broke with traditional practices in the company.

To Tom's surprise, Tanaka did not defend the results of their negotiations, so Tom felt that he had to do that for him with a strong counter speech. However, nobody else supported him, the meeting was postponed shortly afterwards, and a few days later the Japanese firm cancelled the plans for the joint venture.

References

BCF Group (2021). What is the difference between training and coaching? https://bit.ly/3Omi1Ge (last accessed 19 April 2022).

Blanchet, M., Rinn, T., von Thaden, G. & de Thieulloy, G. (2014). *Industry 4.0 – The new industrial revolution – How Europe will succeed*. Munich: Roland Berger Strategy Consultants. Online. https://bit.ly/3vwaGLr (last accessed 19 April 2022).

Blazevski, I. (2018). The relevance of intercultural competence for intercultural management. *KNOWLEDGE*, 26(6), 1681–1686.

Bolten, J. (2003). Phasen des interkulturellen Coachings – Erfahrungen aus der Praxis. *Interculture*, 2(3), 1–7.

Bolten, J. (2006). Interkulturelle Wirtschaftskommunikation. In Tsvasman, L. R. (ed.), *Das große Lexikon Medien und Kommunikation* (pp. 167–170). Würzburg: Ergon.

Bolten, J. (2011). Diversity Management als interkulturelle Prozessmoderation. *Interculture*, 10(13), 25–38.

Bolten, J. (2020). Rethinking intercultural competence. In G. Rings & S. M. Rasinger (eds.), *The Cambridge handbook of intercultural communication* (pp. 56–67). Cambridge: Cambridge University Press.

British Council (2013). Culture at work: The value of intercultural skills in the workplace. Online. https://bit.ly/3rBpcAo (last accessed 19 April 2022).

Brown, P. & Levinson, S. C. (1987). *Politeness: Some universals in language usage.* Cambridge: Cambridge University Press.

Buckley, P. J., Clegg, J. & Tan, H. (2010). Cultural awareness in knowledge transfer in China: The role of Guanxi and Mianzi. In P. J. Buckley (ed.), *Foreign direct investment: China and the world economy* (pp. 165–191). Basingstoke: Palgrave Macmillan.

Buruma, I. & Margalit, A. (2005). *Occidentalism: The West in the eyes of its enemies.* Atlantic Books.

Chang, L.-C., et al. (2021). User-driven business model innovation: An ethnographic inquiry into Toutiao in the Chinese context. *Asia Pacific Business Review*, 27(3), 359–377. DOI:10.1080/13602381.2021.1895492

Chen, G.-M. (2013). A zhong dao model of management in global context. *Intercultural Communication Studies*, 22(1), 1–8.

CORE Languages (2022). Intercultural coaching and training. www.corelanguages.com/blog/intercultural-training-vs.-coaching (last accessed 22 April 2022).

Daxue Consulting (2021). IKEA in China: Big furniture retail adapts to the Chinese market. 13 February. https://daxueconsulting.com/ikea-in-china (last accessed 19 April 2022).

Felser, G. (2010). Intercultural marketing. In A. Thomas, E.-U. Kinast, & S. Schroll-Machl (eds.), *Handbook of intercultural communication and cooperation: Basics and areas of application* (pp. 228–241). Göttingen: Vandenhoeck & Ruprecht.

Gao, H. Z., Ballantyne, D. & Knight, J. G. (2010). Paradoxes and guanxi dilemmas in emerging Chinese–Western intercultural relationships. *Industrial Marketing Management*, 39(2), 264–272.

Holmes, J. & Stubbe, M. (2003). *Power and politeness in the workplace: A sociolinguistic analysis of talk at work.* Harlow: Pearson.

Hooker, J. N. (2012). Cultural differences in business communication. In C. B. Paulston, S. F. Kiesling & E. S. Rangel (eds.) *The handbook of intercultural discourse and communication* (pp. 389–407). Malden, MA: Wiley-Blackwell.

Levy, H. (1931). Sprache und Wirtschaftswissenschaft. *Neuphilologische Monatsschrift*, 2, 35–47.

Lin, L. H. (2011). Cultural and organizational antecedents of Guanxi: The Chinese cases. *Journal of Business Ethics*, 99, 441–451.

Luo, X. (2013). Guanxi competence as intercultural competence in business contexts: A Chinese perspective. *interculture journal: Online-Zeitschrift für interkulturelle Studien*, 12(20), 69–89. https://nbn-resolving.org/urn:nbn:de:0168-ssoar-454271

Luo, X. & Störmer, M. (2018). Chancen und Herausforderungen der Organisations- und Personalentwicklung im Zeitalter der Industrie 4.0 – Bestandsaufnahme und Ausblick. In F. U. Siems & M.-C. Papen (eds.), *Kommunikation und Technik* (pp. 191–209). Wiesbaden: Springer.

Mercer (2020). Worldwide survey of international assignment policies and practices. Online. https://bit.ly/3rCzIYt (last accessed 19 April 2022).

Messing, E. E. J. (1928). Methoden und Ergebnisse der wirtschaftssprachlichen Forschung. In A. W. Sijthoff (ed.), *Actes du premier congrès international de linguistes à La Haye, du 10-15 avril 1928* (pp. 140–142). Leiden: Sijthoff.

Moeller, M. & Harvey, M. (2020). Developing intercultural competency training in global organizations. In D. Landis & D. P. S. Bhawuk (eds.), *The Cambridge handbook of intercultural training* (pp. 475–494). Cambridge: Cambridge University Press.

Montiel Alafont, F. J. (2011). Kulturelle Identität und Place Branding im Internet zwischen Steuerung und Eigendynamik: Der Fall Spanien. In S. Höhne, N. Bünsch & R. P. Ziegler (eds.), *Kulturbranding III: Positionen, Ambivalenzen, Perspektiven zwischen Markenbildung und Kultur* (pp. 203–229). Leipzig: Leipziger Universitätsverlag.

Montiel Alafont, F. J. (2020). Direktheit, Indirektheit und Ironie in der Fremdsprachendidaktik des Spanischen – Über das Konzept der kulturellen Stile und seine Bedeutung für das interkulturelle Lernen im Fremdsprachenunterricht. *Zeitschrift für Interkulturellen Fremdsprachenunterricht*, 25(1), 145–162.

Müller, A. P., Montiel Alafont, F. J. & Lietz, R. (2017). *Country report Germany: Halfway to integration: Observations on recognition, participation, and diversity management practices in the region of Baden.* Karlsruhe: Karlshochschule International University.

Pearce, E. H. (2011). The use of guanxi to minimize business and regulatory risk in China. In J. Reuvid (ed.), *Business Insights China: Practical advice on operational strategy and risk management* (pp. 138–143). London: Kogan Page.

Relocate Editorial (2012). Flexpatriate assignments: Trends and policy implications. 4 December. https://bit.ly/3uZ7jhm (last accessed 19 April 2022).

Said, E. W. (2003 [1978]). *Orientalism*. London: Penguin.

Schirmer, A. (1932). Die Wirtschaftssprache als Spiegel der Wirtschaftsgeschichte. In E. E. J. Messing (ed.), *Zur Wirtschaftslinguistik: Eine Auswahl von kleineren und größeren Beiträgen über Wert und Bedeutung, Erforschung und Unterweisung der Sprache des wirtschaftlichen Verkehrs* (pp. 7–26). Rotterdam: Nijgh U. van Ditmar.

Society for Human Resource Management (2019). *The global skills shortage: Bridging the talent gap with education, training and sourcing.* Alexandria, VA: SHRM Research Department.

Szkudlarek, B., Osland, J. S., Nardon, L. & Zander, L. (2020). Communication and culture in international business – Moving the field forward. *Journal of World Business*, 55(6) 1–9.

Thomas, A., Kinast, E.-U. & Schroll-Machl, S. (eds.) (2010). *Handbook of intercultural communication and cooperation. Vol. 1: Basics and areas of application.* Göttingen: Vandenhoeck & Ruprecht.

Victoria, M. (2009). Power and politeness: A study of social interaction in business meetings with multicultural participation. *ESP Across Cultures*, 6, 129–140.

Wang, T. & Chen L. R. (2009). Commercial guanxi in the context of Chinese native culture: An exploratory research. *Frontiers of Business Research in China*, 3(1), 79–102.

Wong, A. & Tjosvold, D. (2010). Guanxi and conflict management for effective partnering with competitors in China. *British Journal of Management*, 21(3), 772–788.

15 Intercultural Communication in Health Services

In this chapter, we will continue our discussion of intercultural communication in different contexts by looking at healthcare settings. We will begin by exploring the experiences of healthcare professionals and patients, before moving to a discussion of intercultural communication and competence in this setting. We will also touch on linguistic issues and aspects related to translation, drawing parallels to what we discussed in Chapter 7.

AIMS
By the end of this chapter, you will be able to:

1. describe the intercultural experiences of those participating in healthcare settings;
2. explain the role of intercultural competence in the context of healthcare settings;
3. explore linguistic aspects in intercultural healthcare settings.

> **KEY TERMS**
> rituals – intercultural competence – translation

15.1 Cultural Diversity and Healthcare: Illness, Pain and Death

> **TASK**
>
> At what point do you consider it necessary to see a medical or healthcare professional?
>
> Think of the last time you saw a medical or healthcare professional, such as a doctor, nurse, physiotherapist or radiographer. What were the key features of your interaction with them? Which of these features would you describe as due to cultural factors?

Figure 15.1 *Healthcare Communication* by Alíz Kovács-Zöldi

The medical field is one that shows high levels of diversity with regard to the people who operate within it. The National Health Service (NHS) in England, for example, employs 1.3 million people, 22.1 per cent of whom identify as ethnically non-White, and 30.2 per cent of all those in medical roles are of Asian origin (UK Government, 2021). And, of course, patients also come from a wide range of backgrounds: for example, in 2016/17, 41 per cent of the Imperial College Healthcare NHS Trust, which covers parts of London, identified as White, 16 per cent as 'other', 10 per cent as Asian, and 10 per cent as Black (Harrison-White, 2017).

Cultural and linguistic diversity can influence even the most basic concepts that are at the core of medicine and healthcare (Goddard & Ye, 2016), such as 'pain'. Attitudes towards seeking medical help can also vary significantly (Watson et al., 2012). For example, it has been reported that different ethnic groups show different sensitivity to pain stimuli but also have different expectations as to what constitutes pain that requires medical attention: Aboriginal Australians as well as people in rural Nepal, for example, have been found not to consider even prolonged back pain to be a medical condition that requires treatment (Peacock & Patel, 2008). In an experiment on pain perception with African-American and White college students, African Americans rated pain stimuli as more unpleasant than White, and pain coping mechanisms can also differ between cultural groups (Callister, 2016). At the same time, patients of certain ethnic groups, such as Black or Hispanic, are more likely to be under-treated for pain, which suggests stereotyping by race and ethnicity by parts of the medical profession (Peacock & Patel, 2008, p. 7). But this is not just an issue of ethnicity or race, but also professional cultures: pain, and sickness in general, is experienced as a high-context event (see Chapter 8) by patients, and this is met by clinicians who are used to operating in a subculture that prefers low-context communication based on numbers and data (Hallenbeck, 2013).

Racial stereotypes, discrimination and differences in treatment are also prevalent in other areas of healthcare. For example, there is evidence that African Americans in the United States are significantly over-diagnosed with schizophrenia, with Blow and colleagues highlighting 'continued ethnic disparities in diagnostic patterns' and recommending a greater emphasis on cultural competency by healthcare providers (Blow et al., 2004, p. 841). In addition, poor communication can lead to worse treatment (Watson et al., 2012). This is particularly interesting since it illustrates a marked shift in the perception of mental illness and schizophrenia in particular: between the 1920s and 1950s, schizophrenia was often considered a 'white, middle-class housewife illness' (Metzl, 2014, p. 264). This shift from White women to Black men also suggests a culture-gender link already discussed in Chapter 4.

Cultural differences also impact the most fundamental aspects of life: the conceptualisation of death. In Western societies, death is seen as an instant sharp break that demarcates the change from being alive to being not alive (i.e., dead), like a light switch being flipped. In many Southeast Asian cultures however, death is perceived as a process that begins before and can last well beyond the physical end of life and the Western conception of death. Similarly, the Merina people in Madagascar see death as part of a wider process of life that starts with birth and ends only with the total decomposition of the dead body (Bloch, 1996).

Culture, religion and value systems play an important role in end-of-life settings such as those often encountered in Intensive Care Units (ICU). In the UK and other Western countries, a person is legally dead once brain death has occurred, that is, 'when a person on an artificial life support machine no longer has any brain functions' (NHS, 2019). Brain death also constitutes the decision point when it comes to organ donation (other than live donations from blood relatives for example). Brain death, and the resulting withdrawal of medical treatment can, however, be problematic: in some interpretations of Islam, for example, the notion of brain death is controversial as the (rest of the) body is still alive (Bein, 2015): 'many Muslims believe that they are not owners of their own body and have no right to decide on continuing or withdrawing therapy' (Bein, 2017, p. 230). Yet, Islam also puts strong emphasis on helping others, and from this angle, organ donation is considered positive and permissible (Ghaly, 2012; Malagon, 2006).

Similar controversies exist in Chinese and other East Asian cultures influenced by Buddhism, Confucianism and Taoism where *chi* – a 'life force' that permeates the entire body, not just the brain – is more important than brain death; life only ends when 'chi' leaves the body. A human's personality is perceived not by its physical form, but the human body is seen as a 'temporal container' for the ever-rebirthing soul (Bein 2017, p. 230). Death, then, goes beyond the fact that the brain stops working.

Strongly related to illness and death are **rituals**, actions that follow certain set patterns, are strongly symbolic (Mitchell, 1996) and are often performed during crises (Turner, 1969), where they 'may help maintain group solidarity and equilibrium and provide a sense of control over fate and destiny' (Crawford et al., 2015, p. 31). Rituals can play a particularly important part for those in the diaspora, who are away from their original homeland, and being able to carry out cultural and religious practices surrounding death constitutes a crucial link to cultural and religious heritage (Venkatasalu et al., 2014).

TASK

In groups, discuss how your respective cultures conceptualise death. What are the similarities, and what are the differences?

Can you imagine other problems in healthcare settings that may result from the differences?

15.2 Communication in the Healthcare Setting

15.2.1 Cultural Practices and Patient Care

Cultural differences in the conceptualisation and interpretation of key aspects of healthcare settings as outlined above are, unsurprisingly, also mirrored in communicative and wider interactional and behavioural preferences and practices. In some Asian cultures, such as China or Korea for example, it is not uncommon that medical information, especially around terminal illness, is communicated via the patient's family rather than to the patient themselves, even if the patient is fully competent (Hume & Malpas, 2016). This may mean that a patient will not receive all the information about their own health if their family do not consider it appropriate; the communication between doctors and nurses and the patients is hence more indirect than we might expect.

There are also differences in the way care is provided, and nurses and other healthcare and medical professionals need to align their own cultural preferences and practices with those they care for (Almutairi et al., 2015). Nurses in two Swedish ICUs, for example, reported that patients of certain cultural backgrounds tend to receive more visitors, and that family members are keen to be more actively involved in the care of their relatives; this, in turn causes logistical challenges for healthcare staff, including issues of physical space in the ICU. Language barriers further complicate the situation (Listerfelt et al., 2019); we will look at this in more detail later in this chapter.

Intercultural competence is a key skill in the modern healthcare context and requires a skillset that goes well beyond clinical knowledge (Lin et al., 2019). Yet, like any other skill, it is not a given but needs to be learned or acquired (we talk more about the development of intercultural competence in Chapter 17). Training materials provide medical and healthcare professionals in the US with a 'manual' on how to work with patients from particular backgrounds. For example, Chong's *The Latino patient: A cultural guide for health care providers* (Chong, 2002) suggests that healthcare providers caring for Latino patients in the US should make use of Latinos' strong sense of family:

> [S]uggesting that a patient stop smoking for the purpose of improving personal health is not generally an effective way of communicating the message. Rather, appealing to the well-being of the family should be a major component of the message to a patient.
>
> (Chong, 2002, p. 69)

Of course, such handbooks and manuals make use of rather simplistic and essentialist notions of ethnic groups – as we have seen in Chapter 13, Latinos in the US do not constitute a homogeneous group but one that shows considerable internal diversity. Providing culturally sensitive care is important for many healthcare professionals; yet, resources are not always readily available to cater for specific cultural needs, such as accommodating for patients' prayer times, and so on (Ian et al., 2016).

Teal & Street (2009, pp. 537–540) highlight five communication skills that physicians need to operate successfully in an intercultural context: non-verbal behaviour, including active listening; verbal behaviour that allows patients to express their perspectives and responds in a non-judgemental fashion; recognition and exploration of potential cultural differences; incorporation of and adaptation to cultural knowledge; and negotiation and collaboration. Yet, while the importance of intercultural competence is now widely acknowledged, actual support for it is not always forthcoming, and lack of adequate resourcing and systemic support can be stumbling blocks for training (Hagqvist et al., 2020). In addition, Watson and colleagues remind us that overly simplistic approaches to intercultural communication and competence (of the type 'Korean patients are like this'; 'Latino doctors behave like that') are insufficient and argue that explanatory models need to account for the socio-historical background of, and power dimensions behind, intercultural interaction (Watson et al., 2012). We have also seen this line of argument in our discussion of gender roles in Chapter 9.

15.2.2 Intercultural Encounters between Healthcare Professionals

Intercultural issues not only arise in communication between healthcare professionals and patients, but also between professionals. In an Australian study of nurses' and student nurses' experiences with intercultural communication, Henderson et al. (2016) identified four themes that impacted on intercultural communication: prejudice, unfamiliarity with cultural boundaries, stereotyping of cultural behaviours and linguistic problems (2016, p. 73). In New Zealand, Brunton & Cook (2018) compared nurses who trained in NZ with those who had trained abroad, including China, the Philippines and India. Their study found that unfamiliar ways of working and the feeling of being judged, as well as communicative patterns that are different from their own cultural preferences, could lead to tension between the groups. But conflicts were also found around cultural values, such as different understandings and conceptualisations of key aspects such as compassion. These differences manifested themselves in diverse ways such as different preferences when it came to being interrupted in conversations (see our discussion of turn-taking in Chapter 7), or conceptions of what makes a 'caring' nurse.

15.3 Language in the Healthcare Setting

While the sections 15.1 and 15.2 have looked at issues pertaining to communication in medical settings more broadly, this section will consider a few specifically linguistic aspects that may occur.

TASK

Look up the following medical terms: *cephalgia*; *chondromalacia patellae*; *mediastinal emphysema*.

15.3.1   Language and Medicine

In our discussion of pain at the start of this chapter, we have already mentioned that patients and medical professionals operate differently in terms of their communicative preferences (high-context versus low-context). These differences permeate all levels of language, including vocabulary. Even in an *intra*cultural context, the language used by medical professionals at times sounds like a foreign language altogether, and for those new to the field, such as trainee doctors or nurses, the acquisition of medical terminology feels like the learning of a new language (Pamela & Groopman, 2011): *cephalgia* refers to a headache, *chondromalacia patellae* is more commonly known as 'runner's knee', and a *mediastinal emphysema* refers to an injury following a scuba diving accident where air is trapped in the chest cavity between the lungs. While medical terms, usually derived from Latin, make medical language appear inaccessible to laypeople, accurate terminology is vital for accurate diagnoses and effective treatments (Quigley & Shanahan, 2009).

In an intercultural context, and especially where participants speak different languages, or where language proficiency of the patient is considerably lower than that of the medical professional, the above problem is exacerbated. Doctors and nurses caring for cancer patients in New Zealand reported that language barriers were one of the main problems in care interactions and in fact outweigh other cultural differences (Watts et al., 2017). In a study on the East Coast of the United States, Squires et al. (2019) found that dealing with patients with limited English language proficiency added considerably to the workload of those providing medical care, and in turn can have detrimental effects on the care patients receive. The authors suggest the matching of professionals and patients on a language basis. In a similar vein, Schouten et al. (2020, p. 2607) recommend an integrated approach to healthcare that comprises both language lessons and culturally tailored patient education about proper medication use. In their New Zealand study mentioned above, Brunton and Cook found linguistic barriers also amongst healthcare professionals, with New Zealand nurses using slang unfamiliar to international nurses, and international nurses speaking in their own language with each other (Brunton & Cook, 2018).

15.3.2   Bridging the Linguistic Gap: Interpreters in the Medical Context

We have already looked at **translation** and the role of interpreters in our discussion of linguistic approaches to intercultural communication in Chapter 7. In an intercultural medical context, where precision of communication between two parties who do not speak the same language is crucial, interpreters play a unique role. Not only do they serve as 'language converters' or conduits to allow for the successful transmission of messages between patients and medical professionals, but they are also co-participants in the interaction, often taking the role of patient advocates in that they speak *for* the patient and act as mediators in interactions where the balance of power is often skewed towards the medical professionals (Angelelli, 2012). Haffner provides an interesting example from her own interpreting practice where she explains (rather than simply translates) the workings of an epidural block during childbirth to a Mexican (Spanish-speaking) patient, and acts as a negotiator between medical professionals and the patient's cultural beliefs about the treatment (Haffner, 1992).

Access to high quality professional medical interpretation services is important and may include both traditional face-to-face but also remote simultaneous medical interpreting (RSMI), where the interpreters sit outside the physical interaction between the clinician and the patients. In reality, this role is often performed by patients' family, friends, or even children, leading to increased stress for both patients and clinicians (Jones & Gill, 1998). A study by Gany et al. (2007) in New York showed that patients of various linguistic backgrounds evaluated the use of RSMI positively, in particular with regard to a higher level of respect provided by their doctors, suggesting the mediating role that interpreters often have. However, it can often be difficult to ascertain when to provide an interpreter, especially if a patient does not explicitly ask for one (Okrainec et al., 2014).

15.4 In Summary

Illness and death are an unavoidable part of life, and most people will be in contact with the medical profession at some point during their lifetime. In this chapter, we have seen that the various elements of intercultural communication we have discussed in this book so far are also reflected in the medical and healthcare context. Cultural belief systems, stereotypes, unequal power distribution, as well as cultural and linguistic barriers, play an important role in the interaction between patients and healthcare professionals, and intercultural and linguistic competence becomes ever more important.

DISCUSSION QUESTIONS

Take some time to reflect on your own experiences with illness or even death critically, either directly or indirectly through families or friends. How have cultural and/or linguistic aspects affected these experiences? Have you encountered issues similar to those we have discussed in the chapter? Have there been others, too?

CASE STUDY

Spanish nurses in a hospital in southern Spain reported on the (occasional) practice of separating patients by nationality, whereby Spanish and Moroccan patients would be allocated to different rooms (adapted from Plaza del Pino et al., 2013).

What factors can you identify that underlie this practice?

Critically evaluate this practice in the light of intercultural theory.

References

Almutairi, A. F., McCarthy, A. & Gardner, G. E. (2015). Understanding cultural competence in a multicultural nursing workforce: Registered nurses' experience in Saudi Arabia. *Journal of Transcultural Nursing*, 26(1), 16–23. DOI:10.1177/1043659614523992

Angelelli, C. (2012). Medicine. In C. B. Paulston, S. F. Kiesling & E. S. Rangel (eds.), *The handbook of intercultural discourse and communication* (pp. 430–448). Malden, MA: Wiley-Blackwell.

Bein, T. (2015). Interkulturelle Kompetenz: Umgang mit Fremdheit in der Intensivmedizin [Intercultural competence: Management of foreignness in intensive care medicine]. *Der Anaesthesist*, 64(8), 562.

Bein, T. (2017). Understanding intercultural competence in intensive care medicine. *Intensive Care Medicine*, 43(2), 229–231. https://dx.doi.org/10.1007/s00134-016-4432-2

Bloch, M. (1996). Death. In A. Barnard & J. Spencer (eds.), *Encyclopedia of social and cultural anthropology* (pp. 149–151). London: Routledge.

Blow, F. C., Zeber, J. E., McCarthy, J. F., Valenstein, M., Gillon, L. & Bingham, C. R. (2004). Ethnicity and diagnostic patterns in veterans with psychoses. *Social Psychiatry and Psychiatric Epidemiology*, 39(10), 841–851. DOI:10.1007/s00127-004-0824-7

Brunton, M. & Cook, C. (2018). Dis/integrating cultural difference in practice and communication: A qualitative study of host and migrant registered nurse perspectives from New Zealand. *International Journal of Nursing Studies*, 83, 18–24. DOI:10.1016/j.ijnurstu.2018.04.005

Callister, L. C. (2016). Cultural influences on pain perceptions and behaviors. *Home Health Care Management & Practice*, 15(3), 207–211. DOI:10.1177/1084822302250687

Chong, N. (2002). *The Latino patient: A cultural guide for health care providers*. Yarmouth, ME: Intercultural Press.

Crawford, P., Brown, B., Baker, C., Tischler, V. & Abrams, B. (2015). *Health humanities*. Basingstoke: Palgrave.

Gany, F., Leng, J., Shapiro, E., Abramson, D., Motola, I., Shield, D. C. & Changrani, J. (2007). Patient satisfaction with different interpreting methods: A randomized controlled trial. *Journal of General Internal Medicine*, 22(2), 312–318. DOI:10.1007/s11606-007-0360-8

Ghaly, M. (2012). Religio-ethical discussions on organ donation among Muslims in Europe: An example of transnational Islamic bioethics. *Medicine, Health Care and Philosophy*, 15(2), 207–220. DOI:10.1007/s11019-011-9352-x

Goddard, C. & Ye, Z. (2016). *'Happiness' and 'pain' across languages and cultures*: Amsterdam: John Benjamins.

Haffner, L. (1992). Translation is not enough: Interpreting in a medical setting. *The Western Journal of Medicine*, 157, 255–259.

Hagqvist, P., Oikarainen, A., Tuomikoski, A. M., Juntunen, J. & Mikkonen, K. (2020). Clinical mentors' experiences of their intercultural communication competence in mentoring culturally and linguistically diverse nursing students: A qualitative study. *Nurse Education Today*, 87, 104348. DOI:10.1016/j.nedt.2020.104348

Hallenbeck, J. (2013). Pain and intercultural communication. In R. J. Moore (ed.), *Handbook of pain and palliative care: Biopsychosocial and environmental approaches for the life course* (pp. 19–34). Cham: Springer.

Harrison-White, S. (2017). *Annual patient equality and diversity report 2016/17*. London: Imperial College Healthcare NHS Trust.

Henderson, S., Barker, M. & Mak, A. (2016). Strategies used by nurses, academics and students to overcome intercultural communication challenges. *Nurse Education in Practice*, 16(1), 71–78. DOI:10.1016/j.nepr.2015.08.010

Hume, C. & Malpas, P. (2016). A case based reflection on communicating end of life information in non-English speaking patients. *Patient Education and Counseling*, 99(11), 1911–1913. DOI:10.1016/j.pec.2016.06.012

Ian, C., Nakamura-Florez, E. & Lee, Y. M. (2016). Registered nurses' experiences with caring for non-English speaking patients. *Applied Nursing Research*, 30, 257–260. DOI:10.1016/j.apnr.2015.11.009

Jones, D. & Gill, P. (1998). Breaking down language barriers. *British Medical Journal*, 316, 1476.

Lin, M. H., Wu, C. Y. & Hsu, H. C. (2019). Exploring the experiences of cultural competence among clinical nurses in Taiwan. *Applied Nursing Research*, 45, 6–11. DOI:10.1016/j.apnr.2018.11.001

Listerfelt, S., Fridh, I. & Lindahl, B. (2019). Facing the unfamiliar: Nurses' transcultural care in intensive care – A focus group study. *Intensive & Critical Care Nursing*, 55, 102752. DOI:10.1016/j.iccn.2019.08.002

Malagon, S. (2006). Study of the immigrant population's attitude towards organ donation in two groups from Pakistan and Morocco. *Revista de Bioetica Derecho*, 7, 1–4.

Metzl, J. M. (2014). Race and mental health. In T. Jones, D. Wear, L. D. Friedman & K. Pachucki (eds.), *Health humanities reader* (pp. 261–267). New Brunswick, NJ: Rutgers University Press.

Mitchell, J. P. (1996). Ritual. In A. Barnard & J. Spencer (eds.), *Encyclopedia of social and cultural anthropology* (pp. 490–493). London: Routledge.

NHS. (2019). Brain death. Online. www.nhs.uk/conditions/brain-death (last accessed 22 April 2022).

Okrainec, K., Miller, M., Holcroft, C., Boivin, J. F. & Greenaway, C. (2014). Assessing the need for a medical interpreter: Are all questions created equal? *Journal of Immigrant Minority Health*, 16(4), 756–760. DOI:10.1007/s10903-013-9821-9

Pamela, H. & Groopman, J. (2011). The new language of medicine. *The New England Journal of Medicine*, 365, 1372–1373.

Peacock, S. & Patel, S. (2008). Cultural influences on pain. *Reviews in Pain*, 8(2).

Plaza del Pino, F. J., Soriano, E. & Higginbottom, G. M. (2013). Sociocultural and linguistic boundaries influencing intercultural communication between nurses and Moroccan patients in southern Spain: a focused ethnography. *BMC Nursing 2013, 12:14*, 12(1), 14–21.

Quigley, E. M. & Shanahan, F. (2009). The language of medicine: Words as servants and scoundrels. *Clinical Medicine*, 9(2), 131–135.

Schouten, B. C., Cox, A., Duran, G., Kerremans, K., Banning, L. K., Lahdidioui, A., van den Muijsenbergh, M., Schinkel, S., Sungur, H., Suurmond, J., Zendedel, R. & Krystallidou, D. (2020). Mitigating language and cultural barriers in healthcare communication: Toward a holistic approach. *Patient Education and Counseling*. DOI:10.1016/j.pec.2020.05.001

Squires, A., Miner, S., Liang, E., Lor, M., Ma, C. & Witkoski Stimpfel, A. (2019). How language barriers influence provider workload for home health care professionals: A secondary analysis of interview data. *International Journal of Nursing Studies*, 99, 103394. DOI:10.1016/j.ijnurstu.2019.103394

Teal, C. R. & Street, R. L. (2009). Critical elements of culturally competent communication in the medical encounter: A review and model. *Social Science & Medicine*, 68(3), 533–543. DOI:10.1016/j.socscimed.2008.10.015

Turner, V. W. (1969). *The ritual process: Structure and anti-structure*. Ithaca, NY: Cornell University Press.

UK Government. (2021). NHS Workforce. Online. https://bit.ly/3jupIvQ

Venkatasalu, M. R., Seymour, J. E. & Arthur, A. (2014). Dying at home: A qualitative study of the perspectives of older South Asians living in the United Kingdom. *Palliative Medicine*, 28(3), 264–272. DOI:10.1177/0269216313506765

Watson, B., Gallois, C., Hewett, D. G. & Jones, L. (2012). Culture and health care: Intergroup communication and its consequences. In J. Jackson (ed.), *The Routledge handbook of language and intercultural communication* (pp. 510–522). Abingdon: Routledge.

Watts, K. J., Meiser, B., Zilliacus, E., Kaur, R., Taouk, M., Girgis, A., Butow, P., Goldstein, D., Hale, S., Perry, A., Aranda, S. K. & Kissane, D. W. (2017). Communicating with patients from minority backgrounds: Individual challenges experienced by oncology health professionals. *European Journal of Oncology Nursing*, 26, 83–90. DOI:10.1016/j.ejon.2016.12.001

16 Enhancing Intercultural Competence in Military Services

This chapter examines the increasing importance of **intercultural competence** in military services, which draws on recent conceptual discussions of such competence and its increasing role in study abroad, business and health service contexts (Chapters 3, 13, 14 and 15). We will at first concentrate on the related experiences of military service members. We will then move on to the aspects that have been identified as crucial for service members in the twenty-first century (Section 16.2), before we comment on areas for improvement in current training and education (Section 16.3).

AIMS

By the end of this chapter, you should be able to:

1. describe intercultural experiences of military service members;
2. summarise key findings from research on intercultural competence needs in the services;
3. outline intercultural competence deficits in current military training and education and describe potential ways forward.

> **KEY TERMS**
> intercultural competence – counterinsurgency – 6D model – World Cultural Map

16.1 Intercultural Experiences in the Military

Before an audience of war veterans, US President Barack Obama highlighted new cultural trends in the military as follows: 'In the 21st century, military strength will be measured not only by the weapons our troops carry, but by the languages they speak and the cultures they understand' (Obama, 2009). With such remarks he summarised key insights from experiences in armed conflicts, findings from military research and growing popular concerns regarding traditional warfare's civilian and military casualties, many of whom could be avoided through a better understanding of enemies, foreign civilians and allies. The new 'cultural imperative for professional military education and leader development' (Abbe & Halpin, 2010, p. 20) corresponds to advances in intercultural research and its applications elaborated in the preceding chapters, the impact of globalisation and, above all, *changes in military operations* that increasingly include 'multiple engagements around the world with a greater reliance on partner relationships' (2010, p. 30), which could benefit immensely from robust intercultural knowledge, skills and attitudes.

In particular, since the end of the Cold War, the nature and locations of operations have become less predictable, with enemies, foreign civilians and allies often changing significantly within short periods of time. Examples are the Gulf War (1990–1991), the Bosnian War (1992–1995), the 'Global War on Terrorism' (2001–2013), Afghanistan (2001–2014; 2021), Iraq (2003–2011), the intervention in Libya (2011) and the war against the 'Islamic State of Iraq and Syria' (2013–2019). All of these military operations and, overall, most of the larger operations of the last three decades, were conducted by international coalitions, which means there is an enhanced need to cooperate with allies. Finally, armed conflicts with terrorist groups are continuing worldwide, while different forms of state terrorism – from organised mass cyberattacks to bombardments of civilians – are on the rise. Most of these conflicts are nurtured and sometimes triggered by nationalist or other tribalist clashes and this leads to increasing demands for more intercultural competence.

A good starting point for explorations of intercultural experiences in the military are case study collections like Holmes-Eber and Mainz's *Case studies in operational culture* (2014), documentaries like *Restrepo* (Hetherington & Junger, 2010), the *Taking fire* series (Nally & Strickson, 2016), and military academy students' reports that are based on personal experiences, such as *Army leader development for the cross-cultural environment* (Lewis, 2020).

Case studies in operational culture (Holmes-Eber & Mainz, 2014) features numerous cultural challenges during armed conflict in Afghanistan, especially between US American service members and Afghan civilians, although allies are also sometimes given a voice. The challenges range from differences in networking and organisation, for example in Major David Smith's attempt to work without an Afghan Neighbourhood Council, to gender issues outlined by Lieutenant Colonel Eric C. Dill and Major Misty J. Posey. The importance of intercultural competence in such contexts is stressed by Canadian infantry Major Corey J. Frederickson who comments on his experiences in Afghanistan as follows:

> When military forces operate in foreign countries, the inevitable clash of cultures can have a major impact on the success or failure of military operations, particularly when conducting **counterinsurgency** […] or stability operations where the focus is (or at least should be) on the population. People of different cultures may

react differently in the same circumstances, and a lack of understanding of this fact can lead to the undermining of the military effort.

(Holmes-Eber & Mainz, 2014, p. 51)

Frederickson goes on to elaborate on a very basic cultural incident, which caused serious challenges for the assessment of measures in securing an Afghan village. To questions by Canadian soldiers like 'Do you feel secure?' or 'Is the government doing a good job?', which were meant to extract information on the most pressing security issues, Afghan civilians responded predominantly that they felt secure and that everything was fine, which contrasted with security threats in the area. After many misleading information gathering attempts, an Afghan security force partner was consulted, who explained that such misleading feedback was a frequent response when confronted with higher authorities, such as – in this case – the Canadian allies of the Afghan government, who were jointly responsible for security in the region.

The case could be further examined through Hofstede's **6D model** and data highlighted in the **World Cultural Map** as a conflict between civilians in the traditional rural areas of Greater Iran (Persian cultural region), to which Afghanistan belongs, and Canadian soldiers from predominantly urban centres. After all, surveys from the Greater Iran region indicate considerably higher power distance (PDI) and survival values, but lower individualism (IDV) and self-expression scores, than surveys from Canada (see Hofstede Insights, 2021; Wave 6 map in WVS, 2021), to which differences between rural and urban cultures should be added. Differences in interaction styles have also been mentioned, with tendencies towards indirect communication in Afghanistan (Karrer, 2012).

However, national and/or regional essentialisation must be avoided, as Rarick's (2013) relatively low PDI and high IDV scores for Afghan business students from urban centres suggests. His exploratory Hofstede-based survey of forty-six students between 19 and 23 years of age leads to a PDI of 21 and an IDV of 55, which stands in contrast to considerably higher PDI (Pakistan: 55; Iran: 58; Iraq: 95) and lower IDV (Pakistan: 14; Iran: 41; Iraq: 30) in Greater Iran, and in neighbouring Muslim countries like Saudi Arabia (PDI: 95; IDV: 25) and the United Arab Emirates (PDI: 90; IDV: 25). Unfortunately, there are still no reliable cultural value scores for Afghanistan itself, because the country does not appear in maps based on empirical Hofstede or World Values data, which is partially due to decades of internal and external conflicts that continue to obstruct larger research projects. Also, Rarick uses a quantitatively limited sample of a narrow segment of the Afghan population, hence more studies on different groups are needed to develop a robust overview of the cultural spectrum of Afghan society.

The communication difficulties between rural Afghans and urban Canadians described above was eventually solved by a simple rewording of direct questions into the following more indirect task: 'Please prioritize where the government should focus its efforts: security, building schools, the economy, or eliminating corruption.' This then allowed follow-up questions, for example regarding security, without explicit criticism of the Canadians and/or the Afghan government.

Figure 16.1 *Intercultural Competence in Military Services* by Alíz Kovács-Zöldi

INDIVIDUAL TASKS

– Please write down one of your own intercultural experiences from military or non-military life, and summarise exactly how cultural friction was in your case ultimately overcome (or how it could have been overcome if that did not happen at the time).
– Also, elaborate on the impact of that experience, for example on your knowledge, attitudes or skills when dealing with members of that particular culture and/or other cultures.

– If your case study is from a non-military context, explain in what respects it might help service members, from soldiers to cultural attachés, to prepare for deployment.
– Figure 16.1 indicates multiple roles of a service member that could lead to conflicts, for example his tasks in the armed forces and his knowledge of intercultural communication. Compare this to your own multiple roles and the conflicts that might develop from there.

While documentaries like *Restrepo* (Hetherington & Junger, 2010) and the *Taking fire* series (Nally & Strickson, 2016) tend to focus on popular scenes of armed conflict, they also contain interactions between US Americans and Afghans as well as soldiers of different ranks and genders. Particularly interesting in *Restrepo* is a meeting between US captain Kearney and Afghan elders, which could be examined more closely as strong individualism, very direct communication and lecturing style in a far less individualist and more indirect operating Shura context that is traditionally shaped by negotiation (Hetherington & Junger, 2010, 15.00–15.56). The meeting also provides points for a legal debate, for example when Kearney promises to 'wipe the slate clean' regarding unlawful killings in the past (2010, 15.40–15.56). A culminating point of disrespect for Shura elders is reached when the same officer ends a conversation about a missing family member of a village elder with the words 'I don't fucking care' (2010, 38.46–40.20; see also 56.17–57.13).

Finally, in *Army leader development for the cross-cultural environment* (Lewis, 2020), Colonel James M. Lewis presents some of his cultural experiences in a Humanitarian Civic Assistance mission in North Macedonia and he offers his academic interpretation based on intercultural research. At the end of this chapter, we will draw on his insights in our reconstruction of a case study that we would like you to explore in detail.

16.2 Intercultural Competence in the Military

In the context of increasing cultural challenges with often changing enemies, foreign civilians and allies, Sikes and colleagues had already requested in the 1990s better military training and education to 'deal with a diversity of peoples and cultures, tolerate ambiguity, take initiative, and ask questions' in their nearly 70-page long Air Force 2025 research paper (Sikes et al., 1996, p. v). More than twenty years later, this demand has still not been satisfactorily met. Consequently, Mackenzie and Miller have more recently argued again for a shift from the culture-specific focus in established training programmes to 'culture-general training and education' in order to develop 'transferable culture concepts and skills', which service members need to 'interact appropriately and effectively no matter where' (Mackenzie & Miller, 2017, pp. 5, 6). Similarly, Abbe and Halpin challenge the frequent focus on the learning of a particular foreign language as 'the gateway to culture', and recommend instead the triad of regional culture-specific knowledge, foreign language and *cross-cultural competence* as the way forward (Abbe & Halpin, 2010, p. 25), the latter being the more frequent term for intercultural competence in military research (see also Rodman, 2015, Newson, 2020).

In line with Byram's *structural model of intercultural competence* (see Chapter 3), Mackenzie & Miller (2017, p. 6) and Abbe & Halpin (2010, p. 24) agree on the importance of three domains for such competence development: knowledge, affect and skills. There is also agreement that these domains must be linked for successful military deployments, and this is reflected in their definition:

> Knowledge begins with an awareness of one's own culture and includes an
> understanding of culture and cultural differences, but has to progress toward
> an increasingly complex understanding of the sources, manifestations, and

consequences of a particular culture. Affect includes attitudes toward foreign cultures and the motivation to learn about and engage with them. Skills encompass the ability to regulate one's own reactions in a cross-cultural setting, interpersonal skills, and the flexibility to assume the perspective of someone from a different culture.
(Abbe & Halpin, 2010, pp. 24–25)

This implies for example that cultural knowledge might have only a very limited impact if 'rigid interpersonal behavior or ethnocentric attitudes' are not challenged, hence the request to include attitudes and skills training fully (Abbe & Halpin, 2010, pp. 24–25).

Finally, it is recommendable to connect the structural model of intercultural competence more explicitly with *process-oriented models*, as exemplified by Bolten (2020, p. 61; see also Chapter 3). In particular, process-oriented models might help service members to transfer insights from more familiar military training (e.g. on leadership and management) to culturally less familiar situations in military deployments, when faced with differences in meaning, structure and performance of shared concepts like courtesy and respect in leadership and management or negotiation with foreign civilians.

In recent decades, some progress has been made in the development of culture-general training and education. Gallus et al. (2014) argue that intercultural competence has been key for the US American Department of Defense since the beginning of the twenty-first century, and they highlight the development of California's Fort Irwin National Training Center and the courses at Hurlburt Field in Florida (Mackenzie & Miller, 2017, p. 4) as examples of good practice. Abbe & Halpin (2010, p. 23) stress as particularly popular approaches in such centres Hofstede's cultural dimensions (Hofstede, 2001) and the GLOBE study (House, 2004), which attempts to link insights from (back then) Hofstede's five dimensions and Trompenaars and Hampden-Turner's seven dimensions (both are examined in Chapter 5). The Australian Defence Forces piloted Hofstede-based education in 2003 'to enhance generic intercultural skills' (Mills & Smith, 2004), and the Defence Academy in the UK also runs Hofstede workshops next to other culture-general introductions.

However, such training must be underpinned by in-depth contextualisation, critical reflection, open discussion and application of *knowledge* in different scenarios to avoid monocultural homogenisation, essentialisation and separation (see Chapter 1). Better contextualisation might also help to develop the necessary intercultural *affect* and *skills* at *personal, social, strategic* and *specialist* level, which is a focus of process-oriented models of intercultural competence. Since all this is essential for competence development from soldiers to cultural attachés, it is worth double-checking and monitoring if the courses that offer culture-general training allocate enough time to include critical debate of theory and practical applications.

To enhance culture-generic knowledge and develop affect and skills more convincingly, it is also essential to go beyond Hofstede and the related GLOBE study. Power questions raised by critical interculturalists like Nakayama (2020) and identity discussions advanced by evolutionary and positive psychologists might be especially helpful. For example, evolutionary notions of tribalism (Clark & Winegard, 2020) could support discussions of monocultural stereotypes, cultural hierarchies and related paradigms of assimilation and exclusion at different levels, and Peterson and Seligman's exploration of virtues and character strengths (Peterson & Seligman, 2004) have already been applied for so-called transformational leadership development in the US military (Sosik et al., 2018).

As argued in Chapter 4, within and beyond national differences and similarities, there are numerous other cultural aspects worth considering, especially related to class, age, gender and educational background, but there is also the impact of professional cultures (e.g. in air forces, armies and navies) and individual traits. It is, consequently, advisable to opt for a multi-method approach, that is discuss Hofstede in the context of, for example, recent World Values Survey results (2021) and interactive studies. Also, a transcultural approach to Hofstede's dimensions would be recommendable, that is, the use of his dimensions and related questionnaires to examine differences and similarities within and beyond national boundaries. This has effectively been done by many of the more than 400 Hofstede applications explored by Taras et al. (2012), to which we could add Rarick's (2013) study of Afghan students. By suggesting considerably lower power distance and higher individualism for such a group than the average of respondents to Hofstede questionnaires from the wider region, Rarick argues that differences in cultural values might be related to factors like educational knowledge, age and/or urban life experiences. For military service members, it means differentiating more with whom they actually interact – at home or abroad – as the degree of national programming might significantly differ from one collective to the next. However, even in these cases Hofstede's and/or the World Values Survey's dimensions (more than the scores) could be a starting point to categorise potential social behaviour and reactions.

GROUP TASKS

Collect cultural information on three ethnic groups in Afghanistan, such as Pashtuns, Hazaras and Tajiks, and discuss that information with regard to Hofstede's dimensions.

– Which similarities (e.g. high or low power distance) would you expect on average from one group to the next?

– Which differences would you expect within Afghan society as a whole, and to what extent could they be linked to education, gender, age and/or other cultural aspects?

16.3 Areas for Improvement

Unfortunately, research on intercultural competence in the military services remains overwhelmingly US-centric, and there is substantial room for improvement in training and education. Mackenzie & Miller mention courses that continue to focus on short-term culture-specific presentations, while other programmes show a lack of transparency and collaboration across the different services and substantial weaknesses in intercultural competence assessment (2017, pp. 5, 7). Consequently, the US Army Human Dimension Capabilities Development Task Force (2015) suggests the compilation of a basic inventory of intercultural courses to avoid duplication and facilitate access for members of different services, and there are recommendations to amend self-reporting with multi-method approaches, such as the cross-cultural assessment tool discussed by McCloskey et al. (2012).

It is also worth double-checking and monitoring the extent to which and how exactly the growing military literature on intercultural awareness and competence is fully embedded in established programmes. For example, the UK Defence Academy highlights numerous key topics of its courses, from international procurement and leadership to cyberspace operations, but none of them explicitly includes concepts like intercultural/cross-cultural competence for military operations (see Defence Academy of the United Kingdom, 2022), although there are now a few courses that focus on diversity within the British armed forces. This raises concerns regarding the education of British commanders and civil servants, especially in the context of the establishment of the Defence Centre for Languages and Culture at the Defence Academy in Shrivenham (in 2014) and related claims, such as 'Defence really gets this now. The lesson we've learnt from Afghanistan and Iraq, but also from Sierra Leone and Bosnia, is about the importance of language and culture' (Worman in Tickle, 2013).

Ultimately, to be credible, such institutional and verbal statements must be reflected in all major training and education programmes, and they should be crucial for best practice in military selection, promotion and future recruitment. Instead, the Defence Academy of the United Kingdom (2022) continues to focus in twentieth-century tradition on foreign language acquisition for military operations abroad, which is in line with the language focus of the former Defence Centre for Languages and Culture highlighted by the BBC (2014). Furthermore, it could be argued that the proud presentation of Dari, Spanish and Pashto speakers in that short BBC documentary brings us back to the frequent portrayal of foreign language learning in the military as 'the gateway to culture', which Abbe and Halpin had already criticised (2010, p. 25) as insufficient, especially in the context of increasingly more flexible short-term deployments. In particular, there is the danger of reducing a provision that was meant to equip service members for language and cultural challenges in the twenty-first century to a traditional language centre, as the BBC report title seems to suggest: 'Military language centre opened by Prince Michael of Kent' (BBC, 2014). As such, this example might ultimately indicate that the road to intercultural competence in the military is not linear-progressive, but more like a roller-coaster with numerous ups and downs, in which innovative cultural projects are – especially in periods of budget cuts for military service members – often sacrificed to cater for the traditional training and education that tend to receive substantial support from traditional authorities.

To be able to address cultural challenges in the military services more convincingly, training and education programmes might have to be revised, amended and monitored, but they should also be made more transparent in order to facilitate access for members from all services and selected staff beyond these services. The latter could include a wider spectrum of civil servants, which would make the courses more cost-effective, especially when implemented in joint face-to-face and online deliveries where one delivery form only would lead to significant exclusions. Such revisions and amendments would benefit from a continuous input of up-to-date cultural experiences from regions of armed conflicts and diplomatic interactions with allies. Intercultural programmes could include these experiences in the form of case study work, new course books that draw on selected case studies throughout, and other teaching material on cultural tensions in military life, and as such reduce the gap with often substantially more advanced teaching material in intercultural business communication, education and the health services. It is also essential, especially for attitudes and skills development, to explore culture clashes from different perspectives beyond the nationalist gaze, for example by bringing in perspectives from allies as well as foreign civilians. Finally, military research and research-based teaching material should always incorporate recent advances in intercultural studies, which is clearly not the case in the reviewed literature.

The stakes for improvement are high, because better intercultural competence might help to avoid or reduce armed conflicts and related casualties, which is why the United States established the Foreign Service Institute (FSI) in 1947 as one of the earliest applied intercultural communication centres in the world, which led to the pioneering research of one of the institute's educators, Edward T. Hall (see Chapter 2). However, intercultural competence development should now go well beyond diplomatic applications to avoid another world war, and it should go beyond cultural values research by Hall, Hofstede and the GLOBE Study. After all, it is essential to link knowledge, affect and skills development at personal, social, strategic and specialist levels, and it is important to support transfers from general action competence from intercultural competence. If this is achieved, intercultural competence can become a powerful mediator in the pacification of cultural conflicts at local, regional, national and global levels.

16.4 In Summary

In worldwide deployments, military service members have had substantial cultural experiences when sent to armed conflict zones or stationed within the country of an ally. If presented methodologically and according to standards of recent intercultural research, these experiences could help to revise and improve current training and education, for example through the development of appropriate intercultural teaching material. The latter could be reflected in up-to-date course books, case study volumes and documentaries with a cultural focus that might be considerably more helpful for future problem-solving than melodramatic reality series from armed conflicts.

DISCUSSION QUESTIONS

Please go to the website of any military training provider, e.g. in your country, and discuss its current provision of programmes to answer the following questions:

1. To what extent does the provision address the cultural experiences of service members (see Section 16.1) and academic needs assessments for intercultural competence development (Section 16.2)?
2. What should a programme that addresses such experiences and needs look like?
3. What should a website that reflects that programme look like?

Now that you are well aware of potential gaps in intercultural competence development in military services, please read the following case study adapted from Lewis (2020) about a humanitarian civil assistance mission in North Macedonia and answer these questions:

a. How would you explain the following situation?
b. What would you do differently to avoid similar challenges?

CASE STUDY

A one-month-long mission involving nine US American and nine Macedonian engineers was to renovate a school in North Macedonia. Susan, a young US Army First Lieutenant, had thought carefully about the demanding renovation tasks. After introducing herself as officer in charge, she presented an ambitious schedule, with duties from 7 a.m. to 6 p.m.

Neither the Macedonian officer Bogomil, an older special forces Sergeant Major, nor his soldiers showed much enthusiasm. Over the next few days, the Macedonians frequently ignored Susan, expecting instead direction from their Sergeant Major. They also started work later, finished earlier and had numerous coffee breaks with the US American soldiers throughout the day.

Whenever Susan asked if something was wrong, the Macedonians said that everything was fine, but daily targets were hardly ever met, the Macedonians seemed offended and many male American soldiers started to adopt their attitudes.

References

Abbe, A. & Halpin, S. M. (2010). The cultural imperative for professional military education and leader development. *Parameters: Journal of the US Army War College*, 39(4), 20–31.

BBC (2014). Military language centre opened by Prince Michael of Kent. BBC News. 9 April. www.bbc.co.uk/news/av/uk-england-oxfordshire-26948760 (last accessed 20 April 2022).

Bolten, J. (2020). Rethinking intercultural competence. In G. Rings & S. M. Rasinger (eds.), *The Cambridge handbook of intercultural communication* (pp. 56–67). Cambridge: Cambridge University Press.

Clark, C. J. & Winegard, B. M. (2020). Tribalism in war and peace: The nature and evolution of ideological epistemology and its significance for modern social science. *Psychological Inquiry*, 31(1), 1–22.

Defence Academy of the United Kingdom (2022). Find a course. Online. www.da.mod.uk/find-a-course (last accessed 22 April 2022).

Gallus, J. A., et al. (2014, April). *Cross-cultural competence in the department of defense: An annotated bibliography, Special Report 71*. Fort Belvoir, VA: U.S. Army Research Institute for the Behavioral and Social Sciences.

Hetherington, T. & Junger, S. (2010). *Restrepo*. United States: Outpost Films, Virgil Films & Entertainment.

Hofstede, G. (2001). *Culture's consequences* (2nd edition). London: SAGE.

Hofstede Insights (2021). Country comparison. Online. https://bit.ly/3vvDSCC (last accessed 17 April 2022).

Holmes-Eber, P. & Mainz, M. (2014). *Case studies in operational culture*. Quantico, VA: Marine Corps University Press.

House, R. J. et al. (2004). *Culture, leadership, and organizations: The GLOBE study of 62 societies*. Thousand Oaks, CA: SAGE.

Karrer, L. (2012). *Pashtun traditions versus Western perceptions: Cross-cultural negotiations in Afghanistan*. Geneva: Genève Graduate Institute Publications.

Lewis, J. M. (2020). *Army leader development for the cross-cultural environment. Research report*. Montgomery, AL: Air War College.

Mackenzie, L. & Miller, H. W. (2017). Intercultural training in the United States military. In Y. Y. Kim & K. L. McKay-Semmler (eds.), *The international encyclopedia of intercultural communication* (pp. 1–10). Hoboken, NJ: Wiley.

McCloskey, M. J., Behymer, K. J., Papautsky, E. L. & Grandjean, A. (2012). *Measuring learning and development in cross-cultural competence: Technical report 1317*. Fort Belvoir, VA: U.S. Army Research Institute for the Behavioral and Social Sciences.

Mills, V. & Smith, R. (2004). *Short- and long-term effects of participation in a cross-cultural simulation game on intercultural awareness*. Edinburgh, South Australia: Commonwealth of Australia.

Nakayama, T. K. (2020). Critical intercultural communication and the digital environment. In G. Rings & S. M. Rasinger (eds.), *The Cambridge handbook of intercultural communication* (pp. 85–95). Cambridge: Cambridge University Press.

Nally, J. & Strickson, S. (2016). *Taking fire*. United States: RAW.

Newson, R. (2020). Navy SEALS – Crossing cultures: Cross-cultural competence and decision styles. PhD thesis. University of San Diego.

Obama, B. (2009). Barack Obama's address to veterans. *The Guardian*. 17 August. https://bit.ly/38SzTbk (last accessed 20 April 2022).

Peterson, C. & Seligman, M. P. (2004). *Character strengths and virtues: A handbook and classification*. Oxford: Oxford University Press.

Rarick, C., Winter, G., Falk, G., Nickersen, I. & Barczyk, C. (2013). Afghanistan's younger, elite and educated population: A cultural assessment and possible implications for the economic and political future of the country. *Global Journal of Management and Business Research Administration and Management*, 13(4), 1–8. https://bit.ly/39aTmEv (last accessed 22 April 2022).

Rodman, J. (2015). *Cross-cultural competence: Introduction and overview of key concepts*. Human dimension capabilities development task force and mission command. Fort Leavenworth: Homeland Security Digital Library. www.hsdl.org/?view&did=800779 (last accessed 20 April 2022).

Sikes, C. S., Cherry, A. K., Durall, W. E., Hargrove, M. R. & Tingman, K. R. (1996). *Brilliant warrior: Information technology integration in education and training*. Arlington, VA: Air Command and Staff.

Sosik, J. J., Arenas, F. J., Chun, J. U. & Ete, Z. (2018). Character into action: How officers demonstrate strengths with transformational leadership. *Air & Space Power Journal*, 32(3), 4–25.

Taras, V., Steel, P. & Kirkman, B. L. (2012). Improving national cultural indices using a longitudinal meta-analysis of Hofstede's dimensions. *Journal of World Business*, 47, 329–341.

Tickle, L. (2013). Matt Worman: my career in languages. *The Guardian*. 10 October. https://bit.ly/3uXTv6y (last accessed 20 April 2022).

US Army Human Dimension Capabilities Development Task Force (2015). *Cross-cultural competence: Overview of cross-cultural training theory and practice for the army*. Fort Leavenworth, KS: Capabilities Development Integration Directorate Mission Command Center of Excellence.

WVS (2021). World Values Survey. Findings and Insights. Online. www.worldvaluessurvey.org (last accessed 20 April 2022).

17 Intercultural Competence Revisited: Development and Assessment

Throughout the book we have looked at the concept of *intercultural competence*, either directly or indirectly. Unlike Chapter 3, where we first defined the concept, in the current chapter we want to focus on the aspect of measurement.

AIMS

By the end of this chapter, you should be able to:

1. **explain some of the issues behind how we develop intercultural competence;**
2. **and describe some approaches and tools that allow us to assess intercultural competence.**

> **KEY TERMS**
> **intercultural competence – serious gaming/games – assessment –**
> **Developmental Model of Intercultural Sensitivity (DMIS)**

17.1 Intercultural Competence: A Quick Recap

We will start with a very brief recap. In its global competence framework *Preparing our youth for an inclusive and sustainable world*, the OECD identifies four key aspects of **intercultural competence**, which in fact are at the core of many definitions of intercultural competence, and which we have met in Chapter 3: *knowledge, skills, attitudes* and *values*. These factors are inseparably linked:

> For example, examining a global issue (dimension 1) requires knowledge of a
> particular issue, the skills to transform this awareness into a deeper understanding,
> and the attitudes and values to reflect on the issue from multiple cultural perspec-
> tives, keeping in mind the interest of all parties involved.
> (OECD, 2017, p. 12)

What the definitions that include knowledge, skills, attitudes and values have in common is that intercultural competence is considered as something that is primarily located within individuals; very simplistically, this is a bit like driving a car: you need to know the highway code (knowledge) and which pedals to press and levers to move (skills) to make it work. Attitudes and values are also things that are fairly individual features: if we stick to our car example, most of us have certain attitudes towards the use of individual transport (as opposed to public transport), and even the way we value our cars (or bicycles, or motorbikes) varies: for some, these are status symbols which we wash, polish and care for; for others, they are merely ways of getting us from A to B. That said, while these are *primarily* individual features, they are also to an extent influenced by external factors: highway codes act as external regulatory frameworks; the way pedals are arranged in a car is universally agreed (accelerator on the right, clutch on the left, brake in the middle); our attitudes and values towards cars may be heavily influenced by societal attitudes towards individual transport in the light of climate change, and so on. What knowledge, skills, attitudes and values also have in common, though, is that they are *measurable* to an extent, and that they are not static but (can) undergo developmental changes. This leads us to our next section.

TASK

Think about your educational and training experience so far. This may include school, college, university, or other skills such as playing a musical instrument or driving a car.

– What type of testing or assessment did this involve?
– What did the assessment assess? Were there clear-cut pass/fail points?

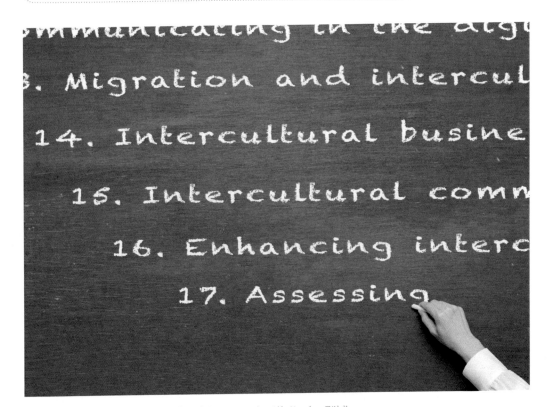

Figure 17.1 *Intercultural Assessment* by Alíz Kovács-Zöldi

17.2 Developing Intercultural Competence

The development of intercultural competence is a life-long process that takes place both inside and outside the classroom, and requires more than just the occasional ad hoc encounter with people from other cultures (Deardorff, 2020). That said, it has become of increasing importance in the educational context. Deardorff argues that developing intercultural competence is a necessity for 'postsecondary institutions seek[ing] to graduate global-ready students' (Deardorff, 2011, p. 76) and explains that in this context, the development of intercultural competence can take place either through the curriculum or co-curricular activities. Saquing, for example, investigated the intercultural competence of undergraduate students of English at a university in the Philippines and suggested that intercultural competence is a key component in the internationalisation of the curriculum (Saquing, 2018).

In particular in a classroom setting, the development of intercultural competence often goes hand in hand with the development of other skills, such as foreign language learning. Al-Jarf, for example, observed how a cross-cultural online writing project with learners of English as a foreign language (EFL) in the Ukraine, Russia and Saudi Arabia helped students develop not only linguistically but also with regard to their attitude towards global cultural issues; students in Al-Jarf's study 'developed a positive attitude towards other cultures and learnt to accept and respect differences in points of views, beliefs and traditions' (Al-Jarf, 2006, p. 24). Similarly, Mekheimer's survey of EFL college students in Saudi Arabia highlighted the 'significance of acculturation as part of second/foreign language acquisition/learning' (Mekheimer, 2011, p. 43). In Chapter 6, we looked at how literature can enhance intercultural understanding; in a similar vein, Nault (2006) showed how teaching literature as part of an EFL class at a Japanese university not only led to students improving their general English reading and discussion skills, but also enhanced their intercultural competence.

TASK

If you have ever learned a second or foreign language at school, college or university: did this include the teaching of the culture of the language, too? Did you find this useful? Did this help with your language learning?

That said, this approach of linking culture to foreign language learning whereby, for example, learners of the English language also learn about English-speaking cultures is not uncontroversial: Mahmoud discusses the relationship between teaching English as a foreign language and culture in the Arab world and concludes that the 'content of EFL texts at Islamic and Arabic schools, institutes, and universities should have cultural relevance to the learners' culture', including material that does 'not clash with Islamic Arabic culture' (Mahmoud, 2015, p. 70). He also recommends that curricula and materials need to avoid stereotypical

'Western' images but present a diverse range; after all, not all 'Westerners' are and think the same, just like not all 'Arabs' are identical.

While a lot of these studies have looked at the development of intercultural competence by students, it is, of course, an equally important skill for teachers. Brodmann Maeder and colleagues analysed communication styles and intercultural competence of both Western instructors and Nepalese trainee mountain rescue instructors during a course in Nepal. They found not only differences in preferred communication styles between the Western instructors and the Nepalese trainees, but also concluded that Western instructors 'should have time and opportunities to become acquainted with the host culture' (Brodmann Maeder et al., 2019, p. 27).

Intercultural competence is of course not only a 'by-product' of other education processes: there is a plethora of specialist training that focuses exclusively on the training of intercultural competence, as revealed by the millions of hits returned by a Google search for 'intercultural training programme'. Many employers, especially those operating globally, provide often mandatory intercultural training for their staff. Organisations such as the Society for Intercultural Education, Training and Research (SIETAR) comprise a membership consisting of academic researchers and professional intercultural trainers with the aim of developing the intercultural training further.

Of course, the teaching and development of intercultural competence has not been unaffected by technological advances: **serious games** are computer games that do not just serve as entertainment, but also have a training and education purpose. Unsurprisingly, serious gaming has entered the teaching and development of intercultural competence, too. Young et al.'s (2012) review of research showed 'very promising impacts' (p. 84) of serious games on educational achievement in general, and this is also found in the context of intercultural competence. Guillén-Nieto and Aleson-Carbonell, for example, used the videogame 'It's a deal' in order to develop students' intercultural competence and concluded that 'it had a large learning effect on intercultural communicative competence' (Guillén-Nieto & Aleson-Carbonell, 2012, p. 435).

From our short review, we can see that the development of intercultural competence is something that plays an important part in a wide variety of settings. Especially in an education context, 'competence' is something that is often 'measured' or 'evaluated', and in Section 17.3, we will look at approaches to assessing intercultural competence.

17.3 Assessing Intercultural Competence

TASK

If we want to assess or evaluate someone's intercultural competence, how could we do this? What would we 'test' or 'measure'?

We are all familiar with the idea of **assessment**, and we all have been assessed multiple times in our lives. In an education context, assessment is about an evaluation or 'measurement' of a particular set of skills or knowledge (as opposed to a clinical assessment that checks whether our bodies function the way they should). Assessments can be simple, for example, checking whether a pre-schooler can count from one to ten in the right order; it can also be complex, especially when assessing complex systems: the *Common European Framework of Reference for Languages: Learning, teaching, assessment* (CEFR) 'describes in a comprehensive way what language learners have to learn to do in order to use a language for communication and what knowledge and skills they have to develop so as to be able to act effectively' (Council of Europe, 2001, p. 1) – so that is a pretty involved way of assessing a complex system! What should be clear from our discussions in this book so far, assessing *intercultural competence* sits more towards the complex CEFR end of the spectrum than that of assessing whether a pre-schooler can count to ten.

Deardorff (2011) states that the assessment of intercultural competence requires not only an assessment of knowledge, but also of skills and attitudes. She identifies five key principles which allow for the systematic assessment of intercultural competence (Deardorff, 2020, pp. 498–499):

1. '*Define* the construct of intercultural competence within its context [...]': this is really the first principle of *any* measurement. We have seen that intercultural competence is a complex construct, with many definitions, so it is important to determine the definition we are going to use.

2. *Prioritise*: the second key principle in any measurement: If we were to measure the size of the car, we would need to decide what 'size' means: its length? Its height? How many seats it has? The size of the engine? The same goes for intercultural competence: what specific aspects are we looking at? Which components do we want to measure?

3. *Align*: this can be a little tricky to get your head round. It relates to whether our measurement actually measures what it is supposed to measure. If we stick to our car size example, valid measurements would be '534 centimetres', '5 seats' or '1.8 litres'; '100 miles per hour', however, would not be (since it relates to speed, not size). With intercultural competence, we are, of course, dealing with knowledge, skills, attitudes or values, or whatever we defined and prioritised for our assessment. In the context of education, we often talk about 'learning outcomes' to describe what a particular course or programme of study wants to achieve (a little bit like the 'aims' at the start of each chapter in this book). 'Alignment' in this context means that the course or programme, the assessment and the outcome all work together.

4. *Identify* evidence: this relates to 'identifying both direct and indirect evidence of desired intercultural changes in the learner and of achievement of stated learning outcomes' (Deardorff, 2020, p. 499), so this is about the actual measurement we are using.

5. *Use*: even though students often perceive it as such, assessment is always forward looking, too; so feed*back* is also a feed*forward*, and any assessment of intercultural competence needs to be used to help students to further develop their competence.

These principles provide us with a useful overarching framework or 'recipe' for researching and assessing intercultural competence in a systematic manner. As with definitions and approaches, there is a myriad of different ways of trying to *measure* intercultural competence (Deardorff, 2016): in the context of study abroad, for example, papers and presentations are used to get students to reflect on their intercultural encounters critically (a bit like the tasks in Chapter 3 and the current chapter), and we can use this as a basis for assessment; interviews work similarly but participants are guided by an interviewer. Portfolios – or, because this is the twenty-first century, increasingly e-portfolios – consist of collections of usually reflective material or 'evidence' relating to a student's intercultural competence, selected by the students themselves (Deardorff, 2011; Jacobson et al., 1999). You might have come across portfolios in other courses where you had to pick a number of the 'best' pieces of work you completed for a course and put these forward for assessment. Fantini (2009) in his chapter provides a very useful list and description of the various tools available for the assessment of intercultural competence and its various components, ranging from the 'Assessment of Intercultural Competence' (AIC) questionnaire, to the 'Multicultural Counselling Inventory' (MCI), which measures intercultural counselling competencies, to 'Tests for Hidden Bias': 'A series of online tests [...] designed to examine unconscious hidden bias' (Fantini, 2009, p. 474). All of these have a slightly different focus and assess different elements of intercultural competence. Deardorff concludes 'that assessment of intercultural competence involves more than observable performance, that it is important to measure the degrees of competence, and that it is important to consider the cultural and social implications when assessing intercultural competence' (Deardorff, 2016, p. 253) – so it is not just about what people *do*, but also what people *know*, even if that knowledge is not overtly visible or observable in their behaviour.

Portalla and Chen developed an Intercultural Effectiveness Scale, a twenty-item self-assessment tool which includes the six components *behavioural flexibility*, *message skills, relationship cultivation, identity management, interactant respect* and *interaction management* (Portalla & Chen, 2010). The tool is based on a series of statements which target the six components, for example:

- 'I am not always the person I appear to be when interacting with people from different cultures.' (behavioural flexibility)
- 'I have problems with grammar when interacting with people from different cultures.' (message skills)
- 'I find it easy to talk with people from different cultures.' (relationship cultivation)
- 'I always show respect for my culturally different counterparts during our interaction.' (interactant respect)

- 'I find I have a lot in common with my culturally different counterparts during our interaction.' (identity maintenance)
- 'I am able to express my ideas clearly when interacting with people from different cultures.' (interaction management)

(Portalla & Chen, 2010, pp. 34–35; includes full list of items)

However, not everyone agrees with the use of such self-assessment tools: Koester and Lustig argue that such tools are inadequate (Koester & Lustig, 2015) as they tend to ignore contextual factors (see our discussion in Sections 17.1 and 17.2), and Collier reminds us that '[i]mpressions of intercultural competence are always contextually contingent and situated in macro structures' (Collier, 2015, p. 10). Measuring complex concepts such as attitudes is notoriously difficult, and the phrasing of questions and statement can also have an impact on how they are interpreted (Rasinger, 2013). Holmes and O'Neil therefore propose the use of a four-stage ethnographic approach which they call PEER – *Preparing, Engaging, Evaluating* and *Reflecting* (Holmes & O'Neill, 2012). At the core of this approach is the idea that 'the student researchers reflected on their own predispositions, culturally held practices, beliefs and attitudes, illuminated through engagement with their Cultural Other' (2012, p. 710); this element of experience-based, critical reflection of students' own intercultural competence is at the very centre of the approach.

TASK

Think about a meeting you have had with someone from a different culture. Critically reflect on this meeting: did it go smoothly? What were the issues? Which of those issues could you attribute to your own behaviour, and which to that of the other person?

We now want to look at what different levels of intercultural competence might look like – after all, if we assess and measure something, there needs to be some sort of 'result' or 'outcome'. Fantini (2000) divides intercultural competence into four developmental levels, from the basic to the specialist: *educational traveller, sojourner, professional* and *intercultural/multicultural specialist*. These levels align with levels of exposure to other cultures: while the *educational traveller* is someone who participates in only short-term activities, and hence has limited exposure to intercultural communication experiences, the *professional* is someone who works or otherwise regularly operates in an intercultural or multicultural context, with the *specialist* being someone at the top of this developmental scale who is involved in the intercultural training and educating of others.

Bennett developed a **Developmental Model of Intercultural Sensitivity** (DMIS for short), which aims at describing intercultural competence as a developmental process not unlike the acquisition of one's first language. The DMIS is a *constructivist* model: 'Constructivism in general holds that people's experience is a function of their perceptual organization of reality' (Bennett, 2017, p. 3). In other words, intercultural competence is something that is developed – or constructed – through our perception of the world around us. Bennett argues that 'dealing with otherness in complex ways is not a natural or historically important part of any culture's adaptive strategy' (2017, p. 3). The DMIS suggests that with changes in our perceptions of others, we move along a continuum from **ethnocentrism**, where we perceive our own culture to be at the centre of our reality, to *ethnorelativism*, which allows us to experience other cultures as 'alternative ways of organizing reality' (Bennett, 2017, p. 4). This development occurs along six stages; these stages are, however, not static categories but manifestations of different levels of development on a spectrum between two opposite poles. Movement from one stage to the other 'depends on the need to become more competent in communicating outside one's primary social context' (2017, p. 4). The six stages of the DMIS are given in Figure 17.2.

Hammer (2007, 2008) developed an 'Intercultural Development Inventory' (IDI), a tool that allows us to assess directly the DMIS stages with the exception of integration. The IDI in its current form (version 3 at the time of writing this book), is a fifty-item questionnaire that can be completed on paper or online; it also includes four open-ended context questions, which 'help further capture the experiences around cultural differences of the respondent' (2008, p. 247).

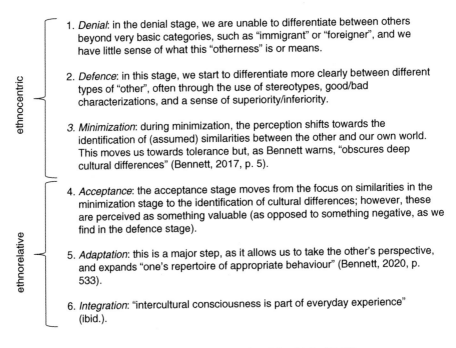

1. *Denial*: in the denial stage, we are unable to differentiate between others beyond very basic categories, such as "immigrant" or "foreigner", and we have little sense of what this "otherness" is or means.

2. *Defence*: in this stage, we start to differentiate more clearly between different types of "other", often through the use of stereotypes, good/bad characterizations, and a sense of superiority/inferiority.

3. *Minimization*: during minimization, the perception shifts towards the identification of (assumed) similarities between the other and our own world. This moves us towards tolerance but, as Bennett warns, "obscures deep cultural differences" (Bennett, 2017, p. 5).

4. *Acceptance*: the acceptance stage moves from the focus on similarities in the minimization stage to the identification of cultural differences; however, these are perceived as something valuable (as opposed to something negative, as we find in the defence stage).

5. *Adaptation*: this is a major step, as it allows us to take the other's perspective, and expands "one's repertoire of appropriate behaviour" (Bennett, 2020, p. 533).

6. *Integration*: "intercultural consciousness is part of everyday experience" (ibid.).

ethnocentric

ethnorelative

Figure 17.2 Developmental Model of Intercultural Sensitivity (DMIS)
Adapted from Bennett (2020, pp. 532–533); line drawing © Sebastian Rasinger.

The results of the IDI place a respondent somewhere along the DMIS stages; this allows 'individuals (e.g., managers) [to] better assess their capability for recognizing and effectively responding to cultural diversity' (2008, p. 254).

17.4 In Summary

The aim of this chapter has been to look at the development and assessment of intercultural competence. We started with a brief recap before moving on to a discussion of how intercultural competence can develop in different contexts and using different methods. We then looked at how we can assess intercultural competence, taking into account different approaches, frameworks and actual tools. Using the DMIS, we also considered what the possible outcomes of stages of competence might look like.

DISCUSSION QUESTIONS

Based on your reading of this chapter and your own experience: should intercultural competence be taught? Why, or why not? Should such teaching be explicit and be part of an independent course, or embedded within another curriculum?

CASE STUDY

Read the following case study, based on Bin Obaid (2015, 2017). How do the various issues pertaining to intercultural competence manifest themselves? Can these issues be measured? How? If you were to design a workshop to address these issues based on your country, what would you include, and why?

University students from Saudi Arabia studying in the UK reported during interviews on a range of challenges they faced at the start of their life and studies in the UK: cultural differences, academic culture, motivation, language difficulties, concerns regarding adaptation to British culture. They included statements such as:

> There are big differences between the culture and religion since I am the only Muslim and Arab in my class. Sometimes, I found it hard especially in winter to find a place in the centre to do my prayers.
> This is my first time to study with females within the same class. In my country they separate between males and females.
> I cannot communicate very well with my classmates because I cannot understand them. Classmates are international such as from China or Italy.

Several workshops on 'British culture' were organised to address these issues. Following these workshops, participants responded as follows:

… the representative from the embassy benefited me in many things, and also about the proverbs, [...]. These things are amazing I didn't expect their proverbs to be like ours. I took a lot from them also the etiquette, rules and regulations and British culture, I mean everything you didn't miss anything.

Information about for example the art of etiquette, we hear a lot [about it] but no one has ever come and explained their use especially for this country, it [is] something good. I didn't know that in [this] country there are laws like ours to be honest; it's a good thing.

References

Al-Jarf, R. S. (2006). Cross-cultural communication: Saudi, Ukrainian and Russian students online. *Asian EFL Journal*, 8(2), 7–32.

Bennett, M. J. (2017). Developmental model of intercultural sensitivity. In Y. Kim (ed.), *International encyclopedia of intercultural communication* (pp. 1–10). Oxford: Wiley.

Bennett, M. J. (2020). A constructivist approach to assessing intercultural competence. In G. Rings & S. M. Rasinger (eds.), *The Cambridge handbook of intercultural communication* (pp. 521–535). Cambridge: Cambridge University Press.

Bin Obaid, L. (2015). Increasing cultural competence for Saudi English Language learners in the UK. *Procedia – Social and Behavioral Sciences*, 192, 695–702.

Bin Obaid, L. (2017). Increasing cultural competence for Saudi English language learners in the UK context. PhD thesis. Anglia Ruskin University.

Brodmann Maeder, M., Saghir, R., Pun, M., Stawinoga, A. E., Turner, R., Strapazzon, G., Exadaktylos, A. K. & Brugger, H. (2019). Intercultural competence of Western teachers for Nepalese rescuers. *High Altitude Medicine and Biology*, 20(1), 22–27. DOI:10.1089/ham.2018.0102

Collier, M. J. (2015). Intercultural communication competence: Continuing challenges and critical directions. *International Journal of Intercultural Relations*, 48, 9–11. DOI:10.1016/j.ijintrel.2015.03.003

Council of Europe. (2001). *Common European framework of reference for languages: Learning, teaching, assessment*. Cambridge: Cambridge University Press.

Deardorff, D. K. (2011). Assessing intercultural competence. *New Directions for Institutional Research*, 149, 65–79. DOI:10.1002/ir.381

Deardorff, D. K. (2016). Identification and assessment of intercultural competence as a student outcome of internationalization. *Journal of Studies in International Education*, 10(3), 241–266. DOI:10.1177/1028315306287002

Deardorff, D. K. (2020). Defining, developing and assessing intercultural competence. In G. Rings & S. M. Rasinger (eds.), *The Cambridge handbook of intercultural communication* (pp. 493–503). Cambridge: Cambridge University Press.

Fantini, A. (2000). A central concern: Developing intercultural competence. *SIT Occasional Papers Series*, 1, 25–42.

Fantini, A. (2009). Assessing intercultural competence: Issues and tools. In D. K. Deardorff (ed.), *The SAGE handbook of intercultural competence* (pp. 456–476). Thousand Oaks, CA: SAGE.

Guillén-Nieto, V. & Aleson-Carbonell, M. (2012). Serious games and learning effectiveness: The case of It's a Deal! *Computers & Education*, 58(1), 435–448. DOI:10.1016/j.compedu.2011.07.015

Hammer, M. R. (2007). *The intercultural development inventory manual (v.3)*. Ocean Pines, MD: IDI, LLC.

Hammer, M. R. (2008). The intercultural development inventory (IDI): An approach for assessing and building intercultural competence. In M. A. Moodian (ed.), *Contemporary leadership and intercultural competence: Understanding and utilizing cultural diversity to build successful organizations* (pp. 245–261). Thousand Oaks, CA: SAGE.

Holmes, P. & O'Neill, G. (2012). Developing and evaluating intercultural competence: Ethnographies of intercultural encounters. *International Journal of Intercultural Relations*, 36(5), 707–718. DOI:10.1016/j.ijintrel.2012.04.010

Jacobson, W., Sleicher, D. & Maureen, B. (1999). Portfolio assessment of intercultural competence. *International Journal of Intercultural Relations*, 23(3), 467–492.

Koester, J. & Lustig, M. W. (2015). Intercultural communication competence: Theory, measurement, and application. *International Journal of Intercultural Relations*, 48, 20–21. DOI:10.1016/j.ijintrel.2015.03.006

Mahmoud, M. M. A. (2015). Culture and English language teaching in the Arab world. *Adult Learning*, 26(2), 66–72. DOI:10.1177/1045159515573020

Mekheimer, M. A. (2011). Impact of the target culture on foreign language learning: A case study. *Cross-Cultural Communication*, 7(1), 43–52.

Nault, D. (2006). Using world literatures to promote intercultural competence in Asian EFL learners. *Asian EFL Journal*, 8(2), 132–150.

OECD. (2017). *Preparing our youth for an inclusive and sustainable world: The OECD PISA global competence framework*. Paris: OECD.

Portalla, T. & Chen, G.-M. (2010). The development and validation of the intercultural effectiveness scale. *Intercultural Communication Studies*, 19(3), 21–37.

Rasinger, S. M. (2013). *Quantitative research in linguistics: An introduction* (2nd edition). London: Bloomsbury.

Saquing, J. (2018). Intercultural communicative competence of Bachelor of Science in Secondary Education (BSED). *Asian EFL Journal*, 20(12), 8–29.

Young, M. F., Slota, S., Cutter, A. B., Jalette, G., Mullin, G., Lai, B., Simeoni, Z., Tran, M. & Yukhymenko, M. (2012). Our princess is in another castle. *Review of Educational Research*, 82(1), 61–89. DOI:10.3102/0034654312436980

18 Reflections on the Future of Intercultural Communication

In this final chapter, we want to reflect briefly on the main developments in intercultural communication and explore opportunities for further research.

AIMS
By the end of the chapter, you should be able to:
1. **critically reflect on what you have learned in this book so far;**
2. **identify possible new avenues of research in intercultural communication.**

TASK

Looking back over what you have read in this book, make notes on these questions:

What do you see as the most pertinent developments in intercultural communication, and why?

Which areas of intercultural communication would you like to see more research in, and why?

18.1 Rethinking the Field: Concepts, Approaches, Contexts

We have questioned key concepts of the field throughout the book: we started by critically interrogating the notion of culture and argued against traditional approaches that have considered cultures as fixed entities. We have argued rather that contemporary conceptualisations – and usage – of culture refer to a dynamic, which leads to the rejection of monocultural perspectives. That dynamic is particularly strong in the era of globalisation, with considerable transnational flows of people and ideas, both in the physical but also, increasingly, in the virtual/digital world.

Figure 18.1 *Rethinking the Field* by Alíz Kovács-Zöldi

Along similar lines, we have argued that intercultural communication is not a simple interaction between people of different cultural backgrounds, but should be seen as a process that focuses on the negotiation of meaning, taking into account similarities and differences. In addition, we have advocated a *critical* approach to intercultural communication: one that considers power as a crucial factor underlying interaction. We have also considered intercultural competence and seen that it is best conceptualised as an open and dynamic concept, influenced by context and power hierarchies.

One of our main aims was to present the full breadth of disciplines that underpin intercultural communication research. Yet, in many ways, current research tends to align with individual disciplines, making intercultural communication a multi- rather than inter- or transdisciplinary encounter: sociologists take predominantly sociological approaches, linguists focus predominantly on language, and so on. For ease of presenting the vast array of different approaches of theories and concepts, we followed this approach to a point in Part II. What all approaches have in common, though, is that power plays an important role. To this end, critical intercultural communication offers a framework that allows for the exploration of intercultural issues through a lens that draws upon a wide repertoire of tools from its constituent disciplines.

Historically, a lot of intercultural communication research focused on international business. However, with globalisation affecting so many parts of our lives, and the dynamics of culture including ethnicity, race, class, age, and gender boundaries, intercultural communication competence should be regarded as part of a wider social action competence that matters to us all. Accordingly, research has started to investigate systematically intercultural communication in a variety of domains, well beyond international business, and we have provided a brief overview of some of these in Part III.

18.2 Moving Forward: The Future of Intercultural Communication Research

In our discussions, we have tried to provide the historical background of intercultural communication research in order to illustrate how the field has emerged from – and in – the various subdisciplines, and to present the state of the art of the field.

The theoretical, methodological and contextual heterogeneity of intercultural communication research offers a vast array of opportunities for further research, but it is this heterogeneity that is also daunting: how can we create new knowledge in the field without losing coherence? Our proposals here broadly follow five suggestions by Szkudlarek et al. (2020), which relate back to what we have discussed so far.

18.2.1 Increasing Focus on Processual Aspects

As we have highlighted throughout the book, intercultural communication is by its very nature a dynamic process, as is the construction of identity (Chapter 1);

yet, much research has tended to look at intercultural communication as something static. This is nicely illustrated by looking at the assessment of intercultural competence (Chapter 17): even if assessment is done at multiple points in time, individual results are snapshots in time. Consequently, as we have seen in Chapters 3 and 17, models such as Bennett's DMIS increasingly focus on processual aspects.

Particularly in a world where digital and virtual communication increasingly plays a role, it is important to shift the focus towards the fluid character of interactional exchanges. Zakaria's analysis of email exchanges as part of global decision-making processes showed how individual communication styles change 'depending on purpose, roles, situation, and people' (Zakaria, 2017, p. 350).

18.2.2 A Focus from Within, not the Outside

The *emic* vs *etic* dichotomy has a long history in the social sciences: the former, emic, is best understood as an 'inside' perspective, the latter as the 'outside' perspective. A considerable amount of intercultural research has taken an etic perspective, analysing cultures from an outsider perspective, often with a view to comparing them (see Chapter 5). For a discipline that partly has its origins in anthropology, with its strong commitment to ethnographic fieldwork with participant observation (see Chapter 8), this is perhaps somewhat unexpected. If the anthropological study of culture relies so heavily on understanding the intricacies of a culture or society and its communicative and behavioural patterns, an emic approach to studying intercultural communication is bound to yield considerable insights. Emic accounts allow us to shift the focus towards the 'thoughts and actions [...] of the actors' self-understanding – terms that are often culturally and historically bound' (Morris et al., 1999, p. 982). It also allows for a nuanced exploration of key cultural concepts such as South African *ubuntu* or Japanese *kizuna* (Chapter 3), which are difficult to grasp fully from an etic perspective.

18.2.3 A Focus on Contextual Richness

We dedicated the whole of Part III of this book to the discussion of the various domains in which intercultural communication has become a major issue. We have also firmly placed our discussion in the critical tradition: one in which power relationships play an important role. In each domain, these power relationships manifest themselves through a variety of means, including cultural, linguistic, historic, social and economic status. All these aspects require careful consideration, and it is worth examining the extent to which they play out differently depending on media involved. As Szkudlarek and colleagues remind us, many of the challenges in intercultural communication can be exacerbated in the virtual world (Szkudlarek et al., 2020, p. 4), but there are also enormous opportunities. For example, during the Covid-19 pandemic many of us saw face-to-face interaction – anything from meetings, seminars, lectures, or socialising with friends and family – move into the digital realm, and communication dynamics as well as behaviours have changed in that context. In teaching online, many of us have seen students preferring text-chat options provided by communication platforms over using a camera and microphone, often leading to several parallel strands of interaction within the same communicative event. It opens opportunities for those more introvert, or those less confident in the oral use of English, and formerly 'quiet' students have become some of the most active. All this indicates the need to consider intercultural communication in context. Thankfully, the study of virtual communities is well established with dedicated methodologies to match (see Pink et al., 2015, and Hjorth et al., 2019, for an introduction), which also provide an excellent starting point for digital intercultural research.

18.2.4 A Move from the Individual to the Relational

Considering that intercultural communication and competence are open, highly dynamic and always depending on context, they are best explored using a dialectical approach. For intercultural competence research, this means placing 'individual competence traits in relational tension with the motivations, knowledge and skills of the others, organizational contexts and the larger cultural contexts' (Martin, 2015, p. 7). This includes personal factors, such as race and gender, and we therefore have to avoid ethnocentric approaches to conceptualising intercultural competence (Yep, 2000; see also Chapters 4 and 9).

18.2.5 From the Organisational to the Interpersonal

Communication is an interactional exchange between at least two people (see Chapter 7), with both linguistic and non-linguistic tools being deployed to do so successfully. While research on organisational level is important, so is the close analysis of communication at local, interpersonal level. Healthcare professionals caring for a patient (see Chapter 15), or migrants seeking to prove their refugee status (see Chapter 7) are not just interactions that take place within the context and constraints of organisational culture (be it healthcare or immigration policy), but interactions between two human beings, each bringing with them a range of individual traits (Section 18.2.4). It is this interpersonal level, explored in an almost Geertzian approach of *thick description* (Geertz, 1993) that allows us to capture and explain the nuances of intercultural communication.

PROJECT

Select an example of intercultural communication. This might be something you have observed yourself, or come across in the media, seen in a film, or read in a book.

1. What concept of culture(s) is the most prevalent one in the example? You may want to refer to chapters in Part I.

2. How does the intercultural communication play out? What seem to be the driving factors and forces? (Part II)

3. How and to what extent does the context play a role? (Part III)

4. If your example includes (unresolved) conflict, what advice would you give to remedy it?

References

Geertz, C. (1993). *The interpretation of cultures: Selected essays*. London: Collins.

Hjorth, L., Horst, H., Galloway, A. & Bell, G. (eds.). (2019). *The Routledge companion to digital ethnography*. Abingdon: Routledge.

Martin, J. N. (2015). Revisiting intercultural communication competence: Where to go from here. *International Journal of Intercultural Relations*, 48, 6–8. DOI:10.1016/j.ijintrel.2015.03.008

Morris, M. W., Keung, K., Ames, D. & Lickel, B. (1999). Views from inside and outside: Integrating emic and etic insights about culture and justice judgment. *The Academy of Management Review*, 24(4), 781–796.

Pink, S., Horst, H., Postill, J., Hjorth, L., Lewis, T. & Tacchi, J. (2015). *Digital ethnography*. London: SAGE.

Szkudlarek, B., Osland, J. S., Nardon, L. & Zander, L. (2020). Communication and culture in international business – Moving the field forward. *Journal of World Business*, 55(6), 1–9.

Yep, G. A. (2000). Encounters with the 'other': Personal notes for a reconceptualization of intercultural communication competence. *The CATESOL Journal*, 12(1), 117–144.

Zakaria, N. (2017). Emergent patterns of switching behaviors and intercultural communication styles of global virtual teams during distributed decision making. *Journal of International Management*, 23(4), 350–366. DOI:10.1016/j.intman.2016.09.002

GLOSSARY

6D model Geert Hofstede's six-dimensional model of national cultural differences and similarities, including individualism, uncertainty avoidance, power distance, masculinity, long-term orientation and indulgence versus restraint.

7D model A seven-dimensional model of national cultural differences and similarities proposed by Fons Trompenaars and Charles Hampden-Turner, which examines individualism versus communitarianism, universalism versus particularism, specific versus diffuse, affective versus neutral, achievement versus ascription, sequential versus synchronic time and inner versus outer directed.

Acculturation Migrants' adjustments to the new environment, including the development of new customs, activities, values and language.

Alli kawsay A concept used by indigenous Kichwa people in Ecuador to mediate key aspects of a 'good life', which includes notions of sustainable societies with a focus on social equality and nature-inclusiveness.

Assessment Systematic evaluation or measurement of a particular set of skills or knowledge.

Bonding social capital Strong and substantive social links, such as with family or close friends, associated with high levels of trust.

Code A collection of symbols and signs that form an orderly system used for communication. A language is a code as it uses linguistic signs to convey information; road signs use visual signs to convey information to road users.

Colonialism A form of cultural and socio-economic exploitation, which developed in the context of globalisation, i.e., post-Renaissance forms of imperialism. Next to European imperialism, researchers examine Japanese, Soviet, Russian and Chinese forms of expansion and exploitation as colonialism.

Communicative competence Coined by Dell Hymes, the ability to use language not only correctly in lexical and grammatical terms, but also appropriately for a given context.

Consumer ethnocentrism Tendency of consumers to purchase national products instead of foreign goods. This is encouraged and enhanced by pressure groups, such as national meat or milk industries, which draw on nationalist narratives to construct hierarchies.

Counterinsurgency Action by a government and/or its allies against non-governmental forces (e.g., guerrillas), including psychological, military and/or political engagement.

Critical intercultural communication Mediation that aims to create mutual understanding between individuals or groups of different cultural backgrounds and considers the extent to which and exactly how this is shaped by existing power hierarchies. That mediation includes the negotiation of common ground and differences by drawing on the cultural, socio-economic, political and legal frameworks, elites, pressure groups and individual human agents that shape interpretations of particular behaviour, norms and institutions.

Cross-cultural management A research field and/or study programme that explores and aims to bridge cultural differences in managerial values, attitudes and practices through comparisons. Especially when including interactive analysis, it is also presented as intercultural management.

Cultural identity In interaction, the mediated and hence dynamic properties that make people from one culture different (or similar) to people from another culture.

Culture Mediated values, beliefs, assumptions and norms common to a larger population that expresses these characteristics in particular patterns of behaviour, artefacts and institutions. Cultures are dynamic, because people retell, rewrite and negotiate cultural narratives.

Culture shock First described by Kalervo Olberg, this refers to the feeling of uncertainty, confusion and anxiety that many people experience when first living in a new country and culture.

Developmental Model of Intercultural Sensitivity (DMIS) A model developed by Milton J. Bennett that describes intercultural competence as a developmental process consisting of six stages. *See also* **intercultural competence**.

Digital divide The fact that not everyone has access to the internet, which can lead to disadvantage. It also refers to the fact that some languages (e.g., English) and cultures dominate the internet and hence marginalise other languages and cultures.

Essentialism In philosophy, the belief that people and objects have an essence, that is a fixed set of characteristics that captures their true nature. This belief is in conflict with contemporary notions of dynamic and socially constructed multiple identities.

Ethics A philosophical concept that describes a set of moral principles and values that determine in a society what is considered good and right ('ethical'), or bad and wrong ('unethical').

Ethnography An approach to studying culture which is based on an in-depth description and analysis of a culture or group, often from extensive observation.

Ethnography of speaking An approach to studying communication between people that assumes that language is an integral part of cultural behaviour, with different cultures using different conventions for linguistic practices.

Expatriates Also known as ex-pats, people who live and/or work long-term in a country that is not their native country. *See also* **flexpatriates** and **inpatriates**.

Face In politeness theory, face refers to the self-image or sense of self that people show or want to show during interaction with others. *See also* **politeness**.

Fake news Fabricated and weaponised false or polarised information that is misleadingly presented as news to claim objectivity, for example, when diminishing particular groups or individuals.

Flash fiction Micro-stories or story miniatures, which tend to range from a six-word story to a maximum 1,500 words, frequently disseminated through open access e-journals or e-(maga)zines.

Flexpatriates People with flexible assignments, including international commuting, rotational mobility and/or extended business travel. *See also* **expatriates**.

Gig economy An economy in which organisations hire people on a self-employed basis often through app-based platforms for short-term work given out in individual pieces or 'gigs'.

Global North and **Global South** Concepts that refer to a North–South divide between socio-economically and politically more and less developed societies. This includes differences when countries are compared, for example the United States and European Union countries in the north and South American and African countries in the south, but also within neoliberal northern countries, which can be referred to as the 'Global South in the north'.

Global or **intercultural citizenship** A concept that goes beyond nationality (i.e., what is on your passport). Global citizens are seen as those who have an understanding of how the world works, and engage at both local and global levels.

Guanxi A Chinese concept that refers to harmony-based relationship marketing associated with long-term engagement, cooperation, trust, loyalty and mutual benefit.

Heterosexism The discrimination against LGBT+ people based on the assumption that heterosexuality is the norm.

High-context culture In high-context cultures, most of the information of a message is located in the physical context or shared cultural knowledge and experiences, so the message does not need to be verbalised explicitly.

Imagology An image studies approach, originally developed in comparative literature to examine stereotypical presentations, which has been transferred to film and media studies.

Inpatriates In business contexts, people that move long-term from subsidiaries to headquarters in another country. *See also* **expatriates**.

Integrative intercultural communication Reorientation of intercultural communication research, which aims to overcome disciplinary boundaries and advance interdisciplinary work to achieve common goals.

Intercultural business communication Mediation aimed at creating mutual understanding between individuals or groups of different cultural backgrounds in business contexts.

Intercultural communication Mediation aimed at creating mutual understanding between individuals or groups of different cultural backgrounds. That mediation includes negotiation of common ground and differences by drawing on the cultural frameworks that shape interpretations of particular behaviour, norms and institutions.

Intercultural competence A concept that refers to an open, dynamic and lifelong process in the development of knowledge, attitudes and skills to build relevant personal, social, strategic and specialist potential for mediation in cultural encounters. This could be achieved through a transfer of comparable aspects in general action competence to unfamiliar situations.

Intercultural identity An identity concept that accepts cultural interconnectedness due to exchange and mediation. The distinction between intercultural and transcultural constructs is gradual, with the former focusing more on differences, while the latter tend to address common ground.

Intercultural management A research field and/or study programme that examines challenges when managing employees, customers or business partners with different cultural backgrounds, which may be caused by differences in interactive styles, values, attitudes and/or practices. Especially when focusing on comparisons of values, attitudes and practices, it is also presented as cross-cultural management.

Intercultural rapport Harmonious relationships between people from different cultural backgrounds.

Internal colonialism A form of cultural and socio-economic exploitation directed against precarious workforces in the home country. It supports imperialist forms (see **colonialism**) through the export of successful models of internal suppression, and vice versa.

Intersectionality First articulated by Kimberlé Williams Crenshaw, a concept that argues that we cannot look at social categories in isolation, but need to consider how they intersect with each other in order to understand individual experiences.

Kizuna A Japanese concept that addresses the desire to establish and maintain social connections by mediation.

Lingua franca A language used by people who do not share the same first language, for example, the use of English to communicate by Spanish and Arabic speakers.

Linguistic relativity The idea that the language we speak influences the way we think about the world. Developed first by Edward Sapir and later by Benjamin Lee Whorf, who argued for what is known as *linguistic determinism* – the view that our language determines the way we see the world.

Low-context culture In low-context cultures, the vast majority of the information is explicitly verbalised, so a message can be understood without contextual information. *See also* **high-context culture**.

Mediation Cultural interpreting, in which cultural frames that shape people's behaviour are compared to facilitate the exploration of common ground for the negotiation of differences.

Monochronism In monochronic societies, people tend to do one thing at a time. *See also* **polychronism**.

Monocultural identity Also known as 'island' or 'container' concepts of cultural identity, in which people are wrongly constructed as members of separate, homogeneous and essentially fixed communities ranging from prehistoric to nationalist 'tribes' in the twenty-first century.

Myth of Return The idea of staying in a host country for only a period of time before returning to a homeland, which is often not actually realised. It can significantly contribute to in-group cohesion in migrant groups.

Network capital This includes intangible assets such as contacts and networking tools (*see also* **symbolic capital**), but also tangible assets such as technological tools that facilitate mobile lifestyles.

Panethnicity A concept that assumes a sense of solidarity and sameness among ethnic subgroups that are perceived to be homogeneous by outsiders. For example, the term 'Asian Americans' groups people of different Asian backgrounds under a single umbrella.

PERMA A model proposed by Martin Seligman to measure individual and social well-being through five key aspects: Positive emotion, Engagement, positive Relationships, Meaning and Accomplishment.

Politeness The use of language that reflects our feelings and attitudes towards, and awareness of, others, and which reflects a range of social dimensions such as power, social distance or solidarity. *See also* **face**.

Polychronism In polychronic cultures, people tend to do several things at the same time. *See also* **monochronism**.

Positive psychology A scientific field of study about what makes life worth living, which includes research on individual and social well-being, and ways of reaching a positive society.

Postcolonialism An academic discipline that examines the impact and ongoing traces of colonialism, which may include contemporary disparities in power and wealth. *See also* **colonialism**.

Precariat A highly diverse and fast-growing class characterised by unstable labour and living conditions, uncertainty due to dependence on insecure wages, and a lack of particular (civil, cultural, social and/or political) rights.

Proxemics Articulated by Edward Hall, a theory about how humans conceptualise personal space.

Push and **pull factors** In the context of migration, economic, environmental and demographic factors that push people out of one location and pull them to another.

Queer theory or queer studies Research across the social sciences and the humanities that explores the experiences of gay, lesbian, bisexual, transgender people and others who do not identify with a heterosexual norm.

Return migration The process of moving back to the original home country; often driven by factors similar to those that triggered the original migration.

Rhizome In botany, plant stems with networks of multiple roots, such as bamboos or ginger. In intercultural studies, the rhizome refers to open, dynamic, interconnected, multiple and non-hierarchical cultural identity concepts, in contrast to presentations of cultures as separate trees growing (homogeneously) from a single root (origin). *See also* **monocultural identity**.

Rituals Actions that follow certain set patterns, and are strongly symbolic.

Serious gaming/serious games Computer games that serve not just as entertainment, but also have an educational and training purpose. For example, games can be used to teach and develop intercultural competence. *See also* **intercultural competence**.

Silaturahmi A Malayan concept that addresses the need to establish mutual respect and trust through mediation between hosts and visitors.

Speech community A group of people who not only speak the same language, but also have agreed norms and conventions on *how* to use it, and how to communicate.

Story circle A methodology of cultural storytelling in social groups or circles elaborated by Darla Deardorff that aims to develop intercultural competence through empathy, respect for others, self-awareness and intercultural relationships.

Symbolic capital Coined by Pierre Bourdieu, these are non-financial assets and resources that are exchanged in day-to-day interaction and which enable access to other resources. Language can be such an asset as speaking a language enables access to other speakers of that language.

Third Space Coined by Homi Bhabha, a hybrid space, in which cultural identities can be negotiated.

Traditional intercultural identity An identity concept that aims to bridge cultural differences through interaction, but continues to construct cultures wrongly as separate, homogeneous and essentially fixed communities. *See also* **monocultural identity**.

Traditional multicultural identity An identity concept that focuses on peaceful cultural coexistence within a society, but continues to construct cultures wrongly as separate, homogeneous and essentially fixed communities. *See also* **monocultural identity**.

Transcultural identity An identity concept that focuses on the interconnectedness, related blurring of boundaries and overlap between cultures through ongoing exchange and mediation between tribal constructs.

Transcultural memory Also known as multidirectional or intercultural memory, a concept that focuses on connections in people's implications of other people's suffering and loss, which facilitates the development of new forms of solidarity and presents alternatives to celebrations and commemorations of supposedly unique historical events in nationalist historiographies.

Translation The process of converting a spoken or written text from one language (the source) to another language (the target). Translation is often more complex than a simple one-to-one conversion, especially with regard to what is culturally appropriate or adequate.

Transnationalism Concept that describes the increasing levels of connectivity between people, whereby networks and activities span a range of countries, societies and cultures.

Tribalism Strong identification with in-group values and interests at the expense of out-groups, which leads to tribal hierarchies, fixed boundary settings and distorted information processing.

Ubuntu Originally a South African concept that refers to intercultural competence at community level with a strong communitarian ethos. *See also* **intercultural competence**.

Value orientations Complex but relatively stable traits held by members of a particular culture; often used as a tool for studying and comparing cultures.

Vishwa roopa darshanam A Hindu concept that addresses the universe as one, with a focus on the need to show respect for man, animals and plants.

Web 2.0 A development of the internet resulting in higher levels of interaction and collaboration between users, and the growth of user-generated content. Social media are a good example of this.

Whānau A Māori concept originally limited to family and/or tribe as an in-group that increasingly includes friends, associates and unrelated people, who show intercultural competence by mediating meaning and offering mutual support, for example in whānau rooms in hospitals. *See also* **intercultural competence**.

World Cultural Map A dynamic map of cultural values that demonstrates developments in traditional versus secular and survival versus self-expression values since 1981. The map is based on data from the World Values Survey (WVS) Association founded by political scientists Ronald Inglehart and Christian Welzel.

Zhong dao Also known as 'middle way', a Chinese concept that addresses the competence to achieve harmonious balance in communication and leadership.

INDEX

Made in the USA
Middletown, DE
01 February 2023

23725849R00148